Thomas Pynchon & the Dark Passages of History

david cowart

thomas PYNCHON & the dark passages of history

THE UNIVERSITY OF GEORGIA PRESS

Athens & London

© 2011 by the University of Georgia Press

Athens, Georgia 30602

www.ugapress.org

All rights reserved

Designed by Walton Harris

Set in 10/14 ITC New Baskerville

Printed digitally in the United States of America

Library of Congress Cataloging-in-Publication Data

Cowart, David, 1947–

Thomas Pynchon and the dark passages of history / David Cowart.

    p.   cm.

Includes bibliographical references and index.

ISBN-13: 978-0-8203-4062-3 (cloth : alk. paper)

ISBN-10: 0-8203-4062-6 (cloth : alk. paper)

ISBN-13: 978-0-8203-4063-0 (pbk. : alk. paper)

ISBN-10: 0-8203-4063-4 (pbk. : alk. paper)

1. Pynchon, Thomas–Criticism and interpretation. I. Title.

PS3566.Y55Z59 2012

813'.54–dc22   2011021936

British Library Cataloging-in-Publication Data available

For Pamela,
Lodestar to *this* wandering bark

Doch alles, was uns unrührt, dich und mich,
Nimmt uns zusammen wie ein Bogenstrich,
Der aus zwei Saiten *eine* Stimme zieht.
Auf welches Instrument sind wir gespannt?
Und welcher Geiger hat uns in der Hand?
O süsses Lied.

— RAINER MARIA RILKE

Think now

History has many cunning passages, contrived corridors

And issues, deceives with whispering ambitions,

Guides us by vanities.

    — T. S. ELIOT, "Gerontion"

CONTENTS

Preface *xi*

Acknowledgments *xv*

Abbreviations *xix*

Introduction: Calibrating Clio *1*

ONE. Prospero's Apprenticeship: *Slow Learner* *25*

TWO. History and Myth: Pynchon's *V.* *40*

THREE. *Streben nach dem Unendlichen*: Germany and German Culture in Pynchon's Early Work *57*

FOUR. Pynchon and the Sixties: The California Novels *82*

FIVE. The Luddite Vision: *Mason & Dixon* *136*

SIX. Pynchon, Genealogy, History: *Against the Day* *159*

SEVEN. The Historiographer Historicized: Pynchon and Literary History *189*

Notes *207*

Books, Pamphlets, and Special Periodical Issues on Thomas Pynchon *221*

Works Cited *227*

Index *237*

PREFACE

I read my first Pynchon novel in Ethiopia, in quarters that lacked electricity and indoor plumbing (actually, there was no outdoor plumbing either). When the daylight faded, I read on by Coleman lantern. If the mantle broke and I had no spare, I could retire early or wend my way through the hyenas to a souk about a mile away. A solitary American in the Horn of Africa, I read rather a lot that season, half-systematically filling gaps in a haphazard undergraduate education. I did not understand Pynchon's *V.*, but it transported me. Reading it became a turning point in my intellectual life.

I read *The Crying of Lot 49* a year or so later, at the behest, if memory serves, of Michael Beard, a couple of years ahead of me in graduate school. After the Peace Corps, a step or two ahead of the draft, I finished a hurried master's degree at Indiana University before receiving the dreaded letter from Selective Service. Like me, the draft board was looking over its shoulder, for conscription was about to end. But that momentous change in the culture came about, as Philip Larkin says, "just too late for me." With the ink still damp on what a certain Jacobean playwright would call the "tegument" of some "hapless mutton," I was inducted into the army in Indianapolis, where, during processing, I found myself in a room full of fellow conscripts, earnestly filling out one of the forms that would facilitate my becoming what the drill sergeants I was presently to meet called an American Fighting Man. I pulled up short over one of the questions: "Have you or any member of your family ever been affiliated with an organization that sought to deny individuals their civil rights?"

I raised my hand to get the attention of the grizzled personage seated at the front of the room. "Excuse me—there's a question here about whether any family member of mine has been in an organization denying people their civil rights. Do I need to state that my grandfather was in the Ku Klux Klan?" The answer was swift: "Hell, boy, *I'm* in the Ku Klux Klan!"

As a soldier, I made Ferdinand the Bull look like Rambo. This American Fighting Man would have been hard pressed to fight his way out of a wet paper bag. I was finishing up my hitch (stationed in Panama, thank goodness, not Vietnam) when *Gravity's Rainbow* appeared. I spent about 6 weeks getting through its 760 pages the first time. When a superb assessment of that novel came out in the *Saturday Review*, I wondered about its author, Richard Poirier—only to find that he directed the doctoral program at Rutgers, where I had just been accepted. (That fall, I would have my one classroom encounter with Pynchon—*Lot 49*—in Poirier's Introduction to Graduate Study course). In those days, we were encouraged to avoid premature specialization, and I actually made a point of not taking courses in my particular interest: twentieth-century American literature. When I completed my doctoral coursework, in fact, I was examined in three historical periods: in one, you were to show comprehensive knowledge; in another, you picked a single genre; and in the last, you did three major figures. I tried to show "comprehensive knowledge" of British writing in the twentieth century; ranged over the English novel in the eighteenth century; and chose Donne, Marlowe, and Sir Thomas Browne from the Renaissance. Comprehensive exams completed, you could strike out in any direction you wanted. I approached Paul Fussell, with whom I had taken no classes, about doing a thesis on Pynchon. Fussell had just won the National Book Award for *The Great War and Modern Memory*, which featured an astute reading of the notorious scene in *Gravity's Rainbow* in which Brigadier Pudding enacts "the ritual of military memory." The dissertation eventually became my first book, *Thomas Pynchon: The Art of Allusion* (1980). Since then, I have continued to read and teach and write about contemporary American fiction—especially the work of Pynchon as it has appeared. In 2013, the world of letters will observe the fiftieth anniversary of *V.*'s publication, and someone (not me) should organize a conference in an appropriate setting. Namibia?

"Some books," Sir Francis Bacon observes, "are to be tasted, others to be swallowed, and some few to be chewed and digested: that is, some books are to be read only in parts, others to be read, but not curiously, and some few to be read wholly, and with diligence and attention." The books of Thomas Pynchon merit inclusion in that exalted last category; those of his critics do not. Vying for space on our shelves and time in our laps, books of criticism and analysis aspire at best (to modify Bacon's gustatory figure) to be *vin ordinaire*, not *grand cru*. One braves no hyenas to get to the end of this or that work of criticism. Indeed, few will read the present effort straight through. I hope anyone who does so will tolerate such occasional repetition of points as would go unnoticed in more sporadic reading, and will recognize that certain points bear repeating because of their centrality to Pynchon's thought.

Upon voyaging (or, ideally, re-voyaging) into successive Pynchon texts, readers may find a critical cicerone desirable company. I offer *Thomas Pynchon and the Dark Passages of History* as a modest vade mecum. I hope that it will interest not only fellow teachers of literature and students at every level, but also the nonacademic Theseus seeking some critical thread through what David Seed calls the labyrinths of Pynchon's daunting but immensely rewarding prose. The reader will encounter relatively little of the terminology that so often risks putting off nonspecialists. I have always felt that the Pynchon text is self-theorizing: it teaches readers to think and perceive and conceptualize in ways that anticipate—with humor and insight and cogency—much that has emerged in the field of literary theory over the past few decades. To be sure, I have profited from my reading of Freud, Lacan, Foucault, Derrida, de Man, Lyotard, Serres, Žižek, and many more philosophers and theorists of discourse, but I have learned more from Pynchon.

Especially about history—history as myth, as rhetorical construct, as false consciousness, as prologue, as mirror, as genealogical trove, as seedbed of national and, yes, literary identities.

A final point: I normally think serious discussion of literature should be undertaken with due notice of prior criticism, but I have conceived this book as a kind of intellectual diary, a record, first, of core samples taken at various points in the career of America's greatest living novelist and, second, of my largely unmediated encounters with Pynchon's later books, one after another, often within minutes of their publication (from *Vineland* on, that is). To be sure, there were usually a few reviews (often quite perspicacious) and early articles to take note of and cite when one's own formal essay got itself written. But I have — for the most part, and with some exceptions — sought to preserve the diary-like aspect of each succeeding chapter here by not attempting any comprehensive engagement with the criticism that has appeared over the last forty-odd years. My subject, after all, is Pynchon and history, not the history of Pynchon criticism. I do, however, cite work of immediate relevance to my own readings.

I have tried, in preparing this book, to make it more than a congeries of essays. Some continuity will, I hope, be seen in my emphasis on the facticity of historical narrative and the historicity of storytelling — and on the relations of both story and history to myth. I have sought to achieve a thoroughgoing assessment of Pynchon's career, with readings informed by many years' scrutiny of literary fashion and its instantiations in current fiction.

As for the novels Pynchon has yet to write, may the hyenas keep their distance.

ACKNOWLEDGMENTS

Part of "Introduction: Calibrating Clio" originally appeared as "Thomas Pynchon," in *Critical Survey of Long Fiction*, 4th ed., edited by Carl Rollyson, 3712–23 (Pasadena, Calif.: Salem Press, 2010); chapter 1, "Prospero's Apprenticeship: *Slow Learner*," subsumes a revised version of "Science, and the Arts in Pynchon's 'Entropy,'" which originally appeared in *CLA Journal* 24, no. 1 (September 1980), 108–15, and parts of "*Slow Learner Early Stories*," originally published in *Magill's Literary Annual 1985*, edited by Frank N. Magill, 830–34 (Pasadena, Calif.: Salem Press, 1985); a version of chapter 2, "History and Myth: Pynchon's *V.*," originally appeared in *Approaches to Teaching Pynchon's* The Crying of Lot 49 *and Other Works*, edited by Thomas Schaub, 88–98 (New York: Modern Language Association Publications, 2008); chapter 3, "*Streben nach dem Unendlichen*: Germany and German Culture in Pynchon's Early Work," incorporates and reworks "Germany and German Culture in the Works of Thomas Pynchon," in *Germany and German Thought in American Literature and Cultural Criticism*, edited by Peter Freese, 305–18 (Essen: Blaue Eule, 1990), "Cinematic Auguries of the Third Reich in *Gravity's Rainbow*," *Literature/Film Quarterly* 6, no. 4 (Fall 1978), 364–70 (reprinted with permission of *Literature/Film Quarterly* @ Salisbury University, Salisbury, MD, 21801), and "Pynchon's Use of the Tannhäuser Legend in *Gravity's Rainbow*," in *Notes on Contemporary Literature* 9, no. 3 (May 1979), 2–3;

chapter 4, "Pynchon and the Sixties: The California Novels," subsumes "Pynchon og tresserne," translated into Danish by Tore Rye Anderson, *Passage* 26 (1997), 55–68 (subsequently published in English as "Pynchon and the Sixties" in *Critique* 41 [Fall 1999], 3–12), "Continuity and Growth: Pynchon's *Vineland*," *Kenyon Review* 12, no. 4 (Fall 1990), 176–90, and "Attenuated Postmodernism: Pynchon's *Vineland*," *Critique* 32, no. 2 (Winter 1990), 67–76; chapter 5, "The Luddite Vision: *Mason & Dixon*," originally appeared in *American Literature* 71, no. 2 (June 1999), 341–63; chapter 6, "Pynchon, Genealogy, History: *Against the Day*," originally appeared in *Modern Philology*; chapter 7, "The Historiographer Historicized: Pynchon and Literary History," originally appeared in *The Cambridge Companion to Thomas Pynchon*, edited by Brian McHale, Inger Dalsgaard, and Luc Herman (New York: Cambridge, 2011).

Writing is a solitary business, but when you emerge, blinking, from your office or study, it's wonderful to find yourself in the company of loving family, congenial colleagues, and friends who tolerate, inspire, and encourage your efforts. My thanks to colleagues in the dynamic Department of English at the University of South Carolina and to an administration (department chair, dean, provost, president) that somehow manages to foster research in the face of every budget cutback known to academe. Thanks, too, to students who have stimulated my thinking in many ways—especially doctoral students who have worked with me in recent years and taught me as much as I have taught them: Carl Jenkinson, Thede Wrede, Laura di Prete, Matthew Miller, Michael Rizza, Jeremey Cagle, Natalie Leppard, Kevin Trumpeter, Paul Plisiewicz, Kevin Kyzer, Michael Overman, Jim Pickard, Matt Childs, Chris Miller, Dawson Jones.

I cannot imagine a more dynamic intellectual community than the one in which Pynchon scholarship flourishes. For their published work on Pynchon and for many stimulating conversations, my thanks to Joseph Slade, Mark Siegel, John Krafft, Deborah Madsen, Donald Greiner, Geoffrey Green, Larry McCaffery, Stacey Olster, Katherine Hayles, Chase Crossingham, Susan Strehle, Hanjo Berressem, Khachig Tölölyan, Steven Weisenburger, Peter Freese, Tiina Käkela-Puumala, M. Angeles Martinez, Samuel Thomas, Rodney Taveira, Nicholas Prescott,

Creon Upton, James M. Mellard, Alan Wilde, Caroline Plowden, Whitney Bolton, Patricia Leighten, Robert McLaughlin, Sally E. Parry, Charles Harris, Victoria Frenkel Harris, Georg Schmundt-Thomas, Joseph Conte, Curtis White, David Thoreen, Edward Mendelson, Zak Smith, John McClure, Paul Fussell, Dwight Eddins, David Leverenz, Niran Abbas, Burhan Tufail, and Zygmunt Mazur. For help with the various chapters of this book, I am especially beholden to Kathryn Hume, Brian McHale, Clifford Mead, Inger Dalsgaard, Luc Herman, Douglas Lannark, Thomas Schaub, Bernard Duyfhuizen, and the readers for the University of Georgia Press, John Krafft (whose corrections and annotations were invaluable), and his anonymous but equally perspicacious colleague.

I could do nothing without the love and support of my family: daughter Rachel, son Chase, wife Pamela. The last effected a great transformation of my spirit in circumstances that I will one day write up for the *New York Times* column "Modern Love."

ABBREVIATIONS

Page numbers for quotations from Pynchon's books appear parenthetically. Publication details appear in the Works Cited.

V.   *V.* (1963)

L49   *The Crying of Lot 49* (1966)

GR   *Gravity's Rainbow* (1973)

SL   *Slow Learner* (1984)

VL   *Vineland* (1990)

MD   *Mason & Dixon* (1997)

ATD   *Against the Day* (2006)

IV   *Inherent Vice* (2009)

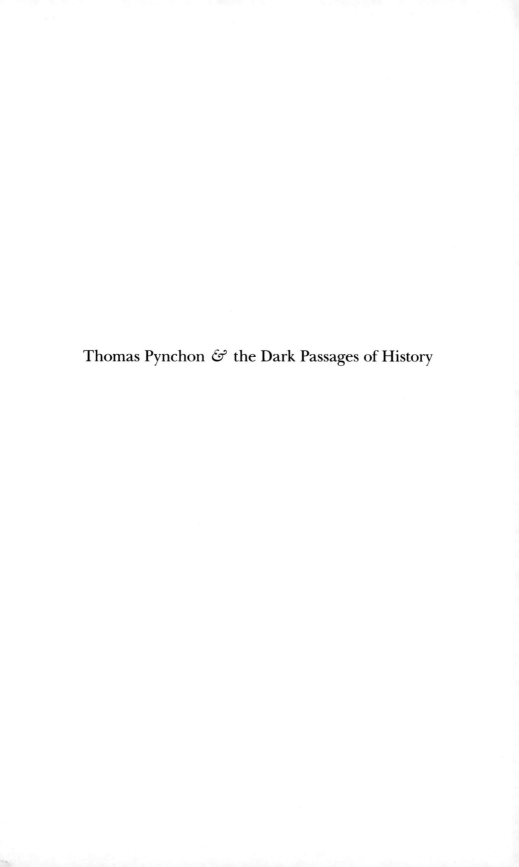

Thomas Pynchon & the Dark Passages of History

History is always written wrong, and so always needs to be rewritten.

—GEORGE SANTAYANA, *Life of Reason: Reason in Science*

INTRODUCTION

Calibrating Clio

Among those contemporary novelists who enjoy both a popular and an academic following, Thomas Pynchon stands out as a near-mythic figure of literary virtù. His novels and stories stand up to the most rigorous critical analysis; they prove, like all great works of art, to be the product of a gifted sensibility and careful craftsmanship. At the same time, Dr. Johnson's "common reader" cheerfully wades through much abstruse matter because this author never fails to delight and instruct with bizarre plots, incandescent language, anarchic humor, memorable characters, powerful insights into the human condition—and an extraordinary grasp of the workings of history.

Pynchon has a large, diverse, and remarkably loyal following. His work has received attention in over eighty monographs and essay collections (see the list appended to the end of this volume), not to mention an enormous body of exegesis in scholarly journals, including the redoubtable *Pynchon Notes*, which has published important articles on this author's oeuvre since 1979, and *Orbit: Writing Around Pynchon*, an electronic serial that will begin publishing in late 2011 or early 2012. Pynchon's reclusive habits have fostered the fascination of readers: he refuses to be interviewed, photographed, or otherwise made into a darling of the media. His domicile remained a matter of speculation for some thirty years after the publication of his first novel. Only toward the end of the last century did it become known that Pynchon made his home in New York City.

Pynchon has been honored with a number of literary awards. He received the 1963 William Faulkner Foundation Award for *V.*, the 1967 Rosenthal Foundation Award of the National Institute of Arts and Letters for *The Crying of Lot 49*, and the National Book Award for *Gravity's Rainbow* in 1974. Though the judging committee unanimously voted to award the Pulitzer Prize in fiction to Pynchon for *Gravity's Rainbow*, they were overruled by an advisory board that found the novel immoral and "turgid." The Howells Medal, awarded once every five years, was offered to Pynchon in 1975, but he declined it. He did so in a letter to Richard Wilbur, fellow of the American Academy of Arts and Letters: "The Howells Medal is a great honor, and, being gold, probably a good hedge against inflation, too. But I don't want it. Please don't impose on me something I don't want. It makes the Academy look arbitrary and me look rude . . . I know I should behave with more class, but there appears to be only one way to say no, and that's no."[1] In 1988, however, Pynchon did accept a MacArthur fellowship—an award that conveys five years of support with "no strings," as the foundation's Web site describes it (current fellows receive five hundred thousand dollars).

Pynchon occupies a place in the front rank of twentieth-century American fiction writers, and more than one distinguished critic has declared him America's finest living novelist.

Life

Because of his passion for privacy, little is known about the life of Thomas Pynchon. His father, Thomas Ruggles Pynchon Sr., was an industrial surveyor who served briefly as supervisor of Oyster Bay, the Long Island township (from 1 January 1963 to 1 January 1964, according to local records). The family also lived in the nearby communities of Glen Cove and East Norwich. Pynchon was sixteen when he graduated from Oyster Bay High School in 1953. He was class salutatorian and winner of an award for the senior attaining the highest average in English. With a scholarship at Cornell University, he first majored in engineering physics but, though he was doing well academically, abandoned that curriculum after the first year. A year later, he decided to do a hitch in the navy before completing his baccalaureate degree. In late 1955 and early 1956, he trained with boot camp Company 84 at Bainbridge, Maryland. He did advanced training as an electrician at Norfolk, Virginia. The two years in the navy, partly spent in the Mediterranean, provided Pynchon with a number of comic situations and characters that he would exploit in "Low-lands," *V.*, *Gravity's Rainbow*, and *Mason & Dixon*. Pynchon finished at Cornell as an English major and graduated in 1959. While at Cornell, the young author studied with M. H. Abrams, Baxter Hathaway, James McConkey, Arthur Mizener, and Walter Slatoff. He may have crossed paths with Vladimir Nabokov, too, though the popular world literature class taught by the author of *Lolita* (published in the United States in 1958) does not, according to those who have seen it, appear on Pynchon's transcript.

Pynchon lived briefly in Greenwich Village and in uptown Manhattan before taking a job with the Boeing Company and moving to Seattle. With Boeing for two and a half years (until September 1962), he worked in the Minuteman Logistics Support Program and, according to Adrian Wisnicki, wrote a number of articles for *Bomarc Service News*. He also wrote for (or was reprinted in) *Aerospace Accident and Maintenance Review*, *Approach: The Naval Aviation Safety Review*, and an air force publication, *Aerospace Safety*.[2] After leaving Boeing in September 1962, he lived in California and Mexico. *V.*, completed in Seattle, was published in 1963 and hailed as a major first novel.

Over the years Pynchon was rumored to be living in various places, including California, Mexico, and Oregon. In the late 1970s, he made a trip to England that was noted in the national newsmagazines. For a long time the author eluded his pursuers, but in the 1980s he supplied a few tantalizing autobiographical facts in the introductory essays he wrote for his *Slow Learner* collection and for the 1983 Penguin reprint of *Been Down So Long It Looks Like Up to Me*, the 1966 novel by his Cornell classmate Richard Fariña.

In 1996, Nancy Jo Sales, writing for the magazine *New York*, traced Pynchon to the Manhattan apartment he shared with his wife, Melanie Jackson (also his agent), and their son. The following year a photograph taken by James Bone appeared in the London *Times Magazine*, and a camera crew from CNN taped Pynchon walking down a street. In these instances, Pynchon fought unsuccessfully to suppress publication or broadcast of his likeness.

Nevertheless, Pynchon sometimes emerges in public. In 2004, for example, he voiced animated depictions of himself for *The Simpsons*. In season fifteen, he appears in episode ten, "Diatribe of a Mad Housewife," which aired 25 January, and in season sixteen, he appears in episode two, "All's Fair in Oven War," which aired 14 November.

Work

Before his novels began to come out, Pynchon published a handful of short stories: "The Small Rain" (1959), "Mortality and Mercy in Vienna" (1959), "Low-lands" (1960), "Entropy" (1960), and "Under the Rose" (1961—an early version of chapter 3 of *V.*). With the exception of "Mortality and Mercy," these stories appear in the 1984 collection *Slow Learner*, which also includes "The Secret Integration," originally published in 1964. Two magazine publications, "The World (This One), The Flesh (Mrs. Oedipa Maas), and The Testament of Pierce Inverarity" (1965) and "The Shrink Flips" (1966), are excerpts from *The Crying of Lot 49*. "A Journey into the Mind of Watts," an essay on the aftermath of the notorious 1965 riots, appeared in *The New York Times Magazine* (1966). Pynchon also published some pieces in the *New York Times Book Review*, including a 1984 meditation on distrust of technology ("Is It O.K. to Be a Luddite?"), a 1988 review of Gabriel García Márquez's *Love in the Time of Cholera*, and a 1993 sketch, "Nearer, My Couch, to Thee," on the sin of sloth (included in the essay collection *Deadly Sins*, by various hands). He penned introductions to a posthumous collection of writings by Donald Barthelme, *The Teachings of Don B.* (1992), and to a reissue of Jim Dodge's 1990 novel *Stone Junction* (1998). Pynchon also wrote liner notes for the albums *Spiked! The Music of Spike Jones* (1994) and *Nobody's Cool*, by the rock group Lotion (1995).

The quest figures prominently in Pynchon's novels—five of them prove to be modern-dress versions of the search for some grail to revive the contemporary wasteland. Pynchon's characters seek knowledge that will make sense of their unanchored lives and their fragmented times; the author hints that questing has a value irrespective of the authenticity of that for which one quests. The quest lends purpose to life, enabling the hapless individual to function, to see the cradle-to-grave journey as worthwhile. At the same time, however, Pynchon invites his more privileged reader to recognize that the ordering principle thus projected is factitious. What is real is the gathering dissolution, the passing of human beings and whole civilizations. Only psychological appetite grounds our attempts to discover or create order and system.

Even so, over the course of Pynchon's career, one notes what may be a tendency to define some grail of his own, an inclination to search for a way out of the cul-de-sac of a metaphysics perhaps unduly in thrall to the principle of entropy (broadly defined as the gradual deterioriation of the universe caused by irreversible thermodynamic equalization). Pynchon's critics disagree sharply on this point. Some maintain that the intimation of counter-entropic orders in *The Crying of Lot 49* and *Gravity's Rainbow* is merely a hook by which to catch the unwary reader, a means of seducing her or him into system making as delusive as that of Herbert Stencil, Oedipa Maas, Tyrone Slothrop, et al. Other critics, unwilling to believe that Pynchon's frequently noted affinity with modern science is frozen at a point attained some time in the 1950s, suspect that he means to hint at transcendent alternatives implicit in the vast mysteries of contemporary astronomy, particle physics, and the genome—not to mention the coming together of "artificial intelligence, molecular biology and robotics" about which he speculates in "Is It O.K. to Be a Luddite?"[3]

Regardless of whether Pynchon is on a grail quest of his own (with, presumably, the spiritual leanings that would foster such an enterprise), he continues to create dark, intricate labyrinths in which the spores of paranoia thrive and grow into religion-like theories of conspiracy. Paranoia is, in fact, the conviction that mighty conspiracies exist, that all things are connected "in spheres joyful or threatening about the central pulse of [one]self" (*L49* 129). Pynchon's protagonists come to believe in this infinite reticulation of conspiracy because it is preferable to the possibility that "nothing is connected to anything" (*GR* 434). Pynchon's readers, by the same token, encounter fictive structures that formally imitate the paranoid premise: all is connected in great, seamless webs of interdependent detail.

The dialectic between order and disorder is the dialectic between art and life, and it is with reference to this neglected commonplace that one should analyze Pynchon's artifice. In art, traditionally, humanity lays claim—sometimes piously, sometimes impiously—to the divine prerogative of creation, the establishment of order where all before was without form and void. Pynchon gives evidence, since the almost nihilistic *V.*, of a fascination with the religious belief that there are "orders behind the visible" (*GR* 188), orders analogous to those found beneath the surface in works of art ostensibly reflecting life in all its chaotic aspects. *Gravity's Rainbow*, for example, strikes one at first as a complete mishmash, a welter of all-too-lifelike confusion, but one subsequently discovers it to be as finely crafted as a Bach fugue or a Fabergé egg. Perhaps Pynchon can best be imagined in the company of such literary predecessors as William Blake, William Butler Yeats, and D. H. Lawrence—visionaries who counter the smugness and complacency of a scientific age with a calculated antirationalism.

These remarks adumbrate the last major thematic pairing in Pynchon's work—science and art. Pynchon knows and makes artistic use of science. He has, if nothing else, dispatched legions of humanists in search of information about modern physics, chemistry, engineering, cartography, and mineralogy—disciplines to which they might not otherwise gravitate. As suggested above, however, science serves vision, not the other way around. Pynchon's work does more than that of any other writer—scientific or literary—to reverse the widening "dissociation of sensibility" that T. S. Eliot identified as a part of the intellectual landscape since the seventeenth century. In Pynchon, and in his readers to a remarkable extent, C. P. Snow's "two cultures" become one again.

In what follows, I will briefly describe Pynchon's major works. The remarks here will be expanded on in later chapters.

V.

Readers of Pynchon's first novel, *V.*, encounter an annunciation of what has become a career-long engagement with history and its fictions. The author, only twenty-six when this novel saw print, brilliantly interweaves two narratives, one in a contemporaneous setting (mid-1950s), the other in the period from 1880 to 1943. The historical narrative, presented obliquely, concerns a mysterious woman who appears originally as Victoria Wren and subsequently under noms de guerre—now Veronica Manganese, now Vera Meroving, now simply V.—who turns up whenever there is bloodshed in the course of the twentieth century. In 1898, for example, she appears at the periphery of the Fashoda crisis in Egypt, where the spies of several nations engage in what Pynchon calls "premilitary activity" (*V.* 53), vying with one another for imperial advantage. This activity continues the following year in Florence. Again, V.—still Victoria Wren—is there, hovering at the edge of an especially violent street action. In 1913, she is in Paris, involved in a bloody theater riot which, like the crises in Egypt and Florence earlier, proves an earnest of World War I—a kind of fulfillment for V. in her early phase. When World War I ends with Western civilization intact, though permanently altered, V. begins to be involved with those elements that will figure in the more satisfying carnage of the century's more comprehensive climacteric, World War II. In 1922, she finds herself in German-colonized southwest Africa, where the decimation of the native Hereros reenacts the even greater massacre of two decades earlier and anticipates the genocide in Europe between 1933 and 1945. On and off after 1918, she is on Malta, consorting with a group sympathetic to Mussolini and his fascists. V. dies in an air raid on Malta in 1943 just as the tide turns against the fascist cause with which she has become increasingly identified.

V.'s affinity with fascism complements a decadent religiosity, and she comes to personify the drift to extinction of Western culture and of life itself. She gradually loses parts of her body and becomes more and more the sum of her prostheses: false eye, false hair, false foot, false navel. She is a brilliant metaphor for entropy and the decline of civilization, and her baleful influence, projected into the novel's present, reveals itself in the decadence of the contemporary characters, most of whom are part of a group called the Whole Sick Crew. The Crew is exemplified by its newest member, the winsome schlemiel Benny Profane. Profane is incapable of love and emotional involvement; he is also perennially at war with inanimate objects. His dread of the inanimate suggests that he intuits the cultural situation as the century wanes. Though he is no thinker, he realizes that he and his fellows are Eliot's hollow men, on the way to their whimpering end. His inability to love is presented in comic terms — though fat, he is doted on by various desirable women, including the Maltese Paola Maijstral and the beautiful Rachel Owlglass. The failure is that of his entire circle, for though there is much sex among the Whole Sick Crew, there is no commitment, no love, no hope. The one baby generated by all the sexual freedom is aborted.

The Whole Sick Crew is what Western civilization has become as a result of entropic processes that are utterly random and mindless. The meaninglessness of entropy is something difficult for the human mind to accept, however, and in Herbert Stencil, a marginal member of the Crew, Pynchon presents what becomes his standard character, a person who must discover conspiracy to deal with the fragmentation of life and culture. It is Stencil who does the mythmaking, the elevating of Victoria Wren from twisted adventuress to something as awesome and as multi-faceted as Robert Graves's White Goddess. Nor is Stencil alone, for the undeniable desire for connectedness is quintessentially human. It is also shared by the sophisticated reader, who, seeking to solve the literary puzzle, becomes *another* Stencil, a quester for meaning in the convoluted plot of *V.* and in the identity of the mysterious personage who gives the novel its name. Pynchon's genius manifests itself in his ability to keep his readers suspended between his two mutually exclusive alternatives: that the clues to V.'s identity are the key to meaning, and that V. is nothing more than a paranoid fantasy, the product of a mind that cannot deal with very much reality.

The fascination with which readers have responded to V. indicates that Pynchon is himself a brilliant mythmaker. Even after one has "solved" the mystery of V. and arrived at an enlightenment that Stencil explicitly rejects as a threat to his emotional and mental stability, one still finds the myth trenchant, moving, even terrifying. The decline of the West is not a new theme, but never has one encountered it so cogently as in this woman who loves death and the inanimate. The real conspiracy, then, is an artistic one; the connectedness is that of the novel, the cabal between author and reader.

The Crying of Lot 49

Pynchon's second novel, *The Crying of Lot 49*, seems slight compared to *V.* and *Gravity's Rainbow*, and Pynchon himself seems to consider it something of a potboiler. Many readers, however, regard it as highly accomplished. It is the story of Oedipa Maas, who is named "executor, or she supposed executrix" (9) of the estate of an ex-lover, the millionaire Pierce Inverarity. In carrying out her duties, she stumbles upon evidence of a conspiracy to circumvent the United States Postal Service. She discovers Tristero, a sub-rosa postal system at war for centuries with all officially sanctioned mail services, first in the Old World, then in the New. Tristero (or Trystero) subsumes an extraordinary number of revolutionary or simply alienated groups. In its New World phase, it seems to bring together all those within the American system who are disfranchised, disaffected, or disinherited—all those defrauded of the American Dream.

Oedipa, like Herbert Stencil, finds that the harder she looks, the more connections to Tristero she discovers, until the connections start revealing themselves in such number and variety that she begins to doubt her sanity. Oedipa's mental condition, in fact, becomes the book's central conundrum. She first confronts the question in a flashback early in the story. She recalls visiting a Mexico City exhibition with Pierce Inverarity and seeing a Remedios Varo painting in which a group of young women, immured "in the top room of a circular tower," embroider a vast tapestry, *el Manto Terrestre*, that "spilled out the slit windows and into a void, seeking hopelessly to fill the void: for all the other buildings and creatures, all the waves, ships and forests of the earth were contained in this tapestry, and the tapestry was the world" (21). That last phrase echoes similar language in Genesis ("and God saw that it was good"), for Oedipa seems to recognize in Varo's painting a parable of cognition grafted onto a surrealist creation myth. Oedipa understands Varo's intimation: imprisoned mentally and perceptually in the tower of individual consciousness, every human being makes the world from moment to moment. External reality, in other words, may be nothing more than what one weaves or embroiders in one's cranial tower. Oedipa weeps at human isolation. Later, tracking down the clues to Tristero (which seems coextensive with Inverarity's estate and enterprises), she cannot free herself from the suspicion that the proliferating connections she is discovering all have their throbbing ganglion in her own mind. She recognizes in herself the classic symptoms of paranoia.

Though Pynchon does not resolve the question of Oedipa's sanity, he hints that becoming sensitized to the problems of twentieth-century American culture (and to the horrors of the spiritual void contingent on certain twentieth-century habits of mind) involves a necessary sacrifice of sanity or at least serenity. At the end, Oedipa is faced with a harrowing choice: either she is insane, or Tristero—with its stupendous reticulation—really exists. When Oedipa attempts to rephrase the dilemma, she finds that the paranoia is somehow inescapable: "[T]here either was some Tristero beyond the appearance of the legacy America, or there was just America and if there was just America then it seemed the only way she could continue, and manage to be at all relevant to it, was as an alien, unfurrowed, assumed full circle into some paranoia" (182). Pynchon implies that Tristero, whatever its status as literal reality, is in effect a necessary fiction, a metaphor for the idea of an alternative to a closed system.

Oedipa's experiences are almost certainly an imaginative version of Pynchon's own. At the time of the novel, 1964, Oedipa is twenty-eight years old—Pynchon was twenty-seven in that year. Like Pynchon, she has attended Cornell and then gravitated to the West Coast. Like Pynchon, too, she comes to view herself as an "alien," unable blithely to embrace the perquisites of her race and class. Thus one can read the novel as Pynchon's account of why he went—and stayed—underground. He has made common cause with America's disadvantaged; in all of his fiction, not to mention his article "A Journey into the Mind of Watts," one notes an obvious sympathy with minorities and something like loathing for the mechanisms of corporate greed responsible for the spoilage of the American landscape, both literal and psychic. One can, in other words, read *The Crying of Lot 49* as spiritual autobiography—in the same tradition as St. Augustine's *Confessions* (397–401 CE) and William Wordsworth's *The Prelude* (1850).

These speculations—the need for an alternative to a closed system, the hints of spiritual autobiography—are supported by Edward Mendelson's brilliant essay "The Sacred, the Profane, and *The Crying of*

Lot 49" (reprinted in Mendelson's *Pynchon: A Collection of Critical Essays*, 1978).[4] Pointing out the high density of language with religious conno-tations, Mendelson argues that what Oedipa really searches for—and with her, twentieth-century humankind—is a new species of revelation, a way out of the agnostic, positivistic cul-de-sac of contemporary rational-ism. He also provides an explanation of the novel's odd title. "Lot 49" is a group of stamps—Tristero forgeries—to be sold as part of the settle-ment of Pierce Inverarity's estate. The novel ends as lot 49 is about to be "cried" or auctioned. Oedipa, present at the auction, expects to con-front some representative of the mysterious Tristero, who will attempt to acquire the evidence of the secret organization's existence. Mendelson suggests that the number forty-nine refers obliquely to the forty-nine-day period between Easter and the descent of the Holy Spirit at Pentecost; the revelation that awaits Oedipa at the crying of lot 49 is symbolically the revelation awaited by the modern world, which so tragically lacks a numinous dimension. Thus Pynchon ends his narrative on a note of expectation, a yearning for some restoration of mystery, some answer to what the narrator calls "the exitlessness, the absence of surprise to life" (170).

Gravity's Rainbow

Pynchon's books teem with bizarre characters and incidents, none more so than *Gravity's Rainbow*. The central character is Lieutenant Tyrone Slothrop, attached to an Allied intelligence unit in World War II London. A Yank Casanova, Slothrop maintains a map of his sexual conquests (or his sexual fantasies; this is kept ambiguous). The pins on the map coin-cide with—indeed, anticipate—the distribution of German V-2 rockets falling on the British capital. A Slothrop erection, that is, *precedes* the arrival of each rocket. This apparent suspension of the principles of causality compounds the terror one experiences in reflecting that a V-2, traveling faster than the speed of sound, is heard falling *after* it has ex-ploded. Pynchon thus dramatizes the clash of two scientific paradigms. The older science, still seldom questioned, models a mechanistic uni-verse that operates according to the laws of cause and effect. The new science, derived from the physics of Werner Heisenberg, Niels Bohr, and

Max Planck, grapples with a universe in which physical phenomena can be plotted and predicted only in terms of uncertainty and probability.

The character associated with the older, Newtonian world view is the sinister Dr. Pointsman, a die-hard Pavlovian who cannot abandon the dream of establishing a mechanical model of the mind and its workings. The character who embraces the more up-to-date world view is the sympathetic Roger Mexico, a statistician. Between these two, poor Slothrop—a kind of Everyman—tries to stay alive and, if possible, free. Pointsman and his minions concoct an experiment with Slothrop; they will provide him with the best information they have on the German rocket and then observe him closely for further revelations. Slothrop, an unwilling pawn, goes AWOL to embark on a private quest to discover the truth of his personal destiny—and perhaps the destiny of his age as well.

Pynchon picks his historical moment carefully, for World War II saw technology's coming of age. Promising humanity complete control of its environment and its destiny, technology offers something very like transcendence—or it offers annihilation. Pynchon's novel is a meditation on the choice, which he conceptualizes as a kind of rocket teleology. Will the rocket enable humanity to go to the stars—or to destroy itself? The answer has been taking shape since the German rocket engineers were sent east and west after World War II, and Pynchon concludes his great narrative with the split second before the ultimate cataclysm: the apocalyptic rocket plunges toward the "theatre" in which the film *Gravity's Rainbow* has unreeled before the reader. Critical opinion is split on the degree of bleakness in this ending. Figuratively, says Pynchon, the world is separated from its end only by "the last delta-t" (760), the last infinitesimal unit of time and space between the rocket and its target. The delta-t, however, is a relative unit of measure. Modern human folly has indeed set in motion the process of destruction, but the process might still be arrested by a reordering of priorities, human and technological.

As for Slothrop, he simply fades away, becomes "scattered" (738), and the word reveals a characteristic aspect of Pynchon's genius. Just as Joyce forced religious and liturgical language to serve his aesthetic ends, Pynchon forces technological language to serve humanistic and spiritual ends. "Scattering," a term from particle physics, refers to the dispersal of a beam of radiation, but it also evokes *sparagmos*, the ritual dismember-ment and dispersal of the divine scapegoat. Slothrop has been associ-ated all along with Orpheus, whose dismemberment became the basis of one of the many fertility cults in the Mediterranean and Near East. In a sense, Slothrop dies for the sins of the modern world, and his scat-tering coincides with the founding of the Counterforce, an anarchic group devoted to resisting or reversing the technology of violence and death. The Counterforce, which has affinities with various countercul-tural movements waxing at the moment of this novel's composition, is not particularly powerful or effective, but it offers hope for a planet hurtling toward destruction.

After *Gravity's Rainbow*, Pynchon published no new fiction for sev-enteen years. During this period, the counterculture retreated as the forces of reaction, complacency, and materialism took over, and perhaps it was this frightening and disheartening development that was behind Pynchon's long silence. He may have abandoned a book or books that came to seem unattuned to the post-1960s Zeitgeist. When the novelis-tic silence was at last broken, it was with a meditation on the historical polarization of the 1960s and the 1980s.

Vineland

In his long-awaited fourth novel, *Vineland*, Pynchon returns to the California setting of *The Crying of Lot 49*. As in *V.*, Pynchon sets up a dual historical focus. He imagines contemporary characters—in the portentous year 1984—trying to come to terms with the period, twenty years earlier, when they and the whole country underwent a searing pas-sage. Broadly, then, Pynchon here reflects on the direction the coun-try's history has taken—from anarchic but healthy hedonism to neo-Puritan repression. These poles are visible in the People's Republic of Rock and Roll, with its ethic of freedom, pleasure, dope, music, and self-expression, and in the Nixonian and Reaganite reactions that put an end to the polymorphous perversity of the 1960s and ushered in the return to materialism and political conservatism.

Vineland is structured—somewhat more loosely than readers of Pynchon's first three novels might expect—around the quest of a girl named Prairie for the mother, Frenesi Gates, who abandoned her shortly after her birth. Prairie's father, Zoyd Wheeler, still loves Frenesi, as does the man with whom she was involved before him—the sinister Brock Vond, a federal agent who had used her to infiltrate and subvert the People's Republic and other radical causes. Zoyd accepts his misery, but Vond will stop at nothing to get Frenesi back in his clutches—not even at kidnapping Prairie, who could be made into an instrument of renewed control. Also involved in the action are female ninja Darryl Louise—DL—Chastain, an old friend of Frenesi, and DL's companion, the "karmic adjuster" Takeshi Fumimota, a kind of Zen private eye.

The centrality of Prairie, Frenesi, and DL, not to mention the narrational attention to Frenesi's mother and grandmother (Sasha Traverse Gates and Eula Becker Traverse), make this novel Pynchon's first real engagement with feminism (V.—the character—merely parodies the kind of matriarchal vision associated with Robert Graves and the White Goddess; Oedipa Maas is an autobiographical conceit.) Somewhat experimental, this feminism enables the author of *Vineland* to move beyond the apocalyptic obsession that characterizes all three of his previous novels, as well as the stories "Mortality and Mercy in Vienna" and "Entropy." *Vineland* ends with a vision of familial harmony—an augury of what an America-wide family might be. Here the reader sees Prairie reunited with her mother and half-brother; nor is her father, Zoyd, left out. Brock Vond alone finds no place in the bosom of this family (his surname is derived from the Dutch word *vondeling*, a foundling—as if to hint at his fated exclusion from hearth and home). The reunion of the Traverse-Becker clans, which seem to center in their women, is Pynchon's Vonnegut-like imagining of the millennium, the era of peace and harmony that ironically succeeds the apocalyptic disruptions everywhere expected in the novel.

Herein, too, lies the significance of Pynchon's setting, the imaginary community of Vineland that provides the novel with its title. Vineland is the name given to the American continent by the Vikings, its first European visitors, circa 1000 CE. This feature of Pynchon's novel reminds American readers of the past's varied perspectives and competing narratives. Indeed, long before Columbus and long before Leif

Ericson, the fresh, green breast of the New World would have beckoned to bands of adventurers making their intrepid way across the land bridge from Asia.

Mason & Dixon

A more proximate past figures in *Mason & Dixon*. Here Pynchon ranges over the eighteenth century, with particular attention to the careers of Charles Mason and Jeremiah Dixon, who are sent by the Royal Society to the far corners of the Earth to observe the 1761 and 1769 transits of Venus. Between these two assignments they accept a commission to establish the much-contested boundary between Pennsylvania and Maryland. The central part of Pynchon's story concerns this project, which occupies his protagonists from 1763 to 1767.

The dates are important: Mason and Dixon do their work on the very eve of the American Revolution. Pynchon looks at the America they traverse for the switching points of the great railroad called history. He sees colonial America as a place where Western civilization paused one last time before following its Faustian course toward more rationalism, greater dependence on technology, and the throwing out of spiritual babies with the bathwater of magic and superstition. The religious freedom it offered notwithstanding, America has always, Pynchon suggests, been a place of struggle between the spiritual and material energies of the West. By the latter part of the eighteenth century, with the Revolution in the offing, the secularizing tendencies of the Enlightenment (notably deism) made America the half-hearted conservator, merely, of an ancient supernaturalism put to flight elsewhere in the West. Though aware that popular religion would always figure prominently in the moral economy of the emergent American nation, Pynchon suggests that some more genuine and legitimate spirituality was elbowed aside by the less-than-idealistic interests that fostered revolution (and he offers largely unflattering sketches of figures such as founding fathers Ben Franklin and George Washington). In the end, invoking the grammatical figure of contingency, Pynchon declares America only "one more hope in the realm of the Subjunctive" (543).

Pynchon seems, in *Mason & Dixon*, to reconceptualize the hallowed myth of a quest for religious freedom. Indeed, he rewrites more than one archetypal American narrative. Thus he intimates, as in *The Crying of Lot 49*, some betrayal of the original American Dream, and thus his protagonists, who twin the American Adam, must like so many of their literary predecessors decide whether to reenact the Fall. Pynchon also revisits the captivity narrative, with emphasis not on the godless savagery of the captors, but on the nefarious scheming of the Europeans they serve. When Native Americans kidnap Eliza Fields of Conestoga, they do so on behalf of evil Jesuits who seek to staff a bizarre convent-brothel called *Las Viudas de Cristo* (The Widows of Christ). Even more bizarre, perhaps, is Fields's escape with Captain Zhang, a Chinese geomancer who objects to the severely rationalistic mensuration (and cartography) of the arch-Jesuit Padre Zarpazo.

Presently joining the crew of lumberjacks, roustabouts, and hangers-on accompanying Mason and Dixon, Zhang provides an important non-Western perspective on their project. He characterizes the Visto (the unnaturally straight ten-yard-wide swath the surveyors cut through the wilderness) as a violation of the sacred Dragon in the landscape—a violation that sooner or later will spawn vast ills, "unto War and Devastation" (615). The American Civil War, a century later, would validate Zhang's prophecy.

Sir Francis Bacon, describing the Idols of the Theater, long ago recognized how received ways of knowing within a given historical period make certain kinds of thinking difficult, if not impossible. Mason, for example, aspires to membership in the Royal Society even as he desperately tries to believe that death—especially the death of his beloved wife, Rebekah—is not final. Yet the scientific calling that he shares with Dixon affords little latitude for such hope. Pynchon ingeniously imagines his protagonists as imperfectly amphibious men of their age. Each struggles to reconcile a propensity for supernatural or magical thinking with professional obligations to the new, rationalist order. Whether in South Africa, on the island of St. Helena, in America, or at the North Cape, Dixon and Mason sense that they are the inconsequential pawns of forces indifferent or hostile to them. Servants of the powerful and remote Royal Society, the surveyors suffer from a paranoia somewhat different from the usual Pynchon article—or perhaps they simply show us, belatedly, the positive side of a putative psychopathology. Pynchon hints, that is, at something admirable, even redemptive, in the paranoia of his eighteenth-century Rosencrantz and Guildenstern. Mason and Dixon resist the coercive intellectual forces of their age.

As brilliantly realized as that age is in these pages, Pynchon delights in anachronistic violations of his historical frame. At a number of points, the reader realizes that some piece of elaborately rendered eighteenth-century foolery actually mirrors a twentieth-century counterpart, for Pynchon frequently circumvents historical constraint to offer droll glimpses of what America and American culture will become. Hilarious, lightly veiled allusions to Popeye, Daffy Duck, the Jolly Green Giant, and *Star Trek* abound, not to mention numerous clever periphrases of a later vernacular. There are no cheap shots here, only the occasional "Inexpensive Salvo" (302). Characters do not get their backs up—they suffer "Thoracick Indignation" (636). Those hoping to keep costs down are reminded that "[*p*]*randium gratis non est*," i.e., there's no such thing as a free lunch (317). The reader smiles, too, at "*téton dernier*" (40), "aviating Swine" (257), "coprophagously a-grin" (427), and (of Fenderbelly Bodine exposing his buttocks to a foe) "Pygephanous" (566).

Pynchon fills his pages with the imaginative conceits his readers have come to expect. There is, for example, a wonderful talking canine, the Learned English Dog. There is also a character who, at the full moon, turns into a were-beaver. An eighteenth-century Valley Girl's every sentence features *as*, rather than the *like* that would characterize the speech of her twentieth-century sister. A chef with the punning name of Armand Allegre fends off the amorous attentions of a mechanical duck—part Daffy, part Frankenstein's monster—invented by Jacques de Vaucanson (1709–82). Such joking has its serious side: de Vaucanson's punch-card technology would be refined in the Jacquard loom and other automated weaving machines that played an important role in the Industrial Revolution, centerpiece of the Enlightenment. Subsequently, punch cards would play their role in the Age of Information.

In *Mason & Dixon*, then, Pynchon characterizes the eighteenth century as the moment in Western history when rationalism became a cultural juggernaut, crushing spiritual alternatives to Enlightenment thinking. As in *V.*, *Gravity's Rainbow*, and the 1984 essay "Is It O.K. to Be a Luddite?," the author focuses on the reification of Faustian appetite for scientific and technological advances, here symbolized in the profoundly unnatural line that, arrowing its way into the mythic American West, consecrates the New World to reason—and to its abuses.

Against the Day

In his 2006 novel *Against the Day*, Pynchon renews his engagement with history. At over one thousand pages, this longest of his works to date resists easy summarizing. Many would characterize it as Pynchon's most demanding fiction—not because they find it hard to understand (one follows the action here, however fanciful, much more readily than that of *V.* or *Gravity's Rainbow*), but because it concedes so little to the kind of propulsive plotting that keeps one turning pages in more popular novels. The reader impatient with a text so vast must understand that originality will not always present itself as entertainment—especially if a writer means to engage and reframe history in fresh and perhaps radical ways. In *Against the Day*, the author has written a kind of "secret history" of the decades in which the most powerful nations of the world competed for colonies, jockeyed for strategic position, entered into secret covenants, engaged in what Kipling called the "Great Game" of espionage, and fanned the endless brushfire conflicts in the Balkans. Pynchon's novel documents the political and cultural currents that swept Western humanity into and through its first world war, but it also suggests that twenty-first century readers might discern in that earlier era a dark mirror of their own historical moment. Hence the title, a phrase that recurs often in the King James Bible, usually with reference to the coming "day" of divine vengeance against the godless. Pynchon implies the imminence, again, of violence such as that which convulsed the world from 1914 to 1918.

One marvels, first, at *Against the Day*'s extraordinary geographical range. Pynchon undertakes to represent, in nothing less than global perspective, the historical events and imagined private experience of the years 1893–1923. He ranges all over the world, sending characters to Iceland, to the arctic, and to great tracts of "inner Asia," including Siberia and a vast region subsuming parts of China, Kazakhstan, Tajikistan, Uzbekistan, and Kyrgyzstan. He escorts readers to remote corners of the moribund Austro-Hungarian Empire and even reproduces examples of the vernaculars spoken there. He anchors these flights in interwoven narratives set in the United States (especially the West), in various parts of Mexico, and in London, Venice, Paris, Göttingen, and the other great cities of European civilization.

To shape his vast narrative, Pynchon focuses on the Traverse family, whose descendents include Frenesi and Prairie in *Vineland*. Indeed, the labor activist Jess Traverse, who so memorably declaims Emerson in the closing pages of that novel, appears as a youth in *Against the Day*, which centers its vast narrative on the lifelong travail of his parents, aunt, uncles, and grandparents. Jesse, as he is called in the later novel, is the grandson of the Adamic Webb Traverse, a miner passionately at odds, late in the nineteenth century, with the owners who employ and exploit him. Webb may or may not be the terrorist dynamiter of mining installations known as "the Kieselguhr Kid" (kieselguhr is diatomaceous earth, an ingredient of blasting powder), but his outspoken labor sympathies bring him to the attention of the loathsome Scarsdale Vibe, a tycoon contemptuous of the working classes and willing to go to any lengths to preserve plutocratic perquisites, privilege, and plunder. The ruthless Vibe, who thinks of unions as havens of anarchy and enemies of civilized order, eventually orders Traverse murdered. Webb's wife Mayva and all but one of their children, including sons Reef, Frank, and Kit, shoulder the burden of bringing violent justice to Vibe and his hired thugs. But Kit allows Vibe to pay his way to Yale, and, in an even more unsettling development, the Traverse daughter, Lake, takes up with and eventually marries Vibe's creature, the vicious Deuce Kindred. Pynchon describes not only the quest for vengeance on the part of Webb's survivors, but also their fanning out into the world, their romantic and marital connections, their shifts for survival in an increasingly complex and dangerous era, and their keeping of the faith against what Emerson called "[a]ll the tyrants and proprietors and monopolists of the world."[5] Carried along on the tide of modernity, Pynchon's characters alternately conspire with and resist forces that will presently define a new era: the American century.

The author rethinks both history and historiography here. Like Henry James or Joseph Conrad, he scrutinizes the growth of international anarchy as a means of resistance to the capitalist Leviathan. He also seeds the past with a host of fanciful and creative conceits that, however factitious, remain curiously faithful to history. Thus readers of *Against the Day* encounter time travel, theosophical cabals, Jules Verne-like vessels for traveling under desert sands in search of Shambhala (Buddhism's mythical holy city), and a band of perennially youthful aeronauts, the Chums of Chance, whose adventures and banter parody those prominent in the various boys' books that became popular in the first years of the twentieth century (the Rover Boys series began in 1899, Tom Swift in 1910, the Hardy Boys and the Ted Scott Flying Stories in 1927). The inclusion of the Chums's antics and melodramatic adventures (all realized with artful burlesque of the "Victor Appleton" or "Franklin W. Dixon" style) is typical of Pynchon's refusal, however serious his theme, to be bound by the conventions of realistic narrative. Indeed, he evidently desires to remind readers of the storytelling that, in the first decades of the twentieth century, commanded a much vaster audience than the age's critically sanctioned realism, naturalism, and emergent modernism. The mixing of styles and repudiation of decorum are hallmarks of the postmodernism that Pynchon, more than any other, has established as literary dominant in the years after World War II. With the Chums of Chance, Pynchon provides his own novelistic airship with the opposite of ballast. They represent a literal puerility that soars above terrestrial events — even as they are imagined as taking some fanciful part in them. The reader may think of the Chums as the embodiment of an innocence that the Great War and the coercions of capital can never quite destroy. The fact that they are figures of romance, however, makes its own comment on the survivability, the real-world viability, of such innocence.

The Chums have counterparts in other countries, notably the Italian "*Amici dell'Azzardo*" and the Russian "*Tovarishchi Slutchainyi.*" Such replications — doubled characters, places, events, and things — figure everywhere in this text. Pynchon recurs with particular emphasis to "the doubly-refracting calcite known as Iceland spar" (114), a crystal through which objects appear dimly twinned (one sees the effect reproduced in the image on the cover of the hardback first editions published by

Penguin and Jonathan Cape). This feature, variously reticulated, seems ultimately to reinforce Pynchon's theme of history itself doubled. *Against the Day* depicts, according to its dust jacket, "a time of unrestrained corporate greed, false religiosity, moronic fecklessness, and evil intent in high places." Readers may recognize in this era what Barbara W. Tuchmann would call a "distant mirror" of their own time. "History repeats itself," said Marx, "first as tragedy, second as farce." Pynchon suggests, to the contrary, that there is little to amuse in what appears to be the world's appalling recapitulation of the international lunacy that precipitated one world war and may yet precipitate another.

Inherent Vice

The character Lew Basnight, in *Against the Day*, appears towards the end to have become a modern private investigator. As such, he is the spiritual ancestor of Larry "Doc" Sportello, protagonist of *Inherent Vice*. The story of Doc's pursuit of an old love and her new paramour, who has — supposedly — been abducted, this novel abounds in catalogs. Pynchon lists bizarre neckties, vehicles on the freeway, places where the missing person has supposedly been seen, sixties television programs, and private eyes who are tougher and more successful than Doc. The lists also include the literally strung-out patients awaiting dubious injections from the Dr. Feelgood who occupies Doc's office building, the mess on a table in his office, and the junky possessions in Doc's lodgings. The book inventories, hilariously, "the unkempt barnyard that was Doc's brain" (267). These lists evoke a dubious idea of repletion — some darkness in the penetralia of the great national horn of abundance. For like Pynchon's other California novels, *Inherent Vice* engages the theme of America and its destiny, especially at the moment when, in the 1960s, the nation made some discoveries and some choices with which it lives to this day.

From novel to novel, Pynchon varies his villains, his depiction of the entities arrayed against those with whom he sympathizes: the "preterite" poor and oppressed. In *Lot 49*, the sprawling Inverarity estate, symbolic of the rapacious appetites of American capitalism, occasions relatively little disquiet on the part of Pierce's ex-lover. Nor does she remember

Pierce as some monster. Even Blicero, in *Gravity's Rainbow*, proves curiously hard to loathe. In *Vineland*, however, the villain becomes much
scarier: where *Lot 49*'s Pierce is likened to the awful Virgin appearing
to a peasant, Brock Vond is nothing less than the Adversary. The author seems similarly to loathe Padre Zarpazo in *Mason & Dixon*. But
in *Inherent Vice*, villainy presents itself as something like the rebar in
society's concrete. One is surprised, in what pretends to be genre fiction
(normally populated with pretty clearly delineated villains), to see such a
complex vision of evil, which discloses itself in a police assassin, in a sinister country-club godfather (a "sensitive tycoon," in the narrator's ironic
view), and in their creatures, chief among them certain veterans of the
Aryan Brotherhood. When, in the novel's climax, Doc overcomes Puck
Beaverton by slamming his head repeatedly against a marble doorsill,
one should remember the swastika tattooed on that head. From Pierce
Inverarity to Scarsdale Vibe, by the same token, each of Pynchon's novels
has its embodiment of capitalist megalomania—sometimes a collective
(the Krupp empire in *Gravity's Rainbow*, the fascists and proto-fascists
in *V.*), but more commonly some such single incarnation of rapacity
as Mickey Wolfmann or Crocker Fenway. Wolfmann, however, reveals
a conscience: experiencing "*arrepentimiento*" (249)—Spanish for moral
regret—he articulates a belated countercapitalist credo that complements Oedipa's notion of redistributing wealth at the end of *Lot 49*.
Fenway suffers no such compunction. A veritable beacon to "class hatred" (347), Fenway is the public face of the dark forces (clearly they go
beyond the actual criminal element) with which lonely Galahads such as
Doc Sportello must do battle. *Inherent Vice* reads at times like an Elmore
Leonard entertainment, but the attention to the "vortex of corroded
history" (110) is all Pynchon.

Pynchon's Historiography

So, half a century in the literary vanguard. How curious, then, that in
a 1963 letter Pynchon declared his wistful admiration for "traditional
realistic" fiction, whose practitioners produce "the only kind of novel . . .
worth a shit."[6] As will be seen, he would occasionally sound a similar note
in later years, for he would have been susceptible, learning his craft in

the 1950s and 1960s, to the James- and Forster-inspired and Leavis- and Watt-ratified gospel of the English novel's supposedly immutable foundation, after emerging out of romance narrative early in the eighteenth century, in the doctrines of realism. But he must always have known the fate of the epigone and so, like the modernists before him, devised an aesthetic of the novel attuned to transformations of the Zeitgeist. Thus Pynchon, instinctively or strategically, committed himself to representation of the postmodern real—of consciousness, of language, of civilization, of history. Obliged to forgo practices compromised by implicit deference to a steadily diminishing number of metanarratives that, perceived as valid or credible, ostensibly ground the traditional realists' understanding of phenomena, Pynchon contrived, early in his career, to make of his often hetero-historiographic narratives a kind of higher mimesis: a realism predicated on the plurality and multivalence of the reality that seems so uncomplicated when Dr. Johnson kicks a stone (that simple, local instantiation of the real) to refute what Boswell calls "the ingenious sophistry" of Bishop Berkeley.[7] To be sure, as his career has progressed, Pynchon has deepened his attention to character and to ways in which it seeds narrative. At the same time, however, he observes with sympathy and humor the many ways in which self, once merely "alienated," has come to lead an increasingly tenuous existence amid the innumerable simulacra that seem, like the Thanatoids, to want company.

Though he recognizes the relentlessness with which, as Baudrillard says, the simulacra "precess," Pynchon nonetheless resists the oft-heard assertion (it originates with Fredric Jameson) that postmodern depthlessness precludes engagement with history, makes for a temporal horizon that does not extend even to yesterday—much less the more remote reaches of the past. As one who read George Santayana's *The Last Puritan* because of the single reference in "Mortality and Mercy in Vienna," I know that Pynchon must think, occasionally, of the famous—and misguided—observation about history for which Santayana is noted ("Those who cannot remember the past" etc.), but I imagine he understands that no amount of historical awareness will preclude our repeating the mistakes of our ancestors. No, one develops a sense of history for other reasons, for it is the cultural or societal analogue of the examined life, the living of which (according to Socrates, its first advocate) leads only to a properly bracing sense of what real education, real knowledge, must be and of how truly extensive is one's ignorance. If study of the past leads to more subtle and varied storytelling (*story* being etymologically the same as *history*), so much the better for the novelist and the reader.

In the present study, I alternate chapters devoted to individual works, notably the short stories, *V.*, *Mason & Dixon*, and *Against the Day*, with chapters that treat the oeuvre more broadly: the sixties as hinge decade in the history of the twentieth century, Germany and its contributions as cultural imaginary, and—the historiographer historicized—the question of tradition and *this* individual talent. I emphasize Pynchon's acute and evolving sense of history, that great river whose upper reaches so few think about or trouble to explore. Fewer still leaven historiography with unwavering attention to the truth of the human heart (which Faulkner eloquently flagged as the literary artist's special preserve). Those who do so come to know why certain wastes and effluents (racism, rapacity, genocide, cracked religiosity) flow by the riparian villages and cities of the present. They can also better understand and appreciate what remains pure in that stream: liberty, tolerance, charity, kindness, and heroic resistance to religious, political, and economic totalitarianism. Thus I argue in the following pages for addition of an important—maybe all-encompassing—title to the various epithets by which criticism characterizes an author generally viewed as the greatest of those living and working in the United States today: more than comic genius, polymath, forger of the postmodern, or deconstructive mythographer, Thomas Pynchon merits recognition as America's greatest historical novelist.

Heat goes to cold. It's a one-way street.
Your tea will end up at room temperature.
What's happening to your tea is happening
to everything everywhere. The sun and the
stars. It'll take a while but we're all going to
end up at room temperature.

— TOM STOPPARD, *Arcadia*

CHAPTER ONE

Prospero's Apprenticeship

Slow Learner

No one would accuse Pynchon of rushing into print. After the publication of his monumental *Gravity's Rainbow* (1973), he remained silent
for a decade—except for the endorsements he occasionally contributed
to the books of other writers. His 1983 introduction to *Been Down So
Long It Looks Like Up to Me* may have marked a turning point, since it
was followed in 1984 by an important essay in the *New York Times Book
Review* ("Is It O.K. to Be a Luddite?") and by *Slow Learner,* a collection of
the author's early stories that included a witty and surprisingly candid
introduction. Here, continuing to play hide-and-seek with curious readers, the publicity-averse author offers up some intriguing hints about
his personal life, notably that he might now be a father (a false intimation, perhaps, for one has since heard only of a son, Jackson, born in
1991). He hints, too, that he has been in analysis (or so one interprets
the reference to a time before "access to my dream life" [20]). He also

discusses the writers and thinkers by whom he was influenced as a young man. He mentions Henry Adams, certain nineteenth-century scientists, Jack Kerouac and the Beats, and Norbert Wiener. For the most part, he confirms the source studies of his critics.

Pynchon comments on his stories (and, incidentally, on his 1966 novel *The Crying of Lot 49*) in a tone of bantering self-disparagement, pointing out what he now considers to be embarrassing or merely funny infelicities of style, plot, and characterization. He emphasizes that only one of the stories ("The Secret Integration") is, in his eyes, anything more than "apprentice work." Nevertheless, *Slow Learner* garnered considerable attention in the popular press, most critics cheerfully accepting the rhetorical ploy of the introduction. Only the occasional reviewer was so churlish as to quote the negative evaluations in the introduction and conclude that the stories are every bit as bad as Pynchon suggests they are. More typical were the confirmations of the respectful judgments of such earlier, scholarly critics as Joseph Slade, William Plater, and Tony Tanner, who had argued the stories' significance, their flaws notwithstanding. In both its daily and Sunday editions, the *New York Times* was especially friendly. Michael Wood, for example, noted the authorial disclaimers but insisted that "what Mr. Pynchon doesn't talk about is how extremely good the stories are for all their faults."[1] Christopher Lehmann-Haupt, similarly, says of the collection that "if it is as much of a failure as Mr. Pynchon insists, then it makes failure positively inviting."[2] Whether one should attribute these critics' generosity to the success of Pynchon's introduction ("forewarned is disarmed," admits Lehmann-Haupt) or to a collective sense that critical discourtesy might, as with J. D. Salinger, forestall the appearance of more recent and more substantive efforts (presumably the fruit of eleven years' labor), *Slow Learner* was well and respectfully received. Indeed, the collection merits critical approbation, for the five stories included teem with Pynchon's characteristic imagination and humor.

A sixth story, "Mortality and Mercy in Vienna," which was published in the Cornell University literary magazine, *Epoch*, in 1959, does not appear in the book, and one is at a loss to explain the omission. The author does not refer to it in his introduction. Though this story is arguably Pynchon's weakest, its shortcomings do not seem graver, really, than those of the stories the author does include. Vincent King has sug-

gested that Pynchon may have been distressed at critical "*perception . . .
that the story validates . . .* violence" on the part of its deranged Native
American, Irving Loon.[3] In the *Slow Learner* introduction, Pynchon notes
his youthful "pose . . . of somber glee at any idea of mass destruction"
(13), but the vision in "Mortality and Mercy" of what Joseph Slade calls
"annihilation as a response to a blighted world" may well have come
to seem irresponsible.[4] One might also speculate that Pynchon simply
felt uncomfortable about his high-handed treatment of Native American
spirituality. For the record, the story rather cleverly restages the act
of surrogacy that Angelo undertakes on behalf of Duke Vincentio in
Shakespeare's *Measure for Measure* (source of Pynchon's title). The main
character, Cleanth Siegel, arrives early at a Washington, D.C., party and
encounters in his host a double: the two men look alike. One is Marlowe,
one Kurtz, it is implied, but which is which remains obscure. Taking
over from the absconding host, Siegel presently exercises the power del-
egated to Angelo in Shakespeare's play. Angelo, one recalls, is eventually exposed as susceptible to the very vices he is supposed to extirpate.
Similarly empowered, Siegel decides against mercy and in favor of mortality for his fellow party guests, denizens of a capital as dark, in its way,
as Shakespeare's Vienna or Conrad's Congo.

Pynchon makes up for the omission of "Mortality and Mercy" by including a rarity, "The Small Rain," which appeared in the *Cornell Writer*
in 1959 and marked (discounting the juvenilia that appeared in the
Oyster Bay High School newspaper, *Purple and Gold*) the author's real
debut as fiction writer.[5] This story, which concerns an alienated soldier
who participates in the relief effort after an especially destructive hurricane, suffers a little from undergraduate pretentiousness, but it is interesting to see the writer learning to deploy motific and symbolic detail.
Pynchon introduces references to *The Waste Land*, the Bible, the Book
of Common Prayer, and, somewhat obliquely, *A Farewell to Arms*. His
protagonist, Nathan Levine, ranks among the alienated, deracinated,
and spiritually dead characters who stalk through the fiction of midcentury. To heighten the bleakness of his vision of the wasteland, Pynchon
weaves in a thematic thread of sexual sterility. More than once he characterizes Levine as a "plowboy" (ancestor, perhaps, of "Old Squalidozzi,
ploughman of the deep," in *Gravity's Rainbow* [447]) but never allows

him to rise above the more trivial or vulgar meanings of an epithet that potentially links him to the earth and its mythic cycles of death and re-birth. Instead, the story closes with Levine copulating woodenly, like "the young man carbuncular" in *The Waste Land*. Aware that photographers from *Life* magazine have covered the hurricane and its aftermath, he produces a sardonic postcoital pun on the familiar prayer-book phrase for "The Burial of the Dead": "In the midst of *Life*. We are in death" (50). One of his fellow soldiers likens him to the seed that, in Christ's parable of the sower, falls on stony ground. He will, in other words, share in no vernal efflorescence; like the rest of his generation, he resists resurrection.

The Waste Land also makes its presence felt in the second story in the collection, "Low-lands," in which Pynchon continues to present images of cultural vitiation. Dennis Flange, the main character, has reached af-fluent middle age, with an expensive house, a thousand-dollar stereo, Mondrians in the belvedere, and a psychiatrist. Thrown out by his un-sympathetic wife, Flange retreats with some disreputable companions to a surreal garbage dump, a Sargasso Sea in which the detritus of a civilization comes at last to rest (one recalls the junk sculpture Pynchon reflects on in his 1966 article "A Journey into the Mind of Watts" or, in *Gravity's Rainbow*, "the garbage trucks . . . all heading north toward the Ventura Freeway, a catharsis of dumpsters, all hues, shapes and batter-ings" [757]).[6] Yet the distinction between a materialist culture and its castoffs proves unstable: full of refrigerators, tires, mattresses, washing machines, and other dead things, the dump effectively mocks American material bounty. Beneath it, in interlacing tunnels built by anarchists in the 1930s, dwells a shadowy group of outsiders, an alternative society undreamed of by the well-adjusted personnel back at Flange's law firm. Here Pynchon experiments with the idea that would eventually become *The Crying of Lot 49*: that of surface and subsurface social realities in America, not to mention the waste that generates discomfort among those doubting the American myth of plenty (and one notes, in passing, how Pynchon anticipates the garbage theme that would exercise Don DeLillo and others later in the century).

"Low-lands" ends with a dream sequence in which Flange encoun-ters a gypsy named Nerissa, a descendent, perhaps, of the "fairy-child" who haunts Sinclair Lewis's Babbitt. A fantasy of female complaisance, Nerissa is associated with all the projections of Dennis's anima: wife, mother, the sea (with which Flange, a navy veteran, has a mystical affinity). Only three and a half feet tall, she is also the child he regrets never having had. But finally she holds a kind of mirror up to Flange's puerility—which, Pynchon wryly concedes, may reflect his own immaturity at the time the story was written.

He takes a more sanguine view of the collection's penultimate story. "Under the Rose," which appears in altered form as chapter 3 of *V.*, is a spy yarn set in the Egypt of 1898, a time when British and German operatives sought to outmaneuver each other as the Great War loomed on the international horizon.[7] The British spies must try to keep hostilities from breaking out between their nation and France as a result of the crisis caused by an encounter between French and British armies at Fashoda, a remote outpost on the Nile. The German spies act as agents provocateurs, hoping to bring off an assassination that will start a war disastrous to their chief European rivals. The British spies prevail, though their leader is killed, and the story ends with a glimpse of his surviving colleague in the crowds at Sarajevo in 1914, hoping once again to forestall apocalypse. In the novel version, Pynchon dispenses with this striking detail, perhaps feeling that it lays too much emphasis on a single war, rather than on a whole century of conflict.

Pynchon admits to finding this story less objectionable than the earlier ones included in *Slow Learner*, and indeed it is masterfully constructed. The local color—cribbed from an 1899 edition of Baedeker's guide to Egypt—is nicely handled, and the allusions, unlike those in "The Small Rain" and its immediate successors, add depth and nuance rather than pretentiousness (a pattern of allusions to Puccini's *Manon Lescaut* highlights the English spymaster's inner struggle with the ethics of his profession). Looking back, the mature author claims to have intended his heroes as authentic Englishmen—he is therefore embarrassed at their clichéd "pip-pip, Old Chap" banter. But the miscalculations of a writer such as Pynchon often prove serendipitous: his stage Englishmen provide a delightful variety of "carry on spying" humor which heightens rather than undercuts the serious theme of Armageddon in the making.

The reader impressed by Pynchon's meditation on the paradoxes of purity and impurity among spies will find even more impressive the related inquiry into innocence and experience in "The Secret Integration," in which winsome kids resist the racism of their parents and their community by small gestures of defiance, notably the adoption of an imaginary black playmate. Throughout, Pynchon artfully minimizes adult perspectives. A coming-of-age story, "The Secret Integration" evokes the clandestine world of preadolescent children with great brilliance and with a comic resourcefulness that recalls some of Frank Conroy's stories. Pynchon's humor, sometimes disparaged as puerile, proves effective in the depiction of literal puerility. Especially deft in Pynchon's handling of the theme here is the gradual modulation from comic and infantile rebellion (sodium bombs in the toilet and such) to the perhaps fatalistic expression of a more substantive resistance within a culture ensnared in racism.

As the author reveals the gulf between the decency of the children and the moral failings of the adults, the narrative takes on a fine, sad, elegiac quality. One might wish for some clearer indication of the actual scope of the adult world's complexity, but Pynchon knows better than to tell readers what they already know. Though the story closes with the hint that these children have begun to acquire knowledge, it defers recognition that they must also fall—become as capable of error, as passionately wrong, on occasion, as their benighted parents. In the nuanced treatment of childhood innocence encountering a corrupt adult world, in any event, Pynchon delivers, as he himself realizes, one of his most accomplished pieces of short fiction.

"Entropy" and the Two Cultures

Also accomplished is the 1960 short story "Entropy," though Pynchon claims to see shortcomings that cause him no small "bleakness of heart" (*SL* 12). The author's diffidence notwithstanding, "Entropy" may strike less captious readers as one of the most durable of these early fictions, a small masterpiece of fluid prose and structural economy. Plater calls it Pynchon's "most successful" story.[8] Pynchon may disparage it in the *Slow Learner* introduction simply to combat the critical tendency to overemphasize the theme of entropy in his work. But that tendency has given way to more subtle readings: in its range of tonalities (including tonalities of humor), moreover, the story augurs some profound changes in literary fashion. Written, as it were, in the looming shadows of Eliot, Hemingway, Nathanael West, and Henry Adams, it germinates a new aesthetic.

In "Entropy" Pynchon seems to invite a scientific analysis of the kind provided by critics like Joseph W. Slade and Anne Mangel. But treatments of the story such as theirs neglect an essential point. Pynchon's theme may be entropy, but he does not make a story of it by recourse to the kind of molecules-in-a-heat-engine examples favored, as Slade points out, by Sir William Dampier and other science historians.[9] Like any other storyteller, he realizes his theme through plot and character. Only a few literati, however, so deftly realize a thematic vision through reference to both science and art. I do not mean to suggest that his early critics were unaware of this allusive breadth—Slade, in particular, discusses the story with admirable catholicity, and Tony Tanner observes that Pynchon, "more . . . than any other living writer," deploys "literary reference" and "intertextuality."[10] Still, they do not always see as clearly as they might that the illustrations from music, art, and literature here greatly outnumber those from science. Thus one has at least a quantitative argument that "Entropy"—once brought forward as another datum in the case for Pynchon's being (by implication) an engineer or physicist who also writes—actually makes a case for Pynchon's being predominantly an artist who happens to take, like John Donne or Percy Bysshe Shelley or Richard Powers, a certain amount of interest in the physical sciences.

One can easily enough mark the essential scientific points. The story demonstrates what one of its characters describes as the spontaneous drift "toward the Condition of the More Probable" (*SL* 87). Set on contiguous floors of an apartment building, "Entropy" unfolds as twinned, complementary narratives. In one of these a man named Callisto has made of his apartment a perfectly balanced ecological system, a hermetically sealed hothouse full of plants and birds that he and his companion, Aubade, never leave. From here they watch the gradual disappearance of fluctuations in the thermometer outside, which has remained at thirty-seven degrees Fahrenheit, as the story begins, for three days running. Musing on entropy, the progressive dissipation of heat energy, Callisto sees the uniformity of the temperature as an augury of the "cosmic heat-death" (87). He also perpends a cultural analogy: Western society, and especially postwar America, suffers its own version of entropy (again, an anticipation of the theme of *The Crying of Lot 49*). Meanwhile, in the apartment below Callisto's, an increasingly chaotic "lease-breaking party" also heads into its third day. The cumulative breakdown of order in the wild party provides a comic illustration of entropy taking its course.

The story ends with an ironic reversal. The downstairs host, Meatball Mulligan, resolves to set about restoring order — thereby reversing entropy in his immediate sphere. Upstairs, simultaneously, Callisto fails in an attempt at literal heat exchange. He has been trying to heal a sick bird by sharing with it the warmth of his own body, and when it dies he concludes that heat-transfer is no longer possible (ironically, he may have hastened its death, unaware that a bird's body temperature is higher than that of a human).[11] Callisto's companion underscores the implied ecological dissolution by breaking a window of their hothouse. In contrast, Meatball, downstairs, handles snowballing disorder with commonsensical resourcefulness. Though there is a sense in which increased order in one place (the party) must be compensated for by increased disorder elsewhere (upstairs), Pynchon seems to be exposing the folly of an obsession with entropy — the very obsession with which he has implicitly been charged. He shows, rather, that Callisto is irrational in his rationality.

Callisto's bleak social prognostication initially seems justified by the wild party going on in the apartment directly below his. Replete with drink, drugs, fights, and broken appliances (not to mention marriages), the party is gradually deteriorating into pure anarchy and randomness. During a lull, the host discusses information theory with one of his guests. Anne Mangel, who notes the correlations between this story and *The Crying of Lot 49* (in which John Nefastis tries to explain both "thermodynamic and informational" [109] entropy to a confused Oedipa Maas), observes that their conversation is itself an illustration of the "noise, redundancy, disorganization, and entropy" of most spoken messages.[12]

This conversation, and one paragraph in which Callisto recalls his undergraduate days, when he learned about thermodynamic entropy studying Gibbs, Clausius, and Boltzmann, comprises, really, all of Pynchon's technical demands on his reader. The bulk of the story's allusions reveal that nontechnical versions of the entropy theme recur continually in the arts, especially in the twentieth century. Outweighing the three scientific names are allusions to *Le Douanier* Rousseau, Mozart, Mussorgsky, Stravinsky, Machiavelli, de Sade, Faulkner, Djuna Barnes, and Henry Miller—as well as a number of famous jazz musicians. Callisto himself seeks artistic parallels for the insight provided by the science of thermodynamics:

> He sought correspondences. Sade of course. And Temple Drake, gaunt and hopeless in her little park in Paris, at the end of *Sanctuary*. Final equilibrium. *Nightwood*. And the tango. Any tango, but more than any perhaps the sad sick dance in Stravinsky's *L'Histoire du Soldat*. He thought back: what had tango music been for them after the war, what meanings had he missed in all the stately coupled automatons in the *cafés-dansants*, or in the metronomes which had ticked behind the eyes of his own partners? Not even the clean constant winds of Switzerland could cure the *grippe espagnole*. Stravinsky had had it, they all had had it. And how many musicians were left after Passchendaele, after the Marne? It came down in this case to seven: violin, double bass. Clarinet, bassoon. Cornet, trombone. Tympani. Almost as if any tiny troupe of saltimbanques had set about conveying the same information as a full pit-orchestra. There was hardly a full complement left in Europe. Yet with violin and tympani Stravinsky had managed to communicate in that tango the same exhaustion, the same airlessness one saw in the slicked-down youths who were trying to imitate Vernon Castle, and in their mistresses, who simply did not care. (93)

A nice touch, those saltimbanques (with admirable indirection, they add Picasso to Callisto's mental inventory of the age). The music Callisto imagines them performing here—that of Stravinsky—seems to bracket the First World War for Pynchon. Much of the Paris chapter in *V.*—which culminates in a version of the riot caused by the premiere of *Le Sacre du Printemps* just before the war—would be a reprise of this passage: the tango, a clockwork dancer, automata, café life, cultural enervation, and a kind of proleptic Great War listlessness.

In the interest of his own artistic ends, Pynchon makes fairly free with the historical character of Stravinsky. Although the war saddened the composer (his brother died of typhus on the Romanian front), he considered himself a Russian "patriot" and was appalled by the disastrous treaty of Brest-Litovsk, by which the Bolsheviks gave up huge tracts of territory to secure peace. Far from being chastened by the costly and inconclusive battles, Stravinsky wanted the war to go on, at least in the east.[13] But in fact the *grippe espagnole* or Spanish influenza did catch up with the composer in Switzerland, as he matter-of-factly records in his *Autobiography*. An epidemic of this particularly virulent type of influenza spread through the world in 1918, killing more, even, than the war. For Pynchon, however, as for Katherine Anne Porter in "Pale Horse, Pale Rider," the Spanish influenza becomes the emblem of a culture-wide spiritual disease, a weltschmerz anchored in the revulsion Europe felt after the horrible spectacle of the war.

Pynchon does not refer to the text of *L'Histoire du Soldat*, but it complements his theme in at least one important point. The eminent music historian William W. Austin locates the "moral" of Stravinsky's fable in the words: "You must not wish to add to what you have what you used to have. You cannot be at once what you are and what you used to be. You must learn to choose. There is no right to have everything; it is forbidden."[14] The formulation sounds rather like Callisto's "mnemonic . . . for remembering the Laws of Thermodynamics: you can't win, things are going to get worse before they get better, who says they're going to get better" (87). Callisto's view of the music is not, however, completely in line with either critical opinion or the historical record. The small orchestra, for example, was dictated by the exigencies of expense and mobility, not the paucity of musical survivors of the war. Stravinsky ingeniously made the ensemble a perfect miniature orchestra by using one bass and one treble instrument from each of the orchestral choirs, plus percussion. One musicologist seems to share Callisto's disgust with the Vernon Castle set: for Richard Anthony Leonard, the composition "satirizes the common music of the dance halls and the vaudeville shows."[15] Austin concedes that the tunes in *Soldat* are "bitterly ironic" and deliberately marked by "an international vulgarity" but maintains that the composition comes to be "transfigured by a spirit that seems . . . more and more compassionate and affirmative."[16]

As Callisto thinks of music, Aubade, his strange mistress, thinks *in* music. Engaged in a unique personal battle against a kind of sound-entropy, Aubade maintains her own mental equilibrium only by a continual transformation of her world into musical metaphor. Realizing this conceit, Pynchon anticipates by many years Michel Serres's aural figurations of the great discordant formlessness that the mind struggles to apprehend. In his 1982 work *Genesis*, Serres grapples with the primal chaos out of which differentiation emerges, the chaos that constantly threatens to swamp apperception. This chaos of "background noise" or "white noise" is precisely what Pynchon's Aubade struggles to integrate and subdue.[17] She receives sensory impressions — sight, smell, touch, taste — as sound, and the "noise" threatens to overpower the "music." The things that make music for her — flowers, wine, lovemaking — cannot really contend with all the nerve-fraying noise she must put up with, so she is constantly in danger of sonic dementia, descent into a chaos of mental noise. Pynchon provides Aubade's every gesture and every sensory impression with either a noise metaphor or a music metaphor; thus, stroking a young mimosa tree, she hears

> a motif of sap-rising, the rough and unresolved anticipatory theme of those fragile pink blossoms which, it is said, insure fertility. That music rose in a tangled tracery: arabesques of order competing fugally with the improvised discords of the party downstairs, which peaked sometimes in cusps and ogees of noise. That precious signal-to-noise ratio, whose delicate balance required every calorie of her strength, see-sawed inside the small tenuous skull . . . (92)

One sees Pynchon's attention to detail in the way he sidesteps a stale expression: Aubade summons "every calorie of her strength," rather than every ounce. The cliché avoided, he renovates the phrase with a word dictated by an aspect of the story's subject — the expenditure of heat.

When Callisto dictates his journal to her, she has difficulty fitting his words into the many other sounds around her that demand integration into personal music:

> Counterpointed against his words the girl heard the chatter of birds and fitful car honkings scattered along the wet morning and Earl Bostic's alto rising in occasional wild peaks through the floor. The architectonic purity of her world was constantly threatened by such hints of anarchy: gaps and excrescences and skew lines, and a shifting or tilting of planes to which she had continually to readjust lest the whole structure shiver into a disarray of discrete and meaningless signals . . . [S]he crawled into dreams each night with a sense of exhaustion, and a desperate resolve never to relax that vigilance. Even in the brief periods when Callisto made love to her, soaring above the bowing of taut nerves in haphazard double-stops would be the one singing string of her determination. (88)

The concluding figure here revises Rilke's image of lovers as adjacent strings on a violin: "Whatever touches you and me / Blends us together just as a bow's stroke / From two strings draws *one* voice."[18] Whether or not he intends the deconstructive echo of Rilke (a major presence in *Gravity's Rainbow* and briefly invoked in the foreword Pynchon wrote for a reissue of Orwell's *1984*), the author of "Entropy" admirably stages recognition of a shocking physiological immediacy lurking just beneath the surface of prose one might dismiss as romance novel impressionism. The word "soaring," which seems to have opposing syntactic relationships with the two halves of the sentence, is a fine example of what rhetoricians call syllepsis (an expression in which one word pretends to double duty). Here the word seems at first to refer to the superincumbency of the lover; then one sees that it refers to the preeminence of the woman's determination never to let noise smother music in the impressions crowding in on her. This determination—being a single string—cannot be double-stopped (the term refers to bowing two strings simultaneously); hence, the phrase "the bowing of taut nerves in haphazard double-stops" makes sense only if it describes Callisto's activity. To clarify the metaphor, the woman is the instrument, Callisto a sexual violinist playing double-stops with the two-stroke motion a violinist and a lover have in common.

The end of the story brings despair for Aubade and Callisto in the conclusion of what Pynchon elsewhere calls "one heart's *andante*."[19] After the heartbeat of the bird Callisto has been sheltering flutters in "a graceful diminuendo down at last into stillness" (97), Aubade breaks a window so that their resistance to fate might not be prolonged. Together they await the final "equilibrium . . . when 37 degrees Fahrenheit should prevail both inside and outside, and forever, and the hovering, curious dominant of their separate lives should resolve into a tonic of darkness and the final absence of all motion" (98). The musical imagery here (the play on "dominant" and "tonic" will recur in *Gravity's Rainbow*) characterizes the death of the bird and the consequences of the broken window less from Aubade's perspective than from that of the narrator. Favoring words like "counterpointing," "recapitulate," "harmony," "rhythm," "components," and "midrange," this narrator has in fact favored a musical and even "high fidelity" vocabulary throughout the story. Pynchon's own acts of musical metaphor making and figuration demonstrate that his linguistic resources are not strained by the requirement he has set for himself to adhere strictly to musical imagery in rendering the neurasthenia of Callisto's companion. Even before the introduction of Aubade, the strange climatic alterations of February in Washington, D.C.—false spring, snow, rain—are described as "a *stretto* passage in the year's fugue" (83). Structurally, "Entropy" is itself a fugue.

The thermo-musical finality of the end of the story, reflecting the despair of the upstairs couple, is countered, as noted before, by Meatball Mulligan's decision to resist the increasing disorder of his party. He begins to work for relative order in the midst of the larger entropic drift—which is exactly what Aubade and Callisto had done prior to giving up. But where they had created an exclusive "enclave of regularity" (83), Meatball now sets about creating something more inclusive. And where their initial withdrawal was basically selfish (not to mention slightly mad), their subsequent passivity seems, in contrast to Meatball's healthy determination not to let chaos prevail, a reprehensibly quietist posture before an inevitability they could not, in fact, live to see. The cosmic heat death will not catch up with the universe for some eons yet.

As will be seen in my final chapter, on Pynchon's place in literary history, the author started out with a keen awareness of the literary figures who reigned at midcentury—from the Hemingway and Eliot he imitates in that first published story, "The Small Rain," to the Fitzgerald he once impersonated at an undergraduate party at Cornell. Eventually he would outgrow these luminaries and invent (or at least assist at the birth of) postmodernism. From a later vantage, it is instructive to balance the modernist affinities with the pre-postmodernist departures. Indeed, the conclusion of "Entropy" shows Pynchon's affinity with and distance from a writer such as Hemingway. Their similarity is immediately evident if one compares Mucho Maas's recurring nightmare of the N.A.D.A. sign against the empty sky in *The Crying of Lot 49* to the waiter's prayer, "Our nada who art in nada," in "A Clean, Well-Lighted Place." Like Hemingway, Pynchon insists—at least in "Entropy"—on the value of the hopeless struggle against the impersonal forces of the cosmos. All things run down, including human beings and their institutions, but humans ennoble themselves by fighting off whatever manifestation of "final equilibrium" they face—by raging, as Dylan Thomas says, against the dying of the light. Aubade and Callisto join the Hemingway characters (the dying writer in "The Snows of Kilimanjaro," Ole Andreson in "The Killers") whose ends come with their ceasing to fight. Meatball Mulligan, meanwhile, is the comic analogue to Hemingway's undefeated bullfighters and marlin fishermen; he even has something besides his dignity to show for his determination, unlike so many of Hemingway's buffeted characters.

The world picture that Pynchon briefly shares with Hemingway and company is hardly unique among writers in our time. Early on, Pynchon plied—or feigned plying—the modern literary mainstream, and a story like "Entropy," which by its title and theme seems to call for a full-blown scientific explication, presents no difficulties to anyone familiar with twentieth-century literature, music, and art. Pynchon is no more abstruse here than Hardy or Wells, with their excursions into Darwinism; or T. S. Eliot, with his filiated platinum in the presence of oxygen and sulphur dioxide; or that first entropist, Flaubert, with his "*fin du monde par la cessation du calorique.*"[20] Pynchon's story is no doubt based on a scientific schema, but the texture derives from the theme's rendering in resonant, aesthetic terms: the "correspondences" (the word echoes Baudelaire, himself a brooder on decay) that both the author and his characters are at such pains to provide. A big part of what makes the story so effective lies in its understated assertion about artists: they have always known, as Pynchon says in *The Crying of Lot 49*, that "death dwell[s] in the cell though the cell be looked in on at its most quick" (129). Whatever the accuracy of Callisto's reflections on Stravinsky, Pynchon is not the only artist of his time to see in the dance of life a sad, sick tango.

In "Entropy," then, a parable about the cosmic heat death unfolds along two complementary lines: upstairs hothouse vs. chaotic conviviality downstairs. Wrongly taken as annunciation of the entropic end, the temperature's hovering at thirty-seven degrees Fahrenheit for three days offers a final insight. In the *Slow Learner* introduction, Pynchon explains that he "chose 37 degrees Fahrenheit for an equilibrium point because 37 degrees Celsius is the temperature of the human body" (13). Consciously or not, Pynchon thereby invites recognition of competing, equally valid paradigms—a recognition that would, in subsequent decades, take on greater and greater importance. From a twenty-first century vantage, by the same token, readers can discern another meaning in the story's dual diegesis: in Callisto, one sees the exhaustion, specifically, of modernism; in his downstairs neighbor, whose guests play both Mussorgsky and Earl Bostic, one sees the eclecticism and rude energy of what would presently begin to call itself postmodernism.

The happiest of women, like the happiest
nations, have no history.
—GEORGE ELIOT, *The Mill on the Floss*

CHAPTER TWO

History and Myth

Pynchon's *V.*

Editions of *V.* ought perhaps to include, as an appendix, the short story
"Under the Rose" (a more straightforward version of the novel's third
chapter, as I have noted previously). First-time readers could consult
the short story if, as seems all too likely, they find themselves at a loss
with regard to just what is going on (or supposedly going on) when
Stencil—in the novel—conjures up Egypt in 1898. Recourse to "Under
the Rose" would allow readers to dispense with the confusion often generated as the author, in *V.*, shifts historical gears for the first time, introducing Victoria Wren and her destiny through the polyhedral lenses of
eight points of view. Readers would have fewer difficulties if they could
be swiftly oriented to what Pynchon does with historical circumstance:
the confrontation of French and British detachments at Fashoda, on
the Nile, in 1898. In both texts, the author imagines that two German
agents, Lepsius and the deceptively named Bongo-Shaftsbury, plot to
assassinate the English consul in Cairo, Lord Cromer. The agents hope
that such a timely assassination, mistaken for French incendiarism, will

precipitate a war between France and England that will weaken both sides, leaving Germany a clear field to realize its own dreams of imperial expansion. Unfortunately, Cromer does not take the threat seriously enough. To make him more cautious, two British agents, Porpentine and Goodfellow, stage a mock-assassination attempt. Although the English agents succeed in foiling the German plot, Porpentine perishes. But only in the short story version does Pynchon include a last glimpse of Goodfellow, partnerless now, scanning the Sarajevo crowd on a fated June morning sixteen years later.

In chapter 3 of the novel, Victoria—or V., as she will come to be known—plays a minor role (she has a liaison with Goodfellow), and this very inconsequence will prove meaningful. But for readers not forewarned to pay careful attention to the appearances of Victoria and her avatars, a chart like the following—a record of appearances by V. under her various noms de guerre—may facilitate understanding:

TIMELINE-CHRONOLOGY: AVATARS AND CONGENERS OF V.
"Victoria was being replaced by V.; something entirely different, for which the young century had as yet no name." (410)

DATE		CHAPTER
1880	born in Lardwick-in-the-Fen, Yorkshire	
1890	sexual encounter with Ralph MacBurgess (later known as Maxwell Rowley-Bugge)	
1898	appears in Alexandria and Cairo during Fashoda crisis, affair with Goodfellow the spy (cf. "Under the Rose")	3
1899	appears in Florence during riot of Venezuelan expatriates, meets Evan and Hugh Godolphin, seduces Sidney Stencil (488)	7
1901	apparently in England, gives birth to Herbert Stencil (489, but cf. 54). Is Sidney the father?	Epilogue
1913	V. in Paris. At Mélanie's death, decamps with Sgherraccio, an Irredentist	14

1914 (ca.)	as Veronica Manganese, arrives on Malta with Sgherraccio, now a Mizzist, to wait out the war	Epilogue
1919	on Malta still, involved in pro-Italian (and proto-fascist) espionage. Evan Godolphin, mutilated, is her companion. Involved with Father Fairing, who later cracks in New York; resumes affair with Sidney Stencil, to his confusion. She has the sapphire and the eye, perhaps a false arm, desires a false foot.	Epilogue
1922	in Fiume with decadent D'Annunzio, much admired by Mussolini and the *fasci di combattimento*	9
1922	in southwest Africa as Vera Meroving; encounters and engenders the corruption—the decadence—of old Godolphin. Weissmann will turn up as an especially perverted Nazi in *Gravity's Rainbow.* (word of V.'s spending a year on Mallorca and appearing in Spain, on Crete, on Corfu, in Asia Minor, in Rotterdam, and in the Roman Campagna [388])	9
1943	qua "bad priest," on Malta again "to wait out" (387) hostilities, evidently dies during air raid, disassembled by callous children (cf. Benny Profane's dream, 39–40). How reliable is Maijstral at this moment?	11
1956	Stencil touches base on Malta, refuses to believe that his quest ends there, yo-yos off to Sweden after another lead. Crises in Hungary, Poland, Suez.	16
1963	Replete with intimations of apocalypse (461, 472, 479–80), Pynchon's novel published, as if to warn readers that presently (in 1965) they would be twenty years beyond World War II—time for another, the most destructive and final of all.	

Various possibilities for mental digestion of this chart present themselves: one can, for example, consider whether shifts in point of view
from chapter to chapter and within chapters raise questions about the
reliability of these sightings. Are some more grounded than others?
Similarly, one can consider whether the scrambling or fragmentation of
the historical sequence is to be understood as a modernist invitation to
reassemble the pieces and so recover a vision of cultural wholeness and
meaning. Readers should note that all the chapters set before 1914 seem
to depict V. in proximity to international fuses, to modify a Pynchon image, looking for the spark that will bring the Great War. The epilogue
and chapter 9 orient V. to the currents that will bring the Second World
War, "whose etiology was also her own" (387). This conflict occupies
the foreground only in chapter 11, closest in time to the novel's present
(1955-56).

One notes again Pynchon's propensity, in the fictions of his early
career, for quest plots and thematic material related to paranoid obsession. But how does such subject matter function thematically? Who
quests here? What is the object of his quest? And what is paranoia?
A quotation from *Gravity's Rainbow* is apropos: "If there is something
comforting—religious, if you want—about paranoia, there is also anti-
paranoia, where nothing is connected to anything, a condition that not
many of us can bear for long" (434). This observation often leads to an
immediate insight or at least a pregnant question or two: does not all
sanity and all civilization require a vision that, like paranoia, involves
the connecting of dots that may, after all, be random? And who con-
nects the dots? Such questions may lead one profitably to compare and
contrast the dot-connecting of science and religion with that of the historian or artist. All such connecting of dots yields meaning—but which
enterprises do so most reliably? Eigenvalue the psychodontist calls into
question the connections made by one especially important viewpoint
character:

> Cavities in the teeth occur for good reason, Eigenvalue reflected. But even
> if there are several per tooth, there's no conscious organization there
> against the life of the pulp, no conspiracy. Yet we have men like Stencil,
> who must go about grouping the world's random caries into cabals. (153)

One should not, however, take Eigenvalue's patronizing observation as definitive. Paranoia in Pynchon frequently symbolizes the process by which human beings organize knowledge, and the category "men like Stencil" includes every philosopher or theologian or scientist who undertakes imaginatively to stitch together the buzzing, blooming confusion of the phenomenal world. Stencil's little quest for V. parodies the more serious system making that, in any age, models reality.

Thus, Pynchon's readers eventually see what complicates any contemporary search for meaning—whether in history or in what Linda Hutcheon calls an "historiographic metafiction" such as this one.[1] They may also see how, as readers, they undertake a quest congruent with or parallel to that of Herbert Stencil. The twinned quests of reader and character involve the pursuit of pattern and meaning, one in a novel, the other in the text of history itself. Some readers will seize on the passages in which Stencil—through the narrator—speculates about what he may be on to: "The Big One, the century's master cabal" (226).

Stencil's very name identifies him as a pattern maker, and, indeed, he attempts to impose a pattern on the mystery of V., the woman he has read about in the journals of his father, Sidney Stencil. Central to the book, Herbert Stencil links the aimless, midcentury present and its immediate historical antecedents, whether World War II or the more generalized currents of violence that rocked the century before and after that conflict. "Born in 1901, the year Victoria died, Stencil was in time to be the century's child" (52). But born to whom, this representative of twentieth-century humanity, this witness to two world wars and the routine carnage of political struggles in forgotten corners of the earth? In the epilogue, in which point of view does not appear to be "Stencilized" (228), the author seems to identify V. as Stencil's mother. Even if one takes the epilogue as free indirect discourse grounded, still, in the projections of the younger Stencil, the suggestion regarding a baleful maternal parent seems nonetheless valid. The conceit of being mothered by some terrible idea of violence will recur in *Gravity's Rainbow*, where Roger Mexico declares, "My mother is the war" (39). Indeed, in the twentieth and twenty-first centuries, she is the mother of us all.[2]

As the book unfolds, then, Stencil's quest for V. becomes the quest of contemporary humanity to understand the violence of our times. In V.

Stencil discovers (or thinks he discovers) an embodiment of the Zeitgeist, an emblem of the age's love affair with carnage. Those who come into contact with her are presently ruined (Ralph MacBurgess), corrupted (the Goldolphins, father and son), or destroyed (the English agent Porpentine, the ballerina Mélanie, Father Fairing, "Ugo Medichevole, a minor magician" [388], and perhaps the Sidney Stencil who runs disastrously afoul of V.-shaped bad weather—a waterspout—in the Mediterranean). Through Stencil fils, Pynchon shows modern human-ity trying to give history itself a shape, a structure, a myth, a meaning. But neither meaning nor myth is more than mirage.

To provide some cross-disciplinary contextualization here, one needs to consider the way history is conceptualized in postmodern historiog-raphy—as, for example, in the work of Hayden White, author of the monumental *Metahistory* (1973), the argument of which *V.* anticipates by a decade.[3] Influenced by Northrop Frye's *Anatomy of Criticism*, White demonstrates how written history, like literature, tends to take on certain formal qualities—to be, in the work of Ranke, Michelet, Tocqueville, and Burckhardt, now comic, now tragic, now romantic, now ironic. The implications are obvious. Historians shape their material: the writing of history, like the writing of fiction, involves selection, subjectivity, "em-plotment." White distils this point in a 1986 article:

> In literature we have no difficulty thinking of a number of stories that have been *emplotted* in a variety of ways: the Faust and Oedipus legends are only the most obvious. It is more difficult to think that a given set of historical events might be variously but equally plausibly emplotted; yet this is exactly what we have to take account of when we encounter what appear to be mutually exclusive *narrative interpretations* of the same his-torical phenomenon. We are inclined to say that *certain* sets of historical events are intrinsically tragic, or comic, or epic, or farcical in nature and that, therefore, they will admit of one and only one mode of emplotment for the truthful representation of their real meaning. But real events are tragic or comic or epic or farcical only when viewed from the *perspective* of the interests of specific agents or groups involved in them. Tragic, comic, epic, and farcical are not categories *descriptive* of real events. As applied to real events, such categories are at best *interpretive*, which is to say, ways

of imputing meaning to such events by emplotting them as stories of a recognizable, but culturally specific, kind. No set of real events, even those comprising an individual life, displays the kind of formal coherency met with in what we conventionally recognize as a story. We may seek to give our lives a meaning of some specific kind by telling now one and now another kind of story about them. But this is a work of construction rather than of discovery—and so it is with groups, nations, and whole classes of people who wish to regard themselves as parts of organic entities capable of living storylike lives. Neither the reality nor the meaning of history is "out there" in the form of a story awaiting only a historian to discern its outline and identify the plot that comprises its meaning.[4]

Not quite the "distillation of rumor" of which Carlyle speaks, but even the simplest, most uninterpreted compilation of facts tends to be compromised by the disappearance from the record of other facts. Such considerations would force historiography into its own kind of postmodern self-consciousness. Not since history was an art with, in Clio, its own muse, has the work of mythographers and historians seemed so congruent.

Pynchon, who seems always to have understood the implications of a postmodern conceptualization of history, introduces in Herbert Stencil a kind of latter-day Herodotus—a thorough researcher with a storyteller's delight in narrative. As historian, however, Stencil produces a picture of V. that is too shapely, too fictive. The mythic V. that he produces betrays the shapeless, uncentered actuality of the past.

But what kind of mythographer is Pynchon himself? How does his "mythical method" differ from that of Joyce or Eliot? Readers need to see how, under its fragmented surface, Pynchon's narrative at once coheres with machined precision and subverts or betrays that wholeness. They should recognize in this seeming conundrum something of how postmodernism differs from modernism. Ideally, they will know a modernist text or two (*To the Lighthouse? The Waste Land?*) against which they can gauge the new aesthetic. If Pynchon does not share one's mental library with a modernist exemplar such as Joyce, Woolf, or Eliot, one can derive the same benefit from brief consideration of significant work to which Pynchon himself alludes: *The Education of Henry Adams* (especially the

famous chapter 25, "The Dynamo and the Virgin"), which goes far toward clarifying both the immediate meanings and the larger cultural significance of Pynchon's novel. Adams at once participates in the modernist exploitation of myth (as universal, instinctive truth) and anticipates its
postmodern debunking. He salutes the divine female principle in Western
history: the Venus of the ancients, the Virgin of medieval Christianity. But
the West, he says, has declined from cultural unity to chaos. Thus both
Venus and Virgin, quondam embodiments of sexual energy and fertility,
find themselves sidelined in the modern age, vitiated, emptied of power.
In 1900, Adams can no longer affirm spiritually grounded meanings for
terms such as *force* or *energy*. Nor can he affirm any direction or telos to
history.

Where Adams ruefully concedes the displacement of the numen by
the forces that positivist science describes, another mythographer insists
that, however neglected, the goddess abides. This second major referent
for Stencil's mythmaking is Robert Graves, explicitly mentioned (along
with Adams) at the beginning of chapter 3. Given its resistance to ex-
cerpting, a brief account of the premise of Graves's *The White Goddess*
might be helpful. More seriously than E. O. James, Erich Neumann, Jane
Harrison, or Johann Jakob Bachofen (author in 1861 of *Myth, Religion
& Mother Right*), Graves argues for the supremacy of a female deity disastrously eclipsed, early in the preclassical West, by the rise of the male-
dominated Greek pantheon. Further eclipsed with the rise of patriarchal
Christianity, the White Goddess remains potent, and like repression itself she exacts a terrible price for humanity's whoring after—no, pimp-
ing for—strange gods. In Graves's view, this apostasy, this deference to
divine usurpers, has warped the course of more than two thousand years
of history.

Like Adams or Graves, Pynchon takes a keen interest in the history
of his times, but he views historiographic mythopoesis with great skepticism. His V. is a *parody* of history's divine female principle, the variously
named goddess that Adams and Graves see as an icon of cultural continuity. The twentieth century's character can be seen in its mythic avatar,
then, but where both Adams and Graves could look back to a prior
standard of cultural wholeness against which to measure (and by which
to rebuke) their present; where they could, at least by implication, envi-

sion some recovery of a cultural arche-order, whether preclassical, classical, or medieval-Christian, Pynchon's V. embodies by contrast only the darker, entropic, self-destructive energies of a civilization on its last legs. Thus Pynchon foregrounds a factitious historical myth only to subvert it—and with it all such mythopoesis.

As V. parodies various female archetypes, so is she recursively parodied by the secondary female figures in the story, and in this feature one discerns the depth of Pynchon's craft. Again, one offers a little chart, this one with Victoria Wren and her avatars, each adopted in particular times and places, on the left, and other women on the right. The side-by-side configuration may promote attention to the ways in which the female characters and V.'s avatars complement one another, all subsisting in the same fictional universe:

WOMEN IN *V.*

Victoria Wren (Cairo, Florence—see 209, riot)	Fortune, La Donna Libertá
	Mélanie l'Heuremaudit
	Mara the sorceress/spirit, "Maltese for woman"
V. at 1913 theater riot ("Nobody knew her name in Paris" [406])	(461); Veronica (1930s New York sewer rat, wants to become nun [121], as had Victoria; cf. Elena Xemxi)
Veronica Manganese (on Malta)	Hedwig Vogelsang
	"Sarah" (southwest Africa, 1904)
Vera Meroving (southwest Africa, 1922)	Mrs. Buffo
	Paola (notice her as the anti-V. at the sailors' melee in chapter 1 [16]—cf. V. in Florence
The Bad Priest (besieged Malta)	or Paris—and, at end, reconciling with Pappy on the Valletta docks after yet another riot)
	Rachel Owlglass
	Esther Harvitz
	Lucille at street fair
	Fina (see 144–5, 151)
	Hanky, Panky, Flip, Flop
	Brenda Wigglesworth

Itself in decline, itself subject to entropic drift, the female mythic archetype defined by V. recurs throughout the novel in steady diminuendo. Like V., the secondary female figures gravitate toward either the inanimate or violence. Rachel Owlglass and Esther Harvitz answer the call of the inanimate, the one fetishizing her MG, the other undergoing rhinoplasty and abortion. Josefina Mendoza ("Fina") seems to thrive at the periphery of violence (that of New York's gangs) — but presently she becomes the sexual victim of her whilom acolytes. Gang rape will also be the fate of Sarah, the unwilling concubine of the channeled trooper in Von Trotha's army. Mélanie l'Heuremaudit will become the fetishized object of V.'s passion, serve as another riot's focal point, and perish in an horrifically literal consummation with the inanimate. Mrs. Buffo, whose "dragon-embroidered kimono" (13) recalls the dragon-embroidered tights of both Mélanie (397) and V. (388), presides over Suck Hour as barroom version of the White Goddess. Paola Maijstral Hod hovers, V.-like, near riots at both the beginning and end of the book. She spends a season as the prostitute Ruby before reconnecting with her estranged husband in one of the book's rare sanguine moments.

In considering the women in the novel, one can also pause to solve the puzzle of sometime viewpoint character Benny Profane. Though he evinces a healthy dread of the inanimate, he represents the passivity of clueless, late twentieth-century humanity—small wonder the Whole Sick Crew swiftly clasps him to its decadent bosom. But what, one asks, makes this "fat boy" so appealing to the predatory Mafia Winsome or, for that matter, to her more genuinely attractive sisters — Paola Maijstral, Fina Mendoza, Rachel Owlglass? Pynchon invites the reader to recognize in women's attitudes to Profane some kind of counterparody of the V. phenomenon. He is almost a complete cipher, yet one woman after another "constructs" him according to her own desire for mythic masculinity.

Herbert Stencil, by the same token, constructs V. according to his desire for some key to history's chaos and his own identity. Through Stencil's eyes, the reader sees that Victoria Wren and the personages she becomes (especially the generic V.) have a valence for violence. Riot is her element, "the state of siege" her "natural habitat" (62). Hence the teasing intimations (386, 387, 410, 460–61) that V. somehow explains the century's drift toward greater and greater violence and disorder. The V. antitypes all batten on violence, first crudely, then with a quickening avidity. In Lardwick-on-the Fen the ten-year-old Victoria destroys only one man, then goes on in Cairo (1898), Florence (1899), and Paris (1913) to hover near and perhaps foster, as tutelary spirit, the Great War itself. Subsequently, she finds herself within the orbit of forces that will "improve" on the carnage of that first war (for the horrors of World War II—on and off the battlefield—will put the prior bloodshed into perspective). But does V. really die in 1943, as Fausto Maijstral's testimony seems to affirm, or is her baleful influence everywhere seeking the true apocalypse of World War III? The book will end with Armageddon seemingly at hand in the form of the Suez crisis of 1956 (Egypt again, where V. began her adult career). Though the first readers of this novel knew, in 1963, that the Suez crisis would be defused, they may have been less comfortable when they reflected that World War II began twenty years after the end of World War I. A similar twenty years of fitful interbellum peace would end within a year or two of *V.*'s publication. Would 1965 see the beginning of yet another world war?

Early in the century, Sidney Stencil (Herbert's father) thinks in terms borrowed from Christian eschatology (descent of the Paraclete, Armageddon, apocalypse), but the author himself encourages the reader to question the premises behind such terms: notions about history as something that has form and moves towards a "promised end." Thus Sidney Stencil's theory of "Paracletian politics" (472, 479–80) is exposed as merely the thinking of patternmaker-senior. Both of the Stencils have theories of history, then, and both are mistaken. *Accident* reigns—the kind of accident that, catalogued in a bravura passage in chapter 10 (290–91), claims the life of Sidney in the Mediterranean on the novel's last page. Whether as ultimate war or simple fulfillment of entropic drift (culminating in a triumph of the inanimate, of nothingness), only secular apocalypse looms, an apocalypse of collapse or self-immolation, not biblical fulfillment. The horror that V. legitimately embodies is that humanity repeatedly conspires to promote, rather than resist, this end.

V. organizes and makes sense of the age only in our fevered desire that there be such sense, such a rationale. Early or late one realizes that in fact V. is *not* present for the important violence of the century. Unlike Brigadier Pudding's Domina Nocturna (in *Gravity's Rainbow*), she puts in no appearance at Passchendaele or the killing fields of the Spanish Civil War—nor does she gravitate to Gallipoli, the Somme, the Battle of Britain, Dresden, the Ardennes, or Hiroshima. Even in Cairo, Florence, Paris, German southwest Africa, and the siege of Malta, she figures only at the periphery of such violence as occurs. Once this dawns on readers, they see the novel as a grand demonstration of humanity's enormous need to rationalize the past, the need that forces the historian—Herbert Stencil, for example—into dubious acts of emplotment. Perhaps, too, they see humanity's conceptual crucifixion between history as concatenation of aimless accident and history as coherent narrative (one option impossible to live with, the other false). As a representative figure, Stencil is not to be despised if, last seen en route to Sweden to check out another lead on V., he cannot give up the quest. The human mind cannot live with the wholly random character of history and the phenomenal world.

What, then, does history in the twentieth century move toward? Again, the very question assumes an unwarranted teleology, for in fact history moves toward nothing at all, unless it be oblivion, nothingness, universal inanimateness—perhaps accelerated or preceded by a meaningless holocaust. This drift is entropic, a creeping hegemony of the inanimate, and throughout the book scenes of portentous emptiness or depthlessness hint at or figure the void that awaits: Benny and Paola on the ferry in the snow (20–21), Benny and Rachel at the quarry (26), Herbert Stencil and the Margravine on Mallorca in 1946 (53), Sidney Stencil and Veronica Manganese on Malta in 1919 ("How pleasant to watch Nothing" [487]), Benny and Brenda running into "absolute night" (455). The Egyptian desert in chapter 3 represents another such evocation. Also exemplary are old Godolphin's experience of the void at the heart of things as seen in Vheissu (where the gaudy superficiality of all life is revealed) and Antarctica (an earnest of what is to come). Presently the aesthete Mantissa, who, like so many of his generation, seeks in art a replacement for the Deus absconditus, discovers that even his splendid Botticelli painting masks emptiness (209–10).

The reader's understanding of these elements depends to a large extent on Benny Profane's vague dread or instinctive abhorrence of the inanimate. For Profane, the simplest of acts invites disaster: showering, toweling off, shaving, tying his shoelaces, and so on, he finds himself spectacularly—and comically—at odds with the baleful world of objects (37). His dream of disassembly (39–40) echoes what, during an air raid in Malta, has already happened to V. qua the Bad Priest. His conversations with SHOCK ("synthetic human object, casualty kinematics" [285]) and SHROUD ("synthetic human, radiation output determined" [284]) modulate toward a cyborg vision and hint at the dreadful possibilities of what in *Gravity's Rainbow* Pynchon calls "Immachination" (297). A longtime road worker, Profane is himself a cultural crossroads. Half-Catholic, half-Jewish, he represents, in the book's economy, the decadence of the one and—especially when reduced to inanimate bulldozed bodies, as SHROUD remarks (295)—the victimization of the other.

What Profane resists, others embrace: objectification, surrender to or incorporation of the inanimate, immachination. Rachel Owlglass makes love to her MG. Schoenmaker the plastic surgeon saws and chisels at the human face, as with Esther Harvitz, or incorporates inanimate materials into it (trying, as it were, to improve on the results experienced by poor Evan Godolphin). Similarly, Fergus Mixolydian seeks to become an extension of his TV set (45), and even the sympathetic McClintic Sphere conceptualizes his art and his ethic as set/reset/flip/flop (293). One can trace out the larger meanings in the most seemingly gratuitous details. Bongo-Shaftsbury in 1898 Egypt, terrifying little Mildred Wren with a switch sewn into his arm (80–81), figures as an early apologist for the larger idea that Germany will come to stand for: humanity discarnate and "pure." The widespread and wholesale conversion of living flesh into inanimate matter would seem to be the chief goal of the fascist ideologies that were the political cancer of midcentury.

More broadly than Profane, Pynchon worries about the drift of the animate toward the inanimate. Pausing again to ask how V. herself exemplifies this entropic tendency, one sees that she comes to instantiate a principle of incremental—and deadly—objectification. The pattern here concerns the conversion of living flesh into something mechanical or moribund. The conceit receives its greatest elaboration in V., who seems to delight in inanimate replacements (the wig, the clockwork eye, the navel sapphire, the silver foot) for her own living tissue and so embodies—literally—the love affair with the inanimate. "Even in Florence," the narrator reminds us, Sidney Stencil "had noted an obsession with bodily incorporating little bits of inert matter" (488). She naturally comes also to embody the fascism that promotes the progressive objectification of human beings in this century, notably in the slave-labor camps of German southwest Africa, which prefigure the more dreadful camps in World War II.

By this reasoning, fascism would seem to exemplify the decadence that keeps cropping up here. Profane, reproached for giving his name as Benny Sfacim (*jism*), corrects it to Sfacimento, meaning *destruction* or *decay* (140). Both words seem to pun on *fascismo*. Even as Pynchon squarely faces up to what might be called existential decadence, the human fate articulated by Mehmet, the xebec captain ("The only change is toward death . . . Early and late we are in decay" [460]), he deplores our century's tendency towards the ideological promotion of what in *The Crying of Lot 49* he calls "the irreversible process" (128). Fausto Maijstral defines decadence as "[o]nly a clear movement toward death or, preferably, non-humanity" (321). Similarly, in the reflections of Itague, in 1913 Paris, the reader sees that the decadence theme complements or subsumes the inanimateness theme: "decadence . . . is a falling-away from what is human, and the further we fall the less human we become. Because we are less human, we foist off the humanity we have lost on inanimate objects and abstract theories" (405). Thus fetishism pervades the Paris chapter, as Mélanie, addressed as *fétiche* and known professionally as *La Jarretière* (the garter), pantomimes intercourse with a lay figure, dreams of herself as windup doll, and dances with automatons. In turn, she will become the "object" of V.'s twisted love. Itague's reference to "abstract theories" may reflect proleptically on those of Herbert Stencil (or Mafia Winsome), but it also gestures towards the aestheticism, the artistic decadence, that influences such characters as Evan Godolphin and Rafael Mantissa.

One of the more subtle historical elements of the novel, in fact, is its attention to purely artistic decadence in a variety of forms. The term *dec-*

adence can, for example, refer specifically to the international movement that embraced late-nineteenth-century French and British aestheticism and the Generation of 98 in Spain—or it can refer more generally to any artistic movement's period of exhaustion and decline. Thus the author of *The Crying of Lot 49* characterizes Jacobean drama as decadent, and many would so characterize the Stravinsky-like Porcépic's compositions. Not necessarily inferior, such art features highly unconventional subject matter and a style that can seem by turns chaotic and precious. The term can characterize any period—including, I should think, both modernism and postmodernism—of extreme artificiality and excess. The contemporary "crisis of representation," which fosters a self-referential art disinclined to mimesis and disengaged from reality, can be understood as a postmodernist version of the aesthetic or decadent assertion of art's superiority to nature. One can see why artistic decadence properly figures as subtheme in Pynchon's novel, which constantly resists ideologies that assert the superiority of the inanimate (even art) to living flesh. If one must recognize this rhapsodist of rhinoplasty, this allegorist of cloacal alligator-hunting, as himself a decadent, one must also recognize his profound humanism, decidedly at odds with occasional critical perceptions of alleged postmodernist nihilism.

Decadence, then, has aesthetic meanings both specific and generic, and in the course of his story Pynchon modulates suggestively from the one to the other. Chapters set before World War I include a number of specific allusions to the aesthetes, decadents, and their fellow travelers. With the exception of a brief reference to D'Annunzio in chapter 9 and to Rimbaud in chapter 13, the chapters set after World War II tend to invoke only the generic decadence represented in Roony Winsome ("king of the decky-dance"[220]), the novels of his wife Mafia, and the *Cheese Danish* series of Slab's Catatonic Expressionism. In between, during World War II, Fausto Maijstral weaves together observations about decadence both moral and aesthetic. Fausto, as it happens, is Herbert Stencil's spiritual brother, for Fausto's mother, Carla, would have destroyed herself and her unborn son were it not for the intervention of Stencil's father, Sidney. Seeming to echo Eigenvalue, Fausto observes in his journal what he calls "life's single lesson: that there is more accident to it than a man can ever admit to in a lifetime and stay sane"

(320–21). But Fausto goes on to affirm the artist's responsibility vis-à-vis the accident-filled cosmos:

> Living as he does much of the time in a world of metaphor, the poet is always acutely conscious that metaphor has no value apart from its function; that it is a device, an artifice. So that while others may look on the laws of physics as legislation and God as a human form with beard measured in light-years and nebulae for sandals, Fausto's kind are alone with the task of living in a universe of things which simply are, and cloaking that innate mindlessness with comfortable and pious metaphor so that the "practical" half of humanity may continue in the Great Lie, confident that their machines, dwellings, streets and weather share the same human motives, personal traits and fits of contrariness as they.
>
> Poets have been at this for centuries. It is the only useful purpose they do serve in society: and if every poet were to vanish tomorrow, society would live no longer than the quick memories and dead books of their poetry.
>
> It is the "role" of the poet, this 20th Century. To lie. (325–26)

More than a pose of weary iconoclasm, Fausto's assertion regarding the mendacity of the artist represents an enlightened aesthetic. Pynchon, who shares it, also "lies," but he contrives to tell the truth about life's shaky foundation in accident. In addition to symbolic brothers, in fact, Fausto Maijstral and Herbert Stencil are Pynchon surrogates, types of the artist who spins narrative gold from the straw of life's disconnected circumstances. Only art manages to be comfortable shuttling between formless actuality and the emplotment that makes it graspable. Only the artist, as Keats famously remarked, "is capable of being in uncertainties, Mysteries, doubts, without any irritable reaching after fact & reason."[5] F. Scott Fitzgerald said much the same thing in *The Crack-Up*:

> [L]et me make a general observation—the test of a first-rate intelligence is the ability to hold two opposed ideas in the mind at the same time and still retain the ability to function. One should, for example, be able to see that things are hopeless and yet be determined to make them otherwise.[6]

Artists, then, are uniquely empowered, especially in certain fictions that display their own artifice, "to lie," to recast the world as narrative even as they show that whoever makes history into story must inevitably traduce and misrepresent it. Pynchon calls into question the sense-making discourses, the organizations of data that cohere to explain history. He demolishes historiography and eschatology alike. Further, he deconstructs myth, and with it the modernist pretense of postreligious metanarrative.

Pynchon's novel invites its readers to see history and other forms of system-making as necessary fictions, product of the collective human need for pattern. This recognition animates not only the deceptive pattern of V. sightings but also the author's predilection for the quest plot and the theme of paranoia. Insofar as Pynchon interrogates the fictive emplotment of history, he exposes its foundation in cultural assumptions analogous to (and generally as unexamined) as the hegemony of Gramsci, the ideology of Althusser, or the *doxa* of Bourdieu. For a long time history itself was blind to its own totalizing ideologies. *V.* is one of the works that has obliged recognition of radically different perspectives. In Egypt, Malta, and southwest Africa, the reader of *V.* encounters early postcolonial discourse: counternarratives to the chronicles of victorious colonizers. If Edward Said's *Orientalism* (1978) began postcolonial studies and Hayden White's *Metahistory* (1973) inaugurated postmodern historiography, Pynchon's *V.* was one of their most important harbingers. But intellectual history was ever so: before Freud, Sophocles and Shakespeare; before Said and White, Pynchon.

Zum Rhein, zum Rhein, zum deutschen Rhein,
wer will des Stromes Hüter sein?

— MAX SCHNECKENBURGER, "Die Wacht am
Rhein"

CHAPTER THREE

Streben nach
dem Unendlichen

Germany and German Culture
in Pynchon's Early Work

Though he wrote to Thomas F. Hirsch that he did not know German
at all well, Pynchon displays a remarkable knowledge of German culture.[1] He invokes German art—what Wagner called *heilige Deutsche
Kunst*—from Goethe and Heine to Rilke and Brecht, from Beethoven to
Ludwig Spohr, from Käthe Kollwitz to Fritz Lang. He ponders German
philosophy from Hegel to Marx and German science from Rudolf
Clausius and Werner Heisenberg to Carl Friedrich Gauss and Friedrich
August Kekulé von Stradonitz. He retells *Märchen*, explores little-known
avenues of German colonial history in southwest Africa, and imagines
the peasant life of the Baltic seacoast. Most impressively, he creates a re-

markable range of German characters: the daft psychiatrist Dr. Hilarius, the silent film star Greta Erdmann, the arch-Nazi Captain Blicero, the rocket engineers Kurt Mondaugen and Franz Pökler.

Pynchon sees in German culture a type of Western civilization; moreover, he suggests in his work that the romance of the West with technology, especially in the twentieth century, owes much to the German example. It was German chemistry that inaugurated the technology of plastics, so emblematic of the breathtaking possibilities—and dangers—of tinkering with nature. Pynchon was four when the United States entered World War II, and the years of his boyhood were also those in which German technology announced itself with such wonders as the first jet fighters and the v-1 and v-2 rockets. The last of these, the v-2, became for Pynchon an emblem of technology's simultaneous promise and curse, for the rocket's more sophisticated descendants can either carry humanity into space—or destroy it.

Pynchon recognizes, in other words, that German culture is the product of Faustian appetite crossed with an historical affinity for philosophical idealism and ideas of transcendence. Thus he is struck with the fact that Wernher von Braun, the famous German rocket engineer, seems to have believed in the hereafter, and von Braun's declaration to that effect serves as an epigraph in *Gravity's Rainbow*, Pynchon's encyclopedic novel of World War II and its aftermath. For Pynchon, the West defines itself by a negative capability of ultimately German provenance: a secular dream of total knowledge and power coexists uneasily with a vision of transcendence. To call Western culture Faustian, in fact, is to recognize the extent to which that culture owes its paradoxical mix of boundless desire and grand vision to a specifically German imagination. The *Streben nach dem Unendlichen* of Goethe's Faust, one recalls, proves redemptive in the end. But the tragedy of the West lies in its perpetual subversion of the redemptive or transcendent ideal by the desire to dominate nature—a desire that leads, on the one hand, to laying waste the natural world through destructive technologies and, on the other, to the destruction of human resources through wars that afford proving grounds for ever newer and deadlier technology. These paradoxes of Western culture, the thematic substance of much of Pynchon's work, often find their focus in specific meditations on Germany, German culture, and German intellectual and social history.

Why does he focus on the German example? Pynchon has always had an acute grasp of popular culture and myth. He knows, for example, that the political ideology that held sway in Germany from 1933 to 1945 has afforded the popular mind with a symbol of absolute evil to replace the increasingly attenuated satanic bogey of religious tradition. Pynchon, however, depicts fascism in its full etiology, including its source in a twisted millenarianism that the Protestant West has collectively embraced. Pynchon sees German culture as part of a much broader spectrum that extends to England and America. Moreover, he reminds his readers over and over again that the most splendid and abhorrent features of German ideation replicate themselves throughout the larger Western culture of which Germany is part. Like Nabokov, whom he could have encountered as an undergraduate at Cornell, Pynchon seems at times profoundly hostile to things German. But he knows German culture far too well to despise it simplistically. Unlike Nabokov (or that other anglicized Slav, Conrad), Pynchon has no qualms about indicting the West more broadly.

Pynchon seems to have a German period, a post-German period, and a neo-Continental or global period. During his German phase he produced his first three novels: *V.*, *The Crying of Lot 49*, and *Gravity's Rainbow*. His next work, the long-awaited *Vineland*, represents a new phase in which the almost obsessive attention to German mores seems to have faded. Here the reader encounters only one allusion to Bach, one ex-Nazi (Kommandant Bopp, who puts in a brief appearance suppressing hippies in the late sixties), and occasional references to the affinity of American materialists for Mercedes and BMW automobiles. Much more prominent now are allusions to Japan and the onslaught of Japanese economic and cultural imperialism. In the America of the 1980s, after the triumph of Sony, Nissan, and their congeners, not to mention *Bladerunner* and the cyberpunk fiction it derives from and complements, Pynchon looks East to register both the possibilities of a fiction with global referents and the need to satirize American popular culture (much enamored of *Taipan, Shibumi, Shogun*, endless ninja stories, and Japanese monster movies). Thus in *Vineland,* Japan and Japanese culture bulk as prominently as Germany and German culture in the earlier novels. Pynchon seems to have shifted his focus from Europe to the East.

Yet whatever the direct cultural referents of *Vineland,* its central myth remains German, for Pynchon proves to have woven the archetypal Faustian bargain as deftly into this novel as into *Gravity's Rainbow,* where the quest of Tyrone Slothrop takes him up on the Brocken with a comely witch in explicit parody of an episode in *Faust.* The heroine of *Vineland,* Frenesi Gates, is a Faust of the American 1960s, who sells out her cause to the Mephistophelean Federal Prosecutor Brock Vond. This drama becomes Pynchon's allegory of how American radicalism became subverted and co-opted in the Nixon-Reagan era. German culture, in other words, remains a paradigm for Pynchon.

Written before the burgeoning of Japanese economic and cultural influence in the United States, Pynchon's first California novel, *The Crying of Lot 49,* falls more obviously into the German period. The author makes virtually no references to the land of the rising sun here; instead, as he does more obviously in *V.* and in *Gravity's Rainbow,* he assesses America's cultural debts to Europe—to England, Italy, the Netherlands—and especially Germany. German heritage and influence make themselves felt at a number of points. Oedipa Maas's German psychiatrist, Dr. Hilarius, for example, sounds like her ex-lover Pierce Inverarity doing his comic imitation of a Gestapo officer—perhaps because (as she eventually learns) Hilarius really did formerly work for the ss. Tracing the mysterious Tristero, Oedipa encounters more Teutonica: she learns about the Austro-Italian house of Thurn and Taxis, about German arms at the Lago di Pietà, and about the contemporary German composer Stockhausen. She also learns that fascism is literally right around the corner in her native country: her encounter with Winthrop Tremaine, purveyor of swastika armbands, ss uniforms, and other Nazi regalia, is part of her sensitization to the extent of America's heterogeneity. *Lot 49,* then, is part of a spectrum that includes *V., Gravity's Rainbow,* and *Against the Day.* Early or late in Pynchon's career, these works concern the unfolding of the twentieth century, a century largely shaped by the

Great War of 1914–18 and its second phase, from 1939 to 1945, with Germany a major participant in both.

Pynchon, an historical novelist of especially subtle gifts, probes the past for those moments that define by analogy—or literally shape—the currents of the present. The historical dimensions of *Lot 49* may seem at first a kind of window dressing for Pynchon's parables of epistemology and the American social reality, but the author in fact examines history for clues to the marginalization in the present of whole social categories that, like other forms of the repressed, inevitably "return." The overarching symbol of marginalization in this novel, a collective Other, is the Tristero, a clandestine postal system that began in opposition to the officially sanctioned Thurn and Taxis couriers who dominated European mail delivery for centuries—"until Bismarck bought them out in 1867" (96). As Oedipa Maas discovers the Tristero, the nemesis of Thurn and Taxis, she discovers a legacy of cultural exclusion dating back to the Renaissance. Perhaps the definitive episode involving this historical conceit is that in which the Scurvhamites, a seventeenth-century "sect of most pure Puritans" (155), become aware of the Tristero and construe it as the diabolical counterweight to the divine clockwork, a "blind, automatic anti-God" (165). But one by one the Scurvhamites defect, allow their own version of a repressed reality to take them over, surrendering to its powerful cogency, its historical inevitability.

In her own century, Oedipa discovers a kind of exploded version of this Other in the disaffected groups and individuals that seem to replicate endlessly all around her. In a way, Pynchon's whole program in *Lot 49* is to expose this forgotten reality, this seldom visible but always present America—the one with roots in a host of ethnic cultures that have been marginalized by the dominant Anglo-Saxon institutions. The country as a whole discovered this element in the sixties, the period of the novel's main action. The burgeoning "empowerment" of women and minorities in the decades following demonstrates the prophetic properties of literature, but as Pynchon shows in *Vineland* a quarter of a century later, the integration of power remains problematic.

But I was making a point about Pynchon as historical novelist, and the relevance of Germany to his vision of a global past and present.

Both *V.* and *Gravity's Rainbow* are explorations of the ways in which the dislocations of the twentieth century can be traced to or come to seem contained in some specifically German intellectual and cultural legacies, notably Protestantism (Luther, Zwingli), idealism (Leibniz, Kant, Fichte, Schelling, Schopenhauer, Hegel), and political millenarianism (Marx, Engels). Of course Pynchon is most emphatically an American writer, with a cultural agenda oriented ultimately to his own side of the Atlantic. Yet he knows that the American nation was founded and subsequently shaped by Anglo-Saxon Protestants, part of the same racial stock as their cousins in north-central Europe. He hints, indeed, at a supreme irony: that America, which began as a place of exile for the religious misfits and social detritus of these older nations, would prove heir to the vast rottenness of Europe: its centuries of repression and—from slavery to competing national mythologies of otherness—its manifold instrumentalities of marginalization.

The psychological, social, and historical mechanisms of this marginalization, Pynchon reminds his readers, either become known to the world through German science and philosophy or are actually German in their cultural inception. A German named Martin Luther, for example, invented Protestant theology, and another, Max Weber, described its cultural effects. Weber argued that the traditional Protestant emphasis on hard work, sobriety, and thrift brought material prosperity to the West at the same time that it promoted the smug conviction that the advancement of the world's haves over the world's have-nots reflected a spiritual distinction. Pynchon is especially interested in the way this dichotomy solidifies into the idea of an elect and a nonelect or "preterite" in the Calvinist revision of Lutheran theology.

Slothrop and Tannhäuser

Luther translated the New Testament into German while hiding out at the Wartburg Castle, hereditary seat of the Landgraves of Thuringia. Long before Luther's time, according to legend, the passion of the minnesinger Tannhäuser transpired there. Pynchon undertakes to retell that ancient story in certain of the adventures of Tyrone Slothrop, whose quest helps to structure *Gravity's Rainbow*. The author identifies this character with a number of mythic personages, some decidedly less exalted than others. At times Pynchon hints that we should view his protagonist as a death-confounding Orpheus or vegetation god; at other times the author encourages readers to see him as King Kong, the "sacrificial ape," or as some kind of composite comic book hero. Most often, however, Slothrop appears as a latter-day, parodic Tannhäuser.

Best known in its Wagnerian form, the Tannhäuser legend concerns a medieval knight who, weary of the world, goes to live with the goddess Venus in her submontane retreat. In former times (as one recalls from *Paradise Lost*), the pagan deities were regarded as devils, and in consorting with one of them Tannhäuser dooms his soul. Leaving Venus, he returns to the world and joins his fellow knights and minnesingers at the castle of the Wartburg, where a *Sängerkrieg*—a song contest—is to be held. Its theme is divine love, but Tannhäuser, to the outrage of all assembled, sings of its carnal counterfeit. The pious knights threaten to kill the blasphemer, but Elizabeth, the Landgrave's niece, intercedes, and he is sent on a pilgrimage to Rome to ask forgiveness of the Pope. But in Rome the pontiff declares that the papal staff will sooner bloom than Tannhäuser escape damnation. Wretchedly, Tannhäuser wanders northward again. He arrives in Thuringia again in time for Elizabeth's funeral, and, after praying at her tomb, he too dies. The operatic version of the story ends as a procession of pilgrims enters with the Pope's staff, which has miraculously flowered. Tannhäuser is redeemed.

Tyrone Slothrop's life is also complicated by the demands of the flesh: the pattern formed by his sexual conquests in wartime London seems to coincide with the pattern of v-2 hits in the city, and this sexual affinity with the rocket generates difficulties for him analogous to those of Tannhäuser. Like the minnesinger, he spends a season in the arms of the Zone's debauched Venus, Katje Borgesius, who he thinks "must have come out of the sea" (186) when he first sees her on the Riviera. But he does not go "under the mountain" until he gets to Nordhausen—located, like the Wartburg, in Thuringia. *Stollen*, the word for the great galleries of the underground rocket factory there, happens also to be the musicological term designating the sections—bars—of a minnesinger's song. Amid the *Stollen* devoted to assembly of Hitler's "ven-

geance weapon," Slothrop attends—though he does not perform at—
a songfest whose theme is rather less elevated than "divine love":

> There was a young fellow named Hector,
> Who was fond of a launcher-erector.
> But the squishes and pops
> Of acute pressure drops
> Wrecked Hector's hydraulic connector. (306)

Marvy's Mothers, the singers among whom Slothrop suddenly finds himself, burlesque the pieties of the Wartburg with their obscene limericks.
The sexuality of Pynchon's Tannhäuser, however, is still the target of the
songsters' contumely, for most of their limericks concern attempts to
copulate with rocket parts—a perversion attributable to Slothrop, since
the rocket, for him, is a sexual stimulus. Once Slothrop is recognized
and the chase begins, the sexual innuendo becomes more general, the
apostrophe in "that 'sucker" (as Major Marvy calls him) condensing volumes of homophobic rage.

Slothrop escapes Major Marvy by train, car, and balloon, though
the Mothers and their limericks pursue him even into the skies. Later,
racked with dysentery, he lies in a Berlin cellar listening to his "dumb
idling heart" tell him he is

> no knightly hero. The best you can compare with is Tannhäuser, the
> Singing Nincompoop—you've been under one mountain at Nordhausen,
> been known to sing a song or two with uke accompaniment, and don'tcha
> feel you're in a sucking marshland of sin out here, Slothrop? . . . And
> where is the Pope whose staff's gonna bloom for you? (364, my ellipsis)

A hundred pages further on, this query is answered negatively: "The
Pope's staff is always going to remain barren, like Slothrop's own un-
flowering cock" (470). Yet the reader should not take this statement too
seriously, for a miraculous efflorescence does take place: a movement
called the Counterforce springs up at the end of the war to resist the
oppression and manipulation practiced by the unscrupulous powerful
on preterite pawns everywhere.

As their first mission, members of the Counterforce set out to rescue
Slothrop, who is somewhere in Europe, desperately fleeing the control

of unscrupulous higher-ups in the Allied intelligence bureaucracy. One morning he is awakened by a Counterforce agent flying overhead "in a more or less hijacked P-47, on route to Berlin. His orders are terse and clear, like those of the others, agents of the Pope, Pope got religion, go out 'n' find that minnesinger, he's a good guy after all" (619). The longer Slothrop remains in the Zone, however, the less he can be "found" in the sense of "positively identified and detained" (712). One can only hope that some deliverance or grace will descend on him, as on the legendary minnesinger. The original story, at any rate, suggests that a distant miracle can make all the difference to him and his preterite kind. When, late in *Gravity's Rainbow*, "idiots from villages throughout Germany" celebrate spring in the town of Niederschaumdorf "brandishing . . . their green-leaved poles" (743, my ellipsis), they remember Tannhäuser's miraculous deliverance—and perhaps Slothrop's as well.

Cinematic Auguries of the Third Reich in *Gravity's Rainbow*

Some centuries closer to our time than the Tannhäuser legend, yet still a summons to all who would scrutinize the interface of history and mythology in *Gravity's Rainbow*, early German cinema composes an important part of Pynchon's conceptualization of the consciousness, during certain crucial decades of the twentieth century, of those who came of age in the Weimar era and its National Socialist sequel. As the silent era came to a close, Fritz Lang filmed *Die Frau im Mond* (1929), for which he devised "[t]he countdown as we know it, 10-9-8-u.s.w. . . . He put it into the launch scene to heighten suspense. 'It is another of my damned "touches,"' Fritz Lang said" (*GR* 753, my ellipsis). Steven Weisenburger traces this detail in Pynchon's great novel to Willy Ley's *Rockets, Missiles, and Space Travel* (1959).[2] Lang's movie about a rocket trip to the moon was remembered with fondness and even reverence by the German rocketeers at Peenemünde during World War II. There being no funds available for the development of rockets for space travel such as they dreamed of, many of these scientists and technicians felt themselves to be working on military rockets faute de mieux. Some of them had advised Lang on technical matters during the filming of *Die Frau im Mond*, and they regarded that movie not as fantasy but as prophecy. It is not surprising, then, to discover in Ernst Klee and Otto Merk's *The Birth of the Missile* that the first successfully flown v-2 rocket, launched 3 October 1942, bore the emblem *"Die Frau im Mond."*[3]

Pökler, a fictitious member of the staff at Peenemünde in *Gravity's Rainbow*, greets the movie on its first appearance with something less than total reverence. Seeing it with his wife, "Franz was amused, condescending. He picked at technical points. He knew some of the people who'd worked on the special effects" (159). Yet for all his superiority on this occasion, Pökler takes great pleasure in movies; in fact he dotes on Fritz Lang films, especially those featuring his favorite actor, Rudolf Klein-Rogge.

While Klein-Rogge was not in *Die Frau im Mond*, he did appear in a number of Lang's other films during the 1920s, including *Dr. Mabuse der Spieler* (1922), *Die Nibelungen* (1923–24), and *Metropolis* (1926). These movies, along with Lang's *Der Müde Tod*, are all cited in Siegfried Kracauer's *From Caligari to Hitler* as examples of films that expose "deep psychological dispositions predominant in Germany from 1918 to 1933 . . . dispositions which influenced the course of events during that time."[4] Kracauer argues that characters like the master criminal Dr. Mabuse, or the mad scientist Rotwang (in *Metropolis*), illustrate a growing fascination with or acceptance of the evil genius or tyrant. The fatalistic plot of *Der Müde Tod*, on the other hand, manifests a spirit of passivity before "fate" or "destiny." *Die Nibelungen* also reveals the inexorability of fate, in addition to exciting horror at the anarchic indulgence of instinct and passion.[5] The sociological and political relevance of these "dispositions" will be evident. When Pynchon makes these particular movies the favorites of the politically apathetic cineaste Franz Pökler, he seems to have Kracauer's theories in mind.

Like many of his fellow rocket technicians, Pökler pays little attention to politics—even when the authorities send his leftist wife to a concentration camp. Yet *Metropolis* is described as

> [e]xactly the world Pökler and evidently quite a few others were dreaming about those days, a Corporate City-state where technology was the source of power, the engineer worked closely with the administrator, the masses

labored unseen far underground, and ultimate power lay with a single leader at the top, fatherly and benevolent and just . . . (578, my ellipses)

The picture fits Nazi Germany, with non-Aryan slave labor at the bottom and paternal Führer at the top. Smaller versions of *Metropolis* will flourish under Nazism. Pökler will be one of the engineer-elite in the *Raketen-Stadt* at Peenemünde, whose workers come from Trassenheide, and subsequently in the even more *Metropolis*-like complex at Nordhausen, whose literally underground factory depends for its productivity on slave labor from the Dora camp.

Pynchon's most important references to *Metropolis* and the other Lang movies come when Tyrone Slothrop, still on the run, encounters the derelict Pökler after V-E Day. Slothrop hopes to find out something about the mad scientist who experimented on him in infancy, one Laszlo Jamf, with whom Pökler had studied at the *Technische Hochschule* in Munich before the war. But the half-mad engineer "keeps getting sidetracked off into talking about the movies, German movies Slothrop has never heard of, much less seen . . . yes here's some kind of fanatical movie hound all right" (577, Pynchon's ellipses). Pökler even thinks General Eisenhower on the radio sounds like Clark Gable.

Jamf, Pökler eventually discloses, was an exponent of what Pynchon dryly calls "National Socialist chemistry" (578). Recalling Jamf's injunctions to his students to be not tame technologues but scientific "lions," Pökler is reminded of his personal idol, the actor Rudolf Klein-Rogge, who played Rotwang, the unhinged but leonine scientist of *Metropolis*. Pökler is

taken with Klein-Rogge playing the mad inventor that Pökler and his co-disciples under Jamf longed to be — indispensable to those who ran the Metropolis, yet, at the end, the untamable lion who could let it all crash, girl, State, masses, himself, asserting his reality against them all in one last roaring plunge from rooftop to street. (578)

Pynchon ironically characterizes this monomania, which Pökler finds so attractive, as "[a] curious potency." Far from potency, in fact, it is the wholly negative final gesture of a lunatic. The idea that seems to appeal most strongly to Pökler here is that Rotwang "asserts his reality." Not his individuality or his importance, but his *reality*, and not *to*, but *against* his fellow characters. Since they have no reason to doubt his reality, the phrase must mean that Rotwang asserts his refusal to be dismissed as a two-dimensional illusion to the audience of which Pökler is a part. It is a curious locution, and Pökler probably would not be able to explain it very well, because he has long since ceased making distinctions between movies and life. Movies, dreams, and waking life all flow together for him to make a single phantasmagorical reality.

Thus it does not matter that, watching the nearly seven thousand meters of Lang's *Die Nibelungen*, Pökler periodically dozes:

> He kept falling asleep, waking to images that for half a minute he could make no sense of at all—a close-up of a face? a forest? the scales of the Dragon? a battle-scene? Often enough, it would resolve into Rudolf Klein-Rogge, ancient Oriental thanatomaniac Attila, head shaved except for a topknot, bead-strung, raving with grandiloquent gestures and those enormous bleak eyes. . . . Pökler would nod back into sleep with bursts of destroying beauty there for his dreams to work on, speaking barbaric gutturals for the silent mouths, smoothing the Burgundians into something of the meekness, the grayness of certain crowds in the beerhalls back at the T. H. . . . and wake again—it went on for hours—into some further progression of carnage, of fire and smashing. . . .
>
> On the way home, by tram and foot, his wife bitched at Pökler for dozing off, ridiculed his engineer's devotion to cause-and-effect. How could he tell her that the dramatic connections were really all there, in his dreams? (578–79, Pynchon's ellipses)

One wonders to what extent Pökler's countrymen found their dreams invaded by such images. Pökler himself will probably not even notice the gradual shift of scenes such as these off the screens of movie theaters and sleeping minds onto the stage of the real world. After 1933, movies like this one will seem to be interacting not only with Pökler's dreams, but with the very life of the nation. And by 1939 the "carnage . . . fire and smashing" and the cowed "Burgundians" will have completed the transition into real life.

Pökler's admiration of Attila the Hun and the other Klein-Rogge characters shows readers why he is so dominated by the sadistic and demented Major Weissmann, his superior in the rocket program. Desiring to launch his catamite Gottfried in a v-2, Weissmann assembles a secret team, which includes Pökler, to make the necessary modifications in the rocket. Horst Achtfaden, another of Weissmann's subordinates, reveals under interrogation that all the members of the team "were given code-names. Characters from a movie, somebody said. The other aerodynamics people were 'Spörri' and 'Hawasch.' I was called 'Wenk'" (455). These are characters from Lang's *Dr. Mabuse der Spieler*; as the mad scheme's mastermind, Weissmann would have designated himself Dr. Mabuse. In the movie, Dr. Mabuse was played by Pökler's "lion," Klein-Rogge.

Pynchon's straining of this movie through Pökler's fevered mind makes clear the way in which the exotically mad criminal genius was made an object of fascination in the German cinema, while directors like Lang refused, according to Kracauer, to confer obvious moral superiority on the forces representing the law.[6] Dr. Mabuse's opposite number is State Prosecutor von Wenk, portrayed by "matinee idol Bernhardt Goetzke . . . who played tender, wistful bureaucratic Death in *Der Müde Tod*" (579, my ellipses). Pökler despises the von Wenk character: "too gentle for the jaded Countess he coveted—but Klein-Rogge *jumped in*, with all claws out, drove her effeminate husband to suicide, seized her, threw her on his bed, the languid bitch—*took her!*" (579). Pökler's sadistic vehemence here reveals feelings of impotence and insignificance that were common in Weimar Germany, feelings whose continual exacerbation in the years between the wars made Hitler's violent reassertion of the honor of the Fatherland inevitable. Presumably Pökler is not alone in the delight he experiences when Mabuse rapes the countess; he and his countrymen will feel a similar release at the rape of Czechoslovakia, Poland, and France.

Nor is the rape in *Dr. Mabuse* the only cinematic sadism that thrills Pökler. He experiences the same kind of excitement watching the flagellation and ravishment of another noblewoman, a "captive baroness," in a movie entitled *Alpdrücken*: "yes, bitch—yes, little bitch—poor helpless *bitch* you're coming can't stop yourself now I'll whip you again whip till you *bleed*" (397). This movie is imaginary, as is its director, Gerhardt von Göll, himself an important character in *Gravity's Rainbow*. Von Göll is of special interest, however, because he is apparently modeled on Fritz Lang—the two having more in common than the effect their work has on Franz Pökler. The work of each lends itself, in Pynchon's eyes, to anagogical interpretation. Because the countdown, "10-9-8-u.s.w.," is analogous to the mystic's ten-stage approach to the *Merkabah*, or Throne of God, Pynchon ascribes kabbalistic significance to Lang's *Die Frau im Mond*. Von Göll's staging of double shadows in *Alpdrücken*, on the other hand, he describes as "clever Gnostic symbolism" (429).

The two directors are closest in their difficulties with the Nazi bureaucracy over film titles. *The Mad Kingdom*, one of von Göll's, seems to impugn the Third Reich: "*Das Wütend Reich*, how could they sit still for that? Endless negotiating, natty little men in Nazi lapel pins trooping through, interrupting the shooting" (394). Never mind that the Reich so described is not Hitler's but Ludwig II's. This incident is evidently based on one of Fritz Lang's anecdotes. Denied the use of a studio, Lang got into a heated exchange with a crypto-Nazi:

> at that moment I grabbed his lapel and felt something, I turned it over and there was a swastika button—he was a member of the Nazi Party. And they thought—blindly—that the title, *Murderer Among Us*, meant a picture against the Nazis.[7]

Lang was more fortunate than von Göll. When it came out that the movie was to be about a child-murderer, he was allowed to proceed with the filming. Nevertheless, he changed the title to *M* (1931).

But the film after *M*, a sequel to *Dr. Mabuse der Spieler*, was suppressed altogether, and Lang—again like von Göll—found it politic to leave Nazi Germany. Siegfried Kracauer explains why:

> In 1932, Lang in *The Last Will of Dr. Mabuse*, resuscitated his supercriminal to mirror the obvious Mabuse traits of Hitler. Through this second Mabuse film the first one is revealed to be not so much a document as one of those deep-rooted premonitions which spread over the German postwar screen.[8]

In his treatment of that earlier Mabuse film and its votary, Franz Pökler, one sees Pynchon rendering Kracauer's broad sociology in individual terms. Pynchon's meditation on *Dr. Mabuse der Spieler* and its effect on

Pökler concludes with a singular passage that sums up the engineer's tendency not to distinguish between life, dreams, and movies:

> Mabuse was the savage throwback, the charismatic flash no Sunday-afternoon Agfa plate could ever bear, the print through the rippling solution each time flaring up to the same annihilating white (Piscean depths Pökler has cruised dream and waking, beneath him images of everyday Inflation dreariness, queues, stockbrokers, boiled potatoes in a dish, searching with only gills and gut—some nervous drive toward myth he doesn't even know if he believes in—for the white light, ruins of Atlantis, intimations of a truer kingdom). (579)

The passage confuses slightly by shifting from cinematic terms to those of still-photography. The "Sunday-afternoon Agfa plate" is the picture taken of a bourgeois family group by a photographer. But Mabuse cannot participate in this banal, middle-class ritual. Like the Nazis, he is violently anti-bourgeois, and some powerful, atavistic aura about him defies parlor photography. The print always comes out white—death's color in the chromatic symbology of *Gravity's Rainbow*.

Pökler, in his sleepy movie-watching, has been figuratively swimming in a sea of film-developing solution (his name suggests that he is pickled by it). These depths are "Piscean" because, as his wife has revealed four hundred pages previously (154), Pökler's zodiacal sign is Pisces. From the bottom of this sea, everyday reality comes through to him as photographic "images" among which he seeks the one developing into apocalyptic whiteness, nominally Dr. Mabuse, but ultimately Pökler's personal "white man," Major Weissmann, who, as suggested previously, may have taken *Dr. Mabuse* as an alias. "Blicero," the major's "ss code name," is complementary, for it is derived from "'Blicker,' the nickname the early Germans gave to Death. They saw him white: bleaching and blankness" (322).

In a larger sense the image of bleached death maturing in the *Inflationzeit* is that definitive Klein-Rogge character Adolf Hitler, the historical madman who caps a long line of cinematic ones. Under whatever name, this personification of whiteness reigns in a "truer kingdom," which is both the Third Reich and the Kingdom of Death. The phrase anticipates "that Other Kingdom" (722) to which Weissmann eventually succeeds in dispatching Gottfried. All of Pökler's favorite Klein-Rogge characters, along with his chemistry teacher, court or espouse some transcendent, nonbourgeois death, a death that is at once the ultimate reality and the ultimate suspension of reality. It was in "defiant death" that Rotwang asserted his reality. "Thanatomaniac Attila," too, though Pynchon does not mention it, commits suicide by plunging into his flaming palace.

> Metropolitan inventor Rotwang, King Attila, Mabuse der Spieler, Prof-Dr. Laszlo Jamf, all their yearnings aimed the same way, toward a form of death that could be demonstrated to hold joy and defiance, nothing of bourgeois Goetzkian death . . . (579, my ellipsis)

Bernhardt Goetzke had played a *Weimarische* fantasy of respectable mortality in *Der Müde Tod*: "tender, wistful bureaucratic Death." But the regime that succeeded the Weimar Republic, heralded as it was by the cinematic Corybants of death parading across Pökler's retinae, would bring with it a much less effete conception of mortality. Indeed, an effete attitude toward Thanatos would be the last thing one could ascribe to the Nazi ethos.

This fascination with joyous, defiant death is merely the last and most bizarre of the Pöklerian movie responses that seem to parallel, at every point, those "deep psychological dispositions" which Siegfried Kracauer found reflected in German films of the 1920s and 1930s. Yet in adducing Kracauer to illuminate Pynchon, one risks doing Pynchon's art a disservice, because the relationship between German political destiny and the German cinema of the *Inflationzeit* cannot—one must admit—be as unequivocal as it is made out to be in *From Caligari to Hitler*. Kracauer has been criticized for the somewhat simplistic correlation he draws between a popular entertainment and the psychological tenor—surely not homogeneous—of an entire nation. Pynchon, however, cannot be faulted on this score because he says nothing explicit about sociological and historical issues. Adhering to what Henry James calls the author's instinct for indirect presentation, he is content to show the effect of a few highly suggestive films on the mind of a single confused German engineer. By revealing Pökler's excited responses to sadism, tyranny, and violence on the one hand, and to bourgeois inertia, meekness, and fecklessness on the other, Pynchon speaks volumes about currents abroad in Weimar Germany—without ever descending to facile sociology or to generalizations about the German "collective soul." The author of *Gravity's Rainbow* demonstrates mental proclivities, then, much more persuasively than does Kracauer, who paints with too broad a brush. And while that author may have influenced him, it is to Fritz Lang alone, his fellow artist, that Pynchon turns for his working material—the images he allows to play before the eyes and in the mind of his character, Franz Pökler.

Mental Preterition

Pökler is not the only character in *Gravity's Rainbow* whose mind and dreams prove a tissue of bizarre psychosexual fantasies. One thinks of Pirate Prentice, who manages the fantasies of others—or poor Slothrop, who struggles to bring to consciousness the secret things done to him in infancy. Thus Pynchon naturally engages, with varying degrees of ironic skepticism, another of Germany's intellectual inventions: the psychoanalysis that might be called the science of mental preterition. Based on theories of the Austrian Sigmund Freud and his quondam Swiss colleague Carl Gustav Jung, psychoanalysis concerns the marginal-izing mechanism of repression as it operates in the mind and spreads through human institutions. Yet the Jewish Freud is himself a cultural Other within the German milieu. He articulates a materialist, positivistic science that denies transcendence—a position that German culture, so wedded to idealism, must perceive as a profound threat. Dr. Hilarius, the ex-concentration-camp physician in *Lot 49*, remarks that

> Freud's vision of the world had no Buchenwalds in it. Buchenwald, ac-
> cording to Freud, once the light was let in, would become a soccer field,
> fat children would learn flower-arranging and solfeggio in the strangling
> rooms. At Auschwitz the ovens would be converted over to petit fours
> and wedding cakes, and the v-2 missiles to public housing for the elves.
> (137–38)

Dr. Hilarius does not do justice to Freud, who in fact promised nothing more than to replace neurotic behavior with "ordinary everyday unhappiness." Yet a rationalistic, antimystical bias does characterize Freudian thought.

Pynchon invokes Freud directly and indirectly to remind his readers that their culture is not immune to the insidious passions of fascism and racism. He intimates that racism in particular derives as much from unconscious fears as from social conditioning. The supreme example of racism in this century is of course the Holocaust, which Pynchon declines to characterize as a purely German phenomenon. Though he has been criticized for obscuring the actual horror of the death camps, he prefers to represent Nazi genocide obliquely. Thus in *V.* he describes the extermination of the Hereros and Hottentots in German southwest Africa in 1904 and 1922. General von Trotha, at the turn of the century, issued his own *Vernichtungsbefehl* and "is reckoned to have done away with about 60,000 people. This is only one per cent of six million, but still pretty good" (245). In *Gravity's Rainbow* Pynchon is yet more indirect. Here he describes the slaughter of dodoes in Mauritius by the *Platt-Deutsch* Frans van der Groov (the name, a recurrent Pynchon metaphor for being unbalanced, is mock-Dutch for "out of the groove"). It is his descendant, Katje Borgesius, who applies the term "genocide" to what he does (545).

But from *V.* to *Gravity's Rainbow* the author seems to move towards a stronger realization that Germany does not have a monopoly on racism and genocide. In *Gravity's Rainbow* the racist attitudes of a Major Marvy are hardly more attractive than those of a Goebbels, and even the sympathetic Slothrop proves, in the Abreaction Research Facility, to be a mine of bizarre racial fears. The Soviet operative Tchitcherine, another sympathetic figure, is also a racist, obsessed with destroying his black half-brother, Enzian. Yet this same racially mongrel Enzian, willing victim of an emblematic colonial sodomy, seems to have inspired a genuine love on the part of that charter member of the Nazi party, the Lieutenant Weissmann who would become Captain Blicero. In *Gravity's Rainbow*, if not in *V.*, Pynchon treats racism iconoclastically, understating German guilt on this score while highlighting the larger guilt of Western culture generally. He seems inclined to locate the origins of racism at once in the unconscious and in the unconsciously motivated drift of history.

That drift is also entropic. Individually and collectively, humanity moves towards an inorganic state. How horrible, then, to accelerate this drift with fascist ideologies that reduce human beings to the status of the inanimate. Pynchon probes fascism obliquely when he makes his first novel, *V.*, a meditation on the creeping hegemony of the inanimate, for fascism, which actually defines itself in the reduction of human beings to the status of objects, tends to promote, rather than resist, the universal entropic drift. Thus Pynchon's central metaphor in this novel is a mythic woman who embraces entropy, a woman who has a special affinity for violence, who incorporates more and more pieces of inanimate matter into her body, until she is equipped with false hair, false teeth, a clockwork glass eye, a detachable silver foot, and a sapphire sewn into her navel. "Victoria was being gradually replaced by V.; something entirely different, for which the young century had as yet no name" (411). World War II, "whose etiology was also her own, a war which came least as a surprise to her" (387), is construed by Pynchon as merely the fulfillment of currents that first brought World War I and may yet bring the Armageddon hinted at in the trajectory of the action in *V.*'s narrative present (and in the closing pages of *Gravity's Rainbow*).

But Victoria Wren, who becomes V., is British, not German. Though her dates, 1880–1943, make her the coeval of Hitler and Mussolini, and though Pynchon invites readers to see her as nothing less than the fascist Zeitgeist (even as she mocks our need—projected in Herbert Stencil's mythography—for some such construct), Victoria is the emblem of an ideological cancer that is hardly limited to Germany and the Axis. Pynchon, then, meditating the course of the twentieth century, means ultimately not to taunt Germany for having played host to fascism, but to show how profoundly congenial this politics is to Western and especially Anglo-Saxon culture. As noted previously, Pynchon tends to treat his Nazis with subversive sympathy—he presents Captain Blicero as a curiously sympathetic monster, and Major Marvy as a loathsome representative of heroic American entrepreneurism. Which, he seems to ask, is the truer fascist? In *Vineland*, too, he gauges the extent to which America has embraced a right-wing ideology that, owing to the still abhorrent German example, dares not speak its name.

"Germany and German Culture in Pynchon's Early Work" turns out to be a much broader topic than one might initially think. The author intimates in a variety of ways that racism and fascism are broadly characteristic of a culture that on the one hand derives its ideas from Germany and, on the other, stigmatizes or scapegoats that nation for the unbridled lust with which the larger culture itself embraces these ideas. Thus his most distinguished novel, while unquestionably "about" the great international currents of twentieth-century history, proves especially dense with allusion to German culture. Indeed, much of *Gravity's Rainbow* is set in Germany during the chaotic period after the formal end of hostilities in World War II. Describing a time in which a once-noble civilization first wages aggressive war and genocide, then lies in ruins, Pynchon artfully weaves in an immense range of German cultural reference: everything from evocations of ancient Germania as described by Tacitus to the look and feel of the *Mittelwerke* at Nordhausen and the adjoining Dora camp. One encounters not only the Tannhäuser story but also the Norse myth of Utgarthaloki and other runic lore, *Das Narrenschiff*, "Hänsel and Gretel," Wilhelm Busch's Max and Moritz, and, as we have seen, the world of prewar German film. Pynchon evokes cultural episodes like the *Inflationszeit* of the twenties, too, and he alludes frequently to the German art of poets like Wolfram von Eschenbach, Goethe, Heine, and Rilke—and composers from Heinrich Suso to Beethoven and Wagner. All of this material he jumbles together, fragments shored against ruins, for he sees the Zone as a wasteland in which one can view the disjecta membra of a culture gone supernova. The author of *Gravity's Rainbow* meditates the prospects for the larger culture to self-destruct with even greater and more absolute apocalyptic violence.

One can reassemble only a few sherds here. One set of them composes the "Hänsel and Gretel" vessel. In England, Roger and Jessica take her nieces to a pantomime *Hänsel und Gretel* that is interrupted by a v-2 attack. The missiles are launched from occupied Holland by crews like the one led by Captain Blicero—who plays at the folktale with Gottfried and Katje. He sees the others as "children" to his "witch" and seems to see the oven as his "destiny." But where the classic story eventuates in the children's consigning the witch to the oven for which they have been fattened, Pynchon imagines Hänsel suffering the fate for which he was originally intended. The reader understands, when Blicero packs Gottfried into the specially modified A-4 rocket, that the ending of this story will depart from tradition. Though the chief locus of this twisted tale is Germany, where a nation's children—its soldiery and its Jewish citizens, as well as its literal young—prove helpless to escape their terrible fate, the burning of children is culture-wide. In the English pantomime Gretel interrupts the performance to sing a supposedly comforting song—but the song ends in a more generalized terror:

> And those voices you hear, Boy and Girl of the Year,
> Are of children who are learning to die . . . (175, Pynchon's ellipsis)

The sacrifice of children has traditionally been the supreme image of a transcendental idea gone hopelessly corrupt and malign. It connotes the worship of Moloch. Here Pynchon imagines a whole world of "[m]others and fathers . . . leaving their children alone in the forest" (176, my ellipses) or sending them to the flames. The climax of this vision, the firing of the 00000 rocket, is at once German and trans-German. Indeed, the rocket containing Gottfried becomes the ICBM descending on Los Angeles in the novel's closing pages, and the message is clear: weaponized technology will sooner or later claim all that human beings hold most dear.

An extension of the "Hänsel and Gretel" theme concerns the exploitation of the third world, whose inhabitants are also children in the paternalistic view of the colonial powers. If, again, "[t]he Oven we fattened you for will glow" (751), the question of whether witch or child goes into the oven becomes ambiguous. To be sure, the native Hänsel has been consigned to the colonial oven time and time again, but the example of the *Schwarzkommando* and their apocalyptic weapon hints at third-world measures—notably successes in Algeria and Vietnam and the rise of terrorism elsewhere—that may yet see the witch betrayed into the oven of her own preparing. Pynchon's focus on German colonialism, at any rate, is an especially obvious symbol of general Western practice: before German exploitation of southwest Africa, the Belgians wrought their horrors in the Congo, the Americans theirs in the Philippines, *u.s.w.*

History's Rainbow

Pynchon, then, takes little interest in tracing various cultural horrors to Germany—he suggests rather that Germany distills all that is best and worst in the social and intellectual life of the West. Indeed, as one sees in the career of Fritz Lang, German culture produces counterweights to its own Faustian striving. Thus Lang alternated tendentious fantasies of *Heldengeschichte* (*Die Nibelungen*, 1923–24) and planetary transcendence (*Die Frau im Mond*) with films exposing the corruption and criminality of the Weimar and post-Weimar architects of power: *Dr. Mabuse der Spieler* (1922), *Metropolis* (1926), and *M* (1931). On a grander and more passionate scale, the poet Rilke can at once embrace death as a mystical consummation (an idea worthy of some of the more cracked Nazi apologists), affirm the perspective of eternity (in his Angels), and celebrate the sanctity of the earth:

> Und wenn dich das Irdische vergass,
> Zu der stillen Erde sag: Ich rinne.
> Zu dem raschen Wasser sprich: Ich bin.

> And though Earthliness forget you,
> To the stilled Earth say: I flow.
> To the rushing water speak: I am. (622)

Both Lang and Rilke, of course, are figures in Pynchon's tapestry, and the ambivalence of their art recurs in the author's other allusions to German culture.

The most pervasive ambivalence attaches to the Rocket, but its significance is framed in a wealth of bipolar politics, philosophy, economics, science, and technology that are first German, then global. These products of German ingenuity begin ideally but end corruptly—they suffer betrayals in their first application and in their export. Aromatic polymers, the politics of left and right, even the "German symphonic arc"—all share the Rocket's fundamental ambiguity and rehearse the same agon, the same "betrayal to gravity." Implicated at every stage, the larger culture that subsumes Germany embraces and corrupts its ideas, its science, the local applications of its idealist heritage. It develops the military rocket along with the space rocket, the Nietzschean philosophy of power as well as the Hegelian dialectic (Marxism is a German export no less than fascism), romantic nature worship along with the ruthless exploitation of nature, and tonality in music as well as the attempt of the serialists to free music from earthbound cadences. "You were never immune over there," as the composer Gustav Schlabone says, "from the . . . German symphonic arc" (443).

Arc. Parabola. Rainbow. Each rises on a promise; each is betrayed to gravity. One meaning of the rainbow in the novel's title is bitterly ironic: it is the parabolic ascent and descent of Western civilization. The paradigm holds also for technology, which promises mastery yet flirts with ecological catastrophe. Indeed, the novel opens with an imagined v-2 hit on that Victorian emblem of technology and its promise, the Crystal Palace. But a richer and more important image (perhaps the central trope of the novel) accompanies Kekulé von Stradonitz's oneiric vision of the benzine ring—a dream that proves the annunciation of a radical new technology. The scientist "dreams the Great Serpent holding its own tail in its mouth"—an emblem of eternity or, more immediately, of the perfect harmony of nature. "But the meanness, the cynicism with which this dream is to be used" (412). The knowledge of that naturally balanced circle of carbon atoms opens up the possibility of tampering with or "improving" it. Pynchon makes this celebrated milestone in the history of science a symbol of what technological humanity has wrought: a sustained violation of nature, a failure to see that "Earth is a living critter" (590). Humanity circumvents nature in favor of a transcendent, ideal meta-nature—in this instance the world of plastics and synthetic fibers. The result is the kind of ecological catastrophe that surrounds "the Castle," the petrochemical plant where Imipolex G research goes on. The world chokes on the wastes of industrial processes that give us polyester.

The violation of nature has its mirrors in the political and economic systems of the West. Innovative technologies call into existence the need for new funding for cynical mirror games with whole national economies, and there is considerable attention to Germany's involvement with such devices in the years following World War I. The picture of Hugo Stinnes, Walter Rathenau, Hjalmar Schacht, and the machinations that compounded the hardships brought on by the Treaty of Versailles in 1919 complements the description of new developments in plastics, rocketry, and armaments. The *Inflationszeit* affords at once an abhorrent experience of pan-German marginalization and a fresh instance of an old paradigm: on one side an economic elite represented by Stinnes, Rathenau, and their cronies—on the other a vast preterite composed of those whose lives the inflation blights. Capital, in other words, remains allied to election. The economic elitism, moreover, soon proves international, as the great cartels erect an international order of financial election and preterition. Within a generation a kind of economic cancer spreads throughout the West. Katje Borgesius reflects early in the novel that "[t]he real business of the War"—she is referring to World War II—"is buying and selling . . . The true war is a celebration of markets" (105, my ellipsis). The *Schwarzkommando* think along similar lines:

> this War was never political at all, the politics was all theatre, all just to keep the people distracted . . . secretly, it was being dictated instead by the needs of technology . . . by a conspiracy between human beings and techniques, by something that needed the energy-burst of war, crying, "Money be damned, the very life of [insert name of Nation] is at stake," but meaning, most likely, *dawn is nearly here, I need my night's blood, my funding, funding, ahh more, more.* . . . The real crises were crises of allocation and priority, not among firms—it was only staged to look that way—but among the different Technologies, Plastics, Electronics, Aircraft, and their needs which are understood only by the ruling elite . . . (521, Pynchon's ellipses)

Pynchon rounds off this picture of macro-economic evolution in the postwar deal making between Allied military interests and the surprisingly robust Krupp corporation. This takes place at elite soirees like the dinner party hosted by Stefan Utgarthaloki—a character named for the giant who presides over an eating and drinking contest in Norse mythology. The author hints at the monstrous appetites indulged in the military-industrial feeding frenzy that continued unabated for decades after the war.

Perhaps one can sum up Pynchon's complex view of Germany and German culture in a last detail from *Gravity's Rainbow*. Sailing improbably down the Oder and taking Tyrone Slothrop aboard after one of his picaresque mishaps is a vessel called the *Anubis*, named after the god of death in the pantheon that German archaeology was instrumental in introducing to the modern world. The *Anubis* makes its way along the boundary between Germany and Poland—along the interface, that is, between East and West. Aboard this vessel are representatives of every nation, all engaged in mindless dissipation, indifferent to the destruction all around them. The voyage of the *Anubis* refurbishes a medieval German conceit: *das Narrenschiff,* the ship of fools. It is reminiscent of Foppl's siege party in *V.,* where in 1922, in a burlesque of the League of Nations, representatives of various nations divert themselves while terrible energies mass and spend themselves all around. Foppl, too, is a German, a veteran of von Trotha's campaigns. But in both the siege party of *V.* and the death-ship cruise in *Gravity's Rainbow,* Pynchon emphasizes the international character of the folly—not the incidental German auspices.

Californians are a race of people; they
are not merely inhabitants of a State.
— O. HENRY, "A Municipal Report"

CHAPTER FOUR

Pynchon and the Sixties

The California Novels

Discussions of the literature that began to emerge in the period just
after World War II tend to emphasize the element of post-Joycean reflexivity. With Beckett as one kind of pathfinder and Nabokov as another, writers became increasingly committed to the interrogation of
their medium—the probing, that is, of language and its epistemological
credentials. These credentials had gone largely unchecked by modernist
writers, even those who, like Eliot in "Burnt Norton," recognized and
worried over the tendency of words to betray:

> Words strain,
> Crack and sometimes break, under the burden,
> Under the tension, slip, slide, perish,
> Decay with imprecision, will not stay in place,
> Will not stay still.[1]

The modernists strove to explore consciousness, time, and history—the
very realities most resistant to representation in words. Language

remained for them, nonetheless, an instrument of knowing, and thus Brian McHale has characterized the modernist project as epistemological in its premises, means, and goals. The postmodernists, by contrast, seem to have begun with a recognition of the mimetic and referential shortcomings of language—a perception that led, McHale argues, to a literary art more interested in ontology than epistemology.[2] As John Hawkes once remarked in an interview, "I want to try to create a world, not represent it."[3]

But things are never, of course, this neat. The real shift, as Lyotard argues in *The Postmodern Condition*, is towards representation of the less and less representable. The moderns, he says, sought to represent the unrepresentable; the postmoderns seek to represent the unrepresentable in representation itself. This is not ontology but a more subtle epistemology—a grappling with the problematics of representation. Thus Nabokov, as early as *The Real Life of Sebastian Knight* (1941), invokes a Velázquez-like reflexivity to "illustrate" the self-referential element of an imagined work of literary art: "It is as if a painter said: look, here I'm going to show you not the painting of a landscape, but the painting of different ways of painting a certain landscape, and I trust their harmonious fusion will disclose the landscape as I intend you to see it."[4] Nabokov prepared the ground for writers from Barth to Barthelme who sought parodically to "represent" prior literary efforts at representation in works characterized as fabulation, surfiction, irrealism, and metafiction. Barth himself saluted this nascent postmodernism in his famous (and much misread) essay of 1967, "The Literature of Exhaustion."

It did not take long for complaints to set in, often calling down—as John Gardner does in *On Moral Fiction* (1978)—a plague on the houses of both modernism and postmodernism. Gardner laments what he calls, in a typically pungent phrase, the smart-mouth cynicism of the new writing. Another critic was Charles Newman, who, in *The Post-Modern Aura* (1985), deplored its alleged nihilism. These pundits (especially Gardner) mistook a natural warping of literary fashion for some latter-day Battle of the Books, a late engagement of ancients with moderns: on one side artists willing to engage real-world exigencies, on the other side artists committed only to to endless, self-indulgent, textual play.

I do not propose to argue some kind of large-scale critical *méconnais-sance* of contemporary literature, but I would like to point out a basic misconception among those who see a division of the kind sketched above. The simple fact is that relatively few of the American postmodern-ists actually divorce themselves from moral and social issues. However accomplished they might be as practitioners of the emergent aesthetic, they remain curiously moral—even moralistic—in their outlook. However committed to the free play of the signifier, they constantly critique the very simulacrum they supposedly exploit. Thus Heller, in *Catch-22* (1961), has some perfectly serious things to say about war. Neither Doctorow, in *The Book of Daniel* (1971), nor Coover, in *The Public Burning* (1977), is indifferent to the real-life anguish of the Rosenbergs. Abish, in *How German Is It* (1980), declines to allow the Nazi evil to disappear into some kind of moral relativism. Vonnegut, in novel after novel, quite passionately deplores violence, racism, and economic ex-ploitation. Even Nabokov, whose hermetic work admits of so little by way of social reality (however many motels he describes in *Lolita*), never misses an opportunity to revile totalitarianism and brutality in both their imaginary and real-life forms.

Nowhere is this paradoxical subversion of the postmodern gospel more evident than in the work of Thomas Pynchon, an author who leaves his readers in no doubt regarding his attitude towards racism, oppressive economic practices, genocidal violence, skullduggery in high places, and police-state repression. He expresses, in numerous ways, a profound empathy with what he calls the preterite, the left out, the passed over in every form of election (spiritual, economic, racial, cultural). These are the American Dream's insomniacs, "the poor, the defeated, the criminal, the desperate," as he calls them in his report on Watts in the aftermath of the 1965 riots.[5] Readers can trace the au-thor's sympathy for this element (and, for that matter, his contempt for the complacently elect) to the decade that redefined American political idealism. For a kind of moral touchstone within the Pynchon *oeuvre* one need only consider his 1964 story "The Secret Integration," in which some children deal with the racial prejudice of their elders by adopt-ing an imaginary black playmate. In a typical piece of what used to be called "black humor," Pynchon makes one of the children a member of Alcoholics Anonymous, but when the local chapter of that organization responds to a call from an alcoholic musician by sending this youthful member to sit with him, the boy and his companions find themselves the unwitting instruments of a cruel joke—black humor of a more radical sort. The anger, frustration, and chagrin of the musician, a "Negro," reveal to the children racism's emotional and moral toll. Worse, they discover the power of racism to include them unawares.

Pynchon's novels and other short stories revolve in planetary orbits around the sunlike moral intensity of the 1960s.[6] Much of the work actually inhabits or brackets that decade. *V.*, its framing narrative set in the mid-1950s, came out in 1963, the year Kennedy was assassinated. *The Crying of Lot 49*, set in 1964, came out in 1966. The central character in *Vineland* (1990) reconstructs the story of a sixties film collective headed by the mother who abandoned her. The roots of slavery and genocide that exercise the author in *Mason & Dixon* (1997), finally, became matters of public concern during the sixties—or as a direct result of wounds reopened during that decade.

Readers of *Mason & Dixon* initially think themselves far removed from the present, but Pynchon fills his fifth novel with veiled allusions to the cultural flotsam and jetsam of the twentieth century—from Daffy Duck and Popeye to Valley Girls and a number of amusingly improbable eighteenth-century periphrases of slang unknown as yet to linguistic history. Some of this anachronistic material—an elaborate fantasy about giant vegetables evidently inspired by Jolly Green Giant commercials (654, 747), a reference to *Star Trek* ("Live long and prosper" [485])— derives from the midcentury decade that parallels, at two hundred years' remove, the one in which Charles Mason and Jeremiah Dixon observe the transit of Venus and lay out the boundary line that will make them famous. These small reflections in history's distant mirror highlight a much larger congruence between the 1760s and the 1960s, for Pynchon ultimately reads the eighteenth century much as he reads the twentieth. As in one era the struggle to resist the totalizing tide of reason manifested itself as a taste for Gothic, a nostalgia for magic, and an embattled spirituality, so, in the 1960s, did enormous numbers of American citizens resist the logical-yet-monstrous coercion of Cold-War rationality as embodied in the military-industrial complex, the Vietnam War, the policy of mutual assured destruction, and so forth.

Gravity's Rainbow, another work that seems not to fit into the pattern under review here, provides further evidence of the importance to Pynchon of the sixties. Published a scant three years into the new decade, this novel does not ignore the years in which it was presumably being written. Here Pynchon transforms the counterculture of those years into the Counterforce that he imagines as coming into existence at the end of World War II. Though set in the period just before and just after the end of that war, *Gravity's Rainbow* moves toward a calculated violation of its meticulously constructed temporal frame. Having begun with an incoming v-2 in wartime London (or, rather, with the *sound* of the rocket, which has exploded some seconds before the novel's famous opening line: "A screaming comes across the sky"), it concludes with the descent of a more deadly rocket—an ICBM in contemporary Los Angeles. This augury of nuclear annihilation takes places under the auspices of Richard M. Zhlubb, a thinly disguised Richard M. Nixon, whose presidency, which began in 1969, was well into a second term at the time of this novel's publication.

Pynchon's first novel, *V.,* chronicles—at least in part—the years in which this same Nixon served as Eisenhower's vice president. As I noted in chapter 2, this historical metafiction seems oriented to the year 1965. Pynchon makes a point of drawing the reader's attention to the two-decade period—1918–39—bewtween the end of the First World War and the beginning of the Second. He ends, the air filled with auguries of apocalypse, with the portentous marshaling of forces that took place on the occasion of the Suez crisis of 1956. Readers who knew, in 1963, that the crisis of 1956 did not eventuate in Armageddon may have had a momentary sense of relief or anticlimax—until they reflected that Suez, like Fashoda in 1898 or Sarajevo in 1914, had as it were "tossed sparks in search of a fuse" (*V.* 386). Pynchon implies that the real date to dread was just over the temporal horizon in 1965—when peace would once again have had, as the British say, its twenty-year innings.

Another side to this novel is its transformation of paranoia and conspiracy into aesthetic principles. Influenced by the culture-defining myths of Henry Adams (the Virgin of the twelfth century, the Venus of antiquity) and Robert Graves (the White Goddess), Pynchon projects, in *V.* herself, an embodiment of the age's love affair with carnage, its failure to resist entropic drift. The reader, along with Herbert Stencil ("the century's child" [52]), discovers a terrifying pattern: V. reigns, a kind of tutelary spirit, wherever bloodshed occurs in the years leading up to and away from the Great War. She represents the mythic ratio-nale for an age of steadily increasing violence. But unlike his modernist masters, who exploit the element of universal, instinctive truth in myth, Pynchon reveals such constructs as factitious, merely the projection of humanity's desperate need for order, coherence, and connectedness. To repeat another point made previously, he expects the reader to make a counter-discovery: V.'s presence amid violent incidents and events is acci-dental, and the violence itself is random. Like Frost's poem "Design," in other words, Pynchon's novel seems to confront its readers with equally hideous alternatives—an active principle of evil on the one hand and, on the other, the absence of any ordering principle whatsoever. V. is not, as Pynchon initially invites his reader to think, the fascist Zeitgeist. In *V.* Pynchon ultimately reveals nothing more than the entropic acceleration of disorder. No pattern palliates our plight.

In recognizing the growing human appetite for a denied historical coherence, Pynchon puts his finger on a major anxiety of the 1960s. He saw and charted the way paranoia on the left began to vie with an older, less imaginative paranoia on the right (briefly burlesqued in *Lot 49*'s Peter Pinguid Society, characterized as being to the right of the John Birchers). The 1950s had seen widespread fear of an international communist plot, brainchild of alleged "masters of deceit," as J. Edgar Hoover called them in his 1958 book of that title (from a later histori-cal vantage we know that the true master of deceit—from cross-dressing to political blackmail—was Hoover himself). But it was the 1960s that discovered the often richer vein of domestic conspiracy. Watching the Zapruder film, watching Jack Ruby kill Lee Harvey Oswald, reading the Warren Commission report, and shaking its collective head over the as-sassinations of Malcolm X, Martin Luther King Jr., and Robert Kennedy, the American public began to suspect, like Oedipa Maas in *The Crying of Lot 49*, that "it's all part of a plot, an elaborate . . . *plot*" (31). In the early years of the next decade, movies like *The Parallax View* (1974) and *Three Days of the Condor* (1975) did little to lay this conviction to rest.

Pynchon explores and exploits this atmosphere of paranoia and distrust in *Vineland*, too. Here, as in *V.*, he develops two parallel historical narratives—one in Ronald Reagan's 1984 (not so different from Orwell's, Pynchon suggests), the other in the late 1960s, where a whole counterculture is projected in the People's Republic of Rock and Roll, a breakaway enclave on the California coast. In *Vineland* Pynchon contemplates and transmutes the fate of a generation of hippies, activists, and would-be revolutionaries—a generation subject, like any other, to growing up and reproaching itself for complicity in all it had despised and struggled against. To provide this transition with dramatic urgency, Pynchon structures the novel around a political assassination—perfect emblem of a frantic decade and the seemingly mysterious dissipation of its unique energy. In the novel's primal scene, the charismatic Weed Atman perishes at the hands of associates manipulated by an agent provocateur. Thereafter, lacking courage to gnaw its own foot off, a generation languishes in the late capitalist trap.

It is in *The Crying of Lot 49*, however, that Pynchon gives us his best sixties novel—best because it so perfectly instantiates the literary virtue of indirection. Just as World War II figures only with the greatest economy in *V.* and *Gravity's Rainbow*, so does the explosive social situation of the sixties in America seem at first highly tangential to the quest undertaken by Oedipa Maas. Pynchon renders his perceptions of the historical moment with a set of understated allusions—to actual TV programs like *Perry Mason* and *Bonanza*, to imaginary popular music groups like The Paranoids and Sick Dick and the Volkswagens, and to student activism on the Berkeley campus of the University of California. The reader who looks for more discovers it in one powerful metaphor: the Tristero (sometimes spelled Trystero). A four-hundred-year-old tradition of postal fraud, the Tristero is the clandestine postal service discovered (or hallucinated) by Oedipa Maas. Oedipa discovers, too, the vast preterition that Tristero subsumes: a host of hitherto unnoticed, sometimes alarming, often tremendously pathetic elements curdling America's cream. She starts off as so many did in those days, a picture of white, middle-class, mildly neurotic suburbanite complacency. She even identifies herself as "a Young Republican" (76). She ends up riddled with paranoia and stifled by "the exitlessness, . . . the absence of surprise to life, that harrows the head of everybody American you know" (170). Among the most important passages in the book, therefore, are those in which Oedipa brushes up against America's human misery—as in those glimpses (provided in her husband Mucho's accounts of the clientele at the used car lot where he previously worked) of the "salad of despair" (14) swept from under the seats and dug out of the upholstery of the wretched automobiles traded in by poor people.

Equally important to my case for Pynchon's argument by indirection and understatement is the novel's single, intense glance at the exploding energies of protest in American universities. When Oedipa makes a brief visit to the campus of the University of California, Berkeley, epicenter of sixties student activism in America, Pynchon's prose gradually accelerates towards Ginsbergian supernova:

> It was summer, a weekday, and midafternoon; no time for any campus Oedipa knew of to be jumping, yet this one was. She came downslope from Wheeler Hall, through Sather Gate into a plaza teeming with corduroy, denim, bare legs, blonde hair, hornrims, bicycle spokes in the sun, bookbags, swaying card tables, long paper petitions dangling to earth, posters for undecipherable FSM's, YAF's, VDC's, suds in the fountain, students in nose-to-nose dialogue. She moved through it carrying her fat book, attracted, unsure, a stranger, wanting to feel relevant but knowing how much of a search among alternate universes it would take. For she had undergone her own educating at a time of nerves, blandness and retreat among not only her fellow students but also most of the visible structure around and ahead of them, this having been a national reflex to certain pathologies in high places only death had had the power to cure, and this Berkeley was like no somnolent Siwash out of her own past at all, but more akin to those Far Eastern or Latin American universities you read about, those autonomous culture media where the most beloved of folklores may be brought into doubt, cataclysmic of dissents voiced, suicidal of commitments chosen—the sort that bring governments down. But it was English she was hearing as she crossed Bancroft Way among the blonde children and the muttering Hondas and Suzukis; American English. Where were

secretaries James and Foster and Senator Joseph, those dear daft numina who'd mothered over Oedipa's so temperate youth? In another world. Along another pattern of track, another string of decisions taken, switches closed, the faceless pointsmen who'd thrown them now all transferred, deserted, in stir, fleeing the skip-tracers, out of their skull, on horse, alcoholic, fanatic, under aliases, dead, impossible to find ever again. Among them they had managed to turn Oedipa into a rare creature indeed, unfit perhaps for marches and sit-ins, but just a whiz at pursuing strange words in Jacobean texts. (103–4)

But if the brilliance of *Lot 49*'s parody of revenge tragedy is any indication, the person most at home with Jacobean texts is Oedipa's creator, who in *The Crying of Lot 49* offers readers an indirect glimpse of himself: in his protagonist, that is, Pynchon projects his own anguish at the American denial of diversity. Through her he inhabits and participates in an American social and cultural moment of enormous consequence. It was during the sixties, after all, that privileged Americans learned that hunger in their country had not disappeared after the Great Depression. It was the sixties that brought racial injustice fully before the mainstream American mind, first in the civil rights movement, then in several long hot summers during which one heartland city after another was torched. In the sixties, too, America discovered that, no matter how much ordnance its B-52s could deliver, a certain country in southeast Asia was going to insist on going its own way. In the sixties, finally, the entire nation began to realize that the version of America seen in films and on TV, in advertisements, and, indeed, in its very neighborhoods, was woefully unrepresentative. The country discovered, in short, that its citizens were not all white and prosperous.

One of those literary characters who embody their historical moment, Oedipa Maas resembles Updike's Rabbit Angstrom or the more sentimentalized Forrest Gump. Such characters are often passive—their function is simply to register or reflect the Zeitgeist and its characteristic energies. Robert Zemeckis, putting Winston Groom's Gump on film, intimates satirically that for all the bumbling sweetness of the generation represented by the protagonist, its desires and consciousness seldom rise to the level of actual volition. One discovers the driving force behind recent history in the least informed appetites of the generation coming clumsily of age. Updike, on the other hand, in his four novels and one novella about Rabbit Angstrom, depicts in lapidary detail the turnings of five successive decades. In *Rabbit Redux* (1971), the second volume of the series, he identifies a kind of national hysteria as the defining mood of the late sixties. But Updike's loyalties are to social realism, and this novel can seem remote from the essential character of its historical moment. The documentary gift of Pynchon's fellow chronicler of the times may leave the reader hungry for something more.

In Oedipa, as in these other characters, one recognizes a latter-day, democratized version of an ancient conceit: the mythic king whose health replicates itself in the physical and spiritual condition of his realm. The odd name of Pynchon's heroine invites readers to recognize in her some sixties version of the Sophoclean protagonist who undertakes a quest involving his own past and a diseased social present. America, like Thebes, suffers pestilence—a plague of racism, economic marginalization, and general neurasthenia. Reenacting the passion of Oedipus, Pynchon's character discovers in herself, in her own blindness and complacency, the source of her country's troubles.

Though painful, such recognitions are part of growing up as a nation. We surrender our innocence (so dangerous to ourselves and others) and begin coming to grips with social realities that belie the vision of equality and justice announced in the preamble to the Constitution and echoed in patriotic addresses. Oedipa "had heard all about excluded middles; they were bad shit, to be avoided; and how had it ever happened here, with the chances once so good for diversity?" (181). Yet this fallacy at the heart of the American syllogism invites a creative deconstruction, for it also figures the not-always-recognized positive element in a story that confronts its readers with their own Oedipa-like need either to organize the world around them, to spin or weave or embroider it in their own mental towers—or to attempt to live in a world in which connection forever eludes them. In the powerful closing pages of *Lot 49*, Pynchon depicts his protagonist striving to negotiate mutually exclusive alternatives: "Either Oedipa in the orbiting ecstasy of a true paranoia, or a real Tristero" (182). But in the suggestive metaphor of the excluded middle, the author hints—in 1966, just as Jacques Derrida was presenting a now-famous paper in Baltimore—that either/or thinking tends to reveal epistemic entrapment, that mutually exclusive binaries are always hierarchical and always invite deconstruction.

Lot 49 augurs an era of societal deconstruction. This is not simple nihilistic destruction, though it is often taken as such. Rather it is the exit from Eisenhower complacency and the entry into an endlessly creative free fall. Pynchon would go on to suggest, in *Vineland*, that rigidity would reassert itself in the eighties, and the narrator of *Inherent Vice* seems aware that the arrival of the baby boom presidents—Bill Clinton, George Bush, Barack Obama—will usher in no belated golden age of societal free play and political liberalism. But Pynchon can still take heart from the strength of those who have, through much persecution, persevered, kept the faith. As will be seen, Jess Traverse, the labor activist who appears as an old man in *Vineland* and as a boy in *Against the Day*, remains able to affirm, in literally Emersonian terms, an ultimate, cosmic standard of justice. Pynchon does not undercut the old man's moralizing, which stands as a counterweight to both the ludic features and the dark political vision of the California novels.

One can often judge literary art by the accuracy with which it registers and gauges its cultural moment. But artists must also be the antennae of the race, to paraphrase Ezra Pound, and we therefore expect not only a scrupulous rendering of the moment from them but also some intimation of where that moment might lead and what it might come to mean over time. One expects of literature, in other words, that it reflect on the present in ways that will prove more or less prescient. Somewhat surprisingly, this prophetic dimension is precisely what informs irreal, metafictional, postmodernist fiction. What appears at first as merely a desperate form of innovation (a response, in Barth's formulation, to the exhaustion of literary forms) proves expressive of the age and its formative spirit. In the sixties, in particular, certain cultural phenomena—the decentering of old subjectivities, the abbreviating of the historical horizon by movies and TV—found their most effective representation in an art that problematized objectivity, foregrounded the processes of representation, and expressed the strange idea that reality was never a given, never something one could divorce from the language purporting to render it.

I have argued that Thomas Pynchon proved, early on, an especially good artistic antenna. He takes a longer view than even his most gifted contemporaries (and as Woolf's Lily Briscoe says, distance is all). In *V.* and *Gravity's Rainbow* he charts, with no small prescience, the toll of the West's Faustian appetite for knowledge and power. In *Mason & Dixon* he explores the late eighteenth-century moment of the nation's founding. In *Vineland*, in press as the Berlin Wall came down, his imagination shifts to the post-apocalyptic—indeed, millennial—fulfillments that might follow a generation's coming to terms with its own manifold betrayals. In *Against the Day*, he implicitly cautions against replicating, early in the twenty-first century, the follies that led, early in the twentieth, to a Great War. In *Inherent Vice*, which appeared scant months into the Obama presidency, he seems again to meditate the clash of reactionary and redemptive energies in shaping an American future. In *Lot 49*, finally, as in all of these fictions, he depicts an entire generation's passage, archetypal and American, from innocence to experience. It is fashionable now to nod glumly at pronouncements like those of Bill Gray, the novelist in DeLillo's *Mao II* who says that the literary artist of the late twentieth century can no longer "alter the inner life of the culture,"[7] but I am struck by the acuity with which Thomas Pynchon now chronicles, now anticipates the unsmooth course of his country's maturation, its putting away of childish things.

Vineland: Continuity and Growth

"A screaming comes across the sky." A rocket? Yes, but also a literary career. Seventeen years after the publication of *Gravity's Rainbow*, the novel that opens with those famous words, Thomas Pynchon returns with *Vineland* and reminds his readers that the meteoric transit is also his own. As charismatic as the mythic Rocket of that earlier novel, Pynchon resists "routinization" by scrupulously refusing to submit to the American fame machine and—as the reader of his fourth novel sees—by reshaping his art and lengthening the trajectory of his imagination. One can think of the seventeen-year hiatus between these novels as a suspension of the meteoric transit—a suspension as portentous in its way as that of the ICBM at the conclusion of *Gravity's Rainbow*, arrested at "the last delta-t" (760) before impact. Now both the apocalypse and the career resume, but in altered form. The apocalyptic becomes the millennial as the career resists its own betrayal to gravity. *Vineland* announces phase two of Pynchon's literary career and so merits close scrutiny—especially for those who might think it a flawed production, published merely to break some creative logjam.

As Norman Mailer once remarked: "There was that law of life, so cruel and so just, which demanded that one must grow or else pay more for remaining the same." In *Vineland* one encounters the familiar Pynchon topoi: funny songs, entropy, paranoia, Puritanism, the quest. Again, too, one encounters the metaphysics of film, the politics of dope, the literary re-creation of faraway places, the flights of imagination. But these topics have evolved—sometimes towards greater subtlety and complexity, sometimes towards a condition of near vestigiality. Pynchon's art, in other words, is not static. Moreover, he tries out new inflections, new topoi, new emphases—notably in some surprising variations on the themes of family, feminism, and the fiction of engagement. Continuity, then, and growth.

One can think of a writer's characteristic images and themes as circus animals that, as Yeats once lamented, eventually grow long in the fang or simply desert. Some of Pynchon's circus animals become, in *Vineland,* less lively than others, perhaps because he has belatedly embraced—so he hints in his *Slow Learner* introduction—a version of that old creative writing saw: write about what you know.[8] Perhaps, on the other hand, a deepening seriousness of the type he has hailed in Gabriel García Márquez has made less viable some of the more pyrotechnic touches of old.[9] The postmodern hoops through which the animals jumped—the reflexivity of structures that mocked structure, the representation of representation, the brilliant demonstrations that "meaning" is always projective—seem to have given way to simpler, less mannered displays. The fiction is still surreal and fabulous, parody is still prominent, realism—such as it is—remains "magical," but the literary energy that shaped Pynchon's work in the sixties and seventies seems to be flowing into fresh channels. Something new is going on.

Has anything been lost? Perhaps, here and there. Whether because Pynchon is writing more from personal experience or because of some imaginative vitiation, there are occasional fallings-off. One finds the songs here less amusing than those appearing in the previous works. Indeed, only "Floozy with an Uzi" is as good as "The Penis He Thought Was His Own" or the Rocket limericks from *Gravity's Rainbow*. Similarly, the descriptions of Tokyo and environs impress one less than the rich evocation, in the earlier novels, of places and times remote from the reader's—and the author's—experience: turn-of-the-century Alexandria and Florence, Paris on the eve of the Great War, the stateless German "Zone" in the aftermath of World War II. One misses, too, the rich troves of recondite information—the ethnography of southwest Africa, the mechanics of rhinoplasty, the history of postal systems, the firing sequence for v-2 rockets. Invention, in short, flags. Thanatoids and the Ninja Death Touch do not afford the pleasure or shock of the alligators in the sewer, the parody of Jacobean revenge drama, and Brigadier Pudding's coprophagy.

Happily the wacky humor remains ("check's in the mayo"), with more of this author's wonderfully deft renderings of ethnic speech. Pynchon's Hispanics speak English with Spanish accent marks and punctuation. He presents the speech of Japanese characters as it is experienced by American viewers of Japanese movies: a series of guttural fits and starts, rendered in the subtitles with an abundance of dashes and exclamation points (which can lead readers familiar with the eccentric punctuation of a certain nineteenth-century American poet to think they have wandered into a screening of *Emily Dickinson Meets Godzilla*). The humor includes the usual krazy konceits: a retreat for Ninjettes, a cocaine nose museum, a lawn-care entrepreneur who calls himself the Marquis de Sod, and "the Harleyite Order, a male motorcycle club who for tax purposes had been reconstituted as a group of nuns" (358). Droll names and foreign puns abound, too. The Spanish word for rump— *trasero*—supplies the name of a mythical California county. Its beach is *Las Nalgas* (the buttocks). Lovers meet in *Las Suegras* (the mothers-in-law). Narcs are named *Brock* (Anglo-Saxon for badger) or the more obvious *Hector*. The name of a sinister dentist, Dr. Elasmo, is short for *elasmobranchii*, the order of fish that includes sharks and rays. The name *Prairie* seems also to be part of the charactonymic play. More than hippie arcadianism, the name glances simultaneously towards television culture (Miss Prairie Dawn is a minor

character on *Sesame Street*) and toward classic insurrectionary consciousness. The French revolutionary calendar of 1793 (which Pynchon refers
to in *The Crying of Lot 49*) includes the month Prairial, from French
prairie, a meadow.

Two other features familiar to Pynchon's readers—paranoia and the
quest—have undergone some interesting modifications, evidently in the
service of seriousness and immediacy. Instead of a Herbert Stencil, an
Oedipa Maas, or a Tyrone Slothrop in search of a master key, one tends
in *Vineland* to encounter characters in pursuit of assorted modest grails.
This splintering of the once unitary quest reduces readability, but it may
enhance the fiction's affinities with everyday life and its often less grand
goals—goals more likely to involve the recovery of an old lover or the
finding of a lost parent than the pursuit of the Zeitgeist. By the same token, the discoveries of connectedness that propel and sustain the quest
in Pynchon's earlier work—discoveries that gradually foster a paranoia
of almost religious intensity—give way to more commonplace discoveries of governmental conspiracy. The paranoia in *Vineland* is rooted in the
political here and now. It becomes less metaphysical, more local.

In the previous work, paranoia—what the narrator of *Gravity's Rainbow*
calls "the discovery that everything is connected" (703)—was associated
with the psychological need for order, connectedness, pattern, and purpose. It was also, by an imaginative reversal, associated with the terrifying absence of these desiderata. In *Vineland* Pynchon domesticates these
stark alternatives. On the one hand he assesses the "spores of paranoia"
(239) that follow the betrayals of the late sixties: the omnipresent dread
of surveillance by or persecution from the attorney general's office, the
federal marshals, agents of the Drug Enforcement Agency, or other tentacles of the Department of Justice. On the other hand he imagines the
meaning of complete governmental indifference. The idea of unsleep-
ing surveillance, then, is balanced against the scarcely more attractive
alternative of a new preterition. People long dependent on federal pro-
tection (and largesse) "ain't on the computer anymore" (85). Victims of
governmental "octogenarihexation" (186), they have been "86'd" (218,
342).

Yet the expunging of files makes persecution easier by a Department
of Justice that becomes less and less accountable and more and more

Orwellian. The year *is* 1984, after all. Hector Zuñiga, the not-altogether-loathsome drug agent, tells Zoyd Wheeler that the federal dossier on his ex-wife has been purged as part of "a *real* revolution" (27) — a phrase that, left mysteriously undefined, evidently has something to do with the Reagan retrenchment in domestic spending. But "in art," as Nabokov once remarked, "the roundabout hits the center."[10] Pynchon's credo as a novelist, again, is to represent by indirection; just as, in *V.* and *Gravity's Rainbow*, he represents the holocaust obliquely and analogically, in the genocidal war against the Hereros in turn-of-the-century south-west Africa and in the slaughter of the dodoes in seventeenth-century Mauritius, so here also he declines to depict the most obvious social costs of the Reagan revolution. Indeed, one of the major ironies of this novel — whose present-time setting is the eve, as it were, of Reagan's second four-year term and the consolidation of the new, "Reaganomic" order — is that the case against Reaganomics is made chiefly in terms of cuts at the expense of those who had been bought out or co-opted or "turned" by the ruthless right back in the days of social revolution. Thus one does not see the "Reaganomic ax blades" (90) emptying mental institutions or slashing education subsidies. One does, however, see the ironic curtailment of the federal government's own latitude for manipulating its citizens.

But not enough. The willingness of those in power to conspire continues to justify considerable dread. To reflect this dialectic of low-grade conspiracy and paranoia, Pynchon recalibrates and reimagines his best-known plot device. The quest becomes multiple. Hector Zuñiga wants to make a movie. Zoyd Wheeler wants his house back. Brock Vond pursues, and occasionally possesses, Frenesi Gates. Estranged from Frenesi, he also pursues her daughter Prairie, whom he hopes to make the instrument of renewed control. Prairie, meanwhile, engages in a quest of her own. Like Herbert Stencil, she undertakes a feminized Telemachiad, a search for the mother. This gender reversal of a literary convention, as will be seen, is a part of the novel's ultimately feminist vision.

But a grander and more problematic quest — something closer in spirit to the fictive strategies of *V.*, *Lot 49*, and *Gravity's Rainbow* — provides the backdrop for these personal grails. From the Death to the Pig Nihilist Film Kollective to the Thanatoids, from the Wobbly survivors to the persecuted Zoyd Wheeler, what shapes and animates *Vineland* is the quest for justice in a Nixonian and Reaganite America. Pynchon's work has always had its political edge, for this author commonly expresses a powerful sympathy for the victims of injustice (or indifference). In *Vineland*, too, whether recalling Hollywood union woes in the blacklist fifties or evoking the counterculture of the sixties, Pynchon clearly leans left—but he is too rigorous a thinker to suggest that the course of recent American history is the result of demonic fascism having its way with innocent, politically correct visionaries. Like Lionel Trilling in *The Middle of the Journey*, the author of *Vineland* unsparingly depicts the corruption of left and right. The poles of misguided millenarian desire in Trilling—Communism and Christianity in the thirties and forties—are not so far from the dialectic of radicalism and repression from the sixties to the eighties in Pynchon's fourth novel.

Much of the story's political focus—and thus its concern with the grail of social justice—concerns the abuses that attend on the massive federal campaign to eradicate drugs from American life. In a time when every poll suggested that Americans considered drugs the supreme menace to the republic, Pynchon might have seemed guilty of the worst kind of bad timing. But he did not misjudge the social moment—he wished to enter a dissent, to satirize and correct the "national drug hysteria" (310) and to raise questions about the apparent promotion, by the "antidrug-hysteria leadership" (340), of "a timeless, defectively imagined future of zero-tolerance drug-free Americans all pulling their weight and all locked in to the official economy, inoffensive music, endless family specials on the Tube, church all week long, and, on special days, for extra-good behavior, maybe a cookie" (221–22). Pynchon defies this coercive homogenization by treating the drug culture sympathetically. Hence the suggestion about subversives who rewrite the slogan "DRUG FREE AMERICA" by adding an "s" at the end of the first word (342). Drugs are to *Vineland* what the Tristero is to *Lot 49*—a metaphor serving the vision of a different social reality.

One wonders, nonetheless, why the author makes so little of the genuine destructiveness of drugs. Why no mention of crack houses and babies born burdened with their mothers' addictions (problems that do get noticed in *Inherent Vice*)? The reader must keep in mind that the failure to differentiate truly dangerous substances from relatively harmless ones is precisely what the government was (and still is) guilty of in its loose-cannon war on drugs. Pynchon understands what a character in *Gravity's Rainbow* describes as the "nearly complete parallelism between analgesia and addiction" (348). But addiction and addictive substances are not his real subject here. They properly appear at the periphery of the action—in Mucho Maas's former dependency on cocaine, in Takeshi Fumimota's reliance on amphetamines, and, more broadly, in the addiction of Hector Zuñiga to television.

Pynchon, then, remains less interested in drugs per se than in drugs as a touchstone or gauge of governmental repression. He intimates—more low-grade paranoia—that the government's tendency to lump marijuana together with heroin reveals a dark goal. The federal "war on a botanical species" (271), in other words, is part of a larger government program. It targets "carefree dopers" (222) guilty of little more than indifference to getting and spending. The war on drugs tends to become a convenient excuse to harass the unassimilated, the different, the nonconforming, and the recusant. As such, it is the wrong war, the wrong cause.

The author also invites the perception that the war on drugs is being waged to distract the populace from a desire for some more worthwhile war—perhaps on the economic and social injustice that fills ghetto streets with juvenile crack pushers. The right war, Pynchon implies, is the one against the great Mammon of American materialism. If at times the author strikes the pose of a Hunter S. Thompson, implying that one needs heavy doses of some powerful anodyne or other to deal with the horrors of contemporary America, his larger purpose resembles more closely that of the Beats, whose work impressed him as a young man. Like them he baits the uptight middle class and generally defies a square and repressive society by seeming to promote a drug mystique. Yet the message remains what it was in *Gravity's Rainbow*, at least in part: that a drug culture is the natural corollary to the political and economic exclusion of any social element. Drugs, at once destructive and subversive, correlate to powerlessness.

The century's greatest challenge to the regimentation, the violence, and the materialism of mainstream American culture came not from the Beats but from the hippies, the "counterculture" of the sixties. The soul of this counterculture—or rather its *atman* (for it favored an Eastern spirituality)—was a substance popularly known as "weed," the spiritual distinctions of which were promoted in a radical new music. In *Vineland* this episode of cultural history is rendered symbolically in the rise and fall of The People's Republic of Rock and Roll and its doomed Fisher King, Weed Atman. Pynchon dramatizes the federal government's intolerance of drugs and difference in the subversion of PR³ and in the murder of its leader—the novel's central act of injustice. Weed Atman joins the community of those unjustly deprived of life, the Thanatoids, those "insomniac unavenged" (324) who thirst for some knowledge that justice still operates within the universe.

Thus even the dead have their grail. They, too, pursue justice, assisted by the unlikely duo of Darryl Louise Chastain, a renegade army brat who becomes a "Ninjette" dedicated to the confusion of the unjust, and Takeshi Fumimota—last seen as part of a Laurel and Hardy kamikaze team in *Gravity's Rainbow* (his partner, Ichizo, may have been the kamikaze who disabled the destroyer on which Prairie's grandfather, Hubbell Gates, served during the war). Takeshi and DL fight injustice of various kinds and at various levels. They set up a "Karmology Clinic" in Shade Creek to service the accounts of the Thanatoids, for Takeshi is a "karmic adjuster," a parody of the familiar insurance functionary. Having worked for Wawazume Life & Non-Life before becoming a free lance, he now battles karmic fraud—getting away with injustice—in its most extravagant forms.

In a sequence that parodies Japanese monster movies, Takeshi investigates the destruction of a lab on the coast of Japan belonging to Chipco, a "shadowy world conglomerate" (142). He thinks that the lab was destroyed by a bomb, not the size-twenty-thousand foot of some monster (Professor Wawazume's counterconclusion [169] can be discounted as self-serving, since he was apparently "fading some of the action" [146]). But Takeshi never really identifies the malign entities that have destroyed the lab—they become part of the larger, more metaphysical injustice with which he struggles. His ultimate enemies, in fact, are the "unrelenting forces" that forever confound the human yearning for cosmic justice. "[I]mpassive in pursuit, usually gaining," these forces manifest themselves as

> the faceless predators who'd once boarded Takeshi's airplane in the sky, the ones who'd had the Chipco lab stomped on, who despite every Karmic Adjustment resource brought to bear so far had simply persisted, stone-humorless, beyond cause and effect, rejecting all attempts to bargain or accommodate, following through pools of night where nothing else moved wrongs forgotten by all but the direly possessed, continuing as a body to refuse to be bought off for any but the full price, which they had never named. (383)

Takeshi, then, is a kind of Zen private eye, up against time, death, and entropy. His struggles with these entities, though doomed to failure, cannot be abandoned, for they are the struggles of humanity itself.

Karmic Adjustment, impotent yet resourceful, is a metaphor for art, too, and one can identify Takeshi, finally, as the author's surrogate, a "magician" whose "Act, with its imitations of defiance . . . of gravity and death" (384), will not, in Auden's famous dictum, make anything happen. Yet the supreme quest has always been for some means of circumventing forces like gravity and death, and art has always been the vehicle of that desire. The human thirst for the miraculous—and art's gratification of that thirst—is one of the healthiest manifestations of a resistance to universal mechanization. Indeed, as Pynchon remarks in his 1984 article "Is It O.K. to Be a Luddite?," art exists to front and occasionally defy "the laws of nature," including "space, time, thermodynamics, and the big one, mortality itself."[11]

Not that art fronts these horrors alone. There is also, more problematically, religion. In *Vineland*, as elsewhere in his work (notably *Mason & Dixon*), Pynchon balances the spiritual dimension of art against the cruder appetite for miracle at the heart of conventional religion. Specifically, he assays the distortions effected in American character and consciousness through their early shaping by Puritan theology. Thus the Puritan proclivity to divide humanity into elect and preterite figures obliquely here, as does the Puritan fascination with apocalyptic signs on high. But this time the apocalypse comes in an arrestable form: no triumph of the inanimate, no descending ICBM. Pynchon dismantles the myth of apocalypse to reveal a vision—carefully qualified, it is itself a delicate myth—of elegiac and millennial peace. A further consideration of the presence of Pynchon's Puritan New England heritage will discover fresh instances of continuity and growth. Here, too, the old topoi evolve.

Permutations of Puritanism

Again, a screaming comes across the sky, this time "helicopters descending" (248), latter-day versions of "the sleek raptors that decorate fascist architecture" (287). Brock Vond likes to operate out of "dead-black Huey slicks . . . liable to pop up suddenly over a peaceful ridgeline or come screaming down the road after an innocent motorist" (375). The helicopter, that familiar cinematic symbol of modern evil (as Pauline Kael once pointed out), becomes in the novel's climactic sequence the emblem of federal ruthlessness, a travesty of the power on high so dear to hearts still unable to shake off what a character in *Gravity's Rainbow* calls "the damned Calvinist insanity" (57). In that novel, allusions to Puritan theology help to illustrate the historical and philosophical affinities, notably the similar pretensions to racial election, of all Teutonic peoples—Anglo-Saxon as well as Nordic. Here again Pynchon imagines both sympathetic and villainous characters grappling with the spiritual legacy of Puritanism.

As Max Weber showed in *The Protestant Ethic and the Spirit of Capitalism*, the course of Western history, from the sixteenth century to the twentieth, has been profoundly influenced by cultural changes set in motion by the Reformation. In *Vineland* as in *Gravity's Rainbow*, Pynchon notes the strange tenacity of Calvinist and Puritan values in American culture: the encouragement of sobriety and plain living, the intolerance of idleness and "mindless pleasures," the sanctity of work (which promotes the growth of capital), and especially the distinction between the regenerate saved—a select remnant—and the vast body of the unchosen. Long after the heyday of real Puritans—indeed, long after a general secularization—these values remain part of the fabric of American life, as one sees in the terms in which a counterculture character cautions his fellows: "You're up against the True Faith here, some heavy dudes, talking crusades, retribution, closed ideological minds passing on the Christian Capitalist Faith intact, mentor to protégé, generation to generation, living inside their power, convinced they're immune to all the history the rest of us have to suffer" (232). A Brock Vond, for example, can exemplify a Puritan outlook without being religious. He represents a world of public officials and their narrow views, especially the diehard certainty of election on the part of a certain kind of white Anglo-Saxon Protestant. His victims are the latter-day "preterite," those predestined to define by their victimization the spiritual distinction of the elect. But as Hawthorne shows in "Young Goodman Brown," there is something devilish in Puritan rectitude, and this is certainly true of Vond.

Early American Puritans looked for and responded to signs, and so do their descendants. In *Gravity's Rainbow* Pynchon satirizes this sensitivity in the erections with which Tyrone Slothrop, who evinces "a peculiar sensitivity to what is revealed in the sky" (26), greets the celestial revelation of descending v-2 rockets. In *Vineland* the Puritan sensitivity to aerial revelation—to apocalypse, that is, in its original meaning—again figures centrally, even in scenes culturally remote from the Puritan sphere. Whatever Takeshi Fumimota and his colleagues make of the destruction of the Chipco lab, the narrator invites his Western readers to recognize a trope on the idea of apocalyptic desire, the expectation that justice, whether in the form of annihilation or "rapture" (a word that figures repeatedly in the novel), will come from the sky. Hence the insistent references to helicopters and monsters on high, not to mention monster-helicopters like the aircraft Chipco's employees modify as a joke—or helicopter-monsters like the one that figures in Prairie's near-kidnapping by the copter-crazy Brock Vond. Such entities descend not to deliver but to ravage, to deal "Death From Slightly Above" (375). In the novel's climax, then, the reader "beholds" an arrested apocalypse, as Brock Vond, in an especially outrageous piece of helicopter terrorism, appears in the sky to fulfill the favorite prophecy of those dubious latter-day Puritans, the fundamentalists. As Vond himself says, "The key is rapture" (376).

This apocalyptic tenor is a standard feature of Pynchon's work. The early stories "Entropy" and "Mortality and Mercy in Vienna" conclude with images of annihilation, and both *V.* and *Against the Day* can be read as part of a many-layered meditation on the apocalyptic tendencies of modern and postmodern history. Sidney Stencil, in *V.*, has a theory of "Paracletian politics" (479–80) whereby, as early as 1919, he anticipates the Second World War as

> the Paraclete's coming, the comforter, the dove; the tongues of flame, the gift of tongues: Pentecost. Third Person of the Trinity. None of it was implausible to Stencil. The Father had come and gone. In political terms, the Father was the Prince; the single leader, the dynamic figure whose virtù used to be a determinant of history. This had degenerated to the Son, genius of the liberal love-feast which had produced 1848 and lately the overthrow of the Czars. What next? What Apocalypse? (472).

Lot 49 gives expression to the yearning for some more conventionally defined Paraclete. It ends on a note of sacred *Erwartung*, for the number in the title may refer, as Edward Mendelson has suggested, to the span of days between Easter and Pentecost.[12] Supreme among these apocalyptic visions, of course, is the conclusion of *Gravity's Rainbow*, in which the Rocket descends, bringing universal destruction.

Small wonder, then, that one of the set pieces of *Vineland* is the scene in an Oklahoma motel room where Brock Vond suborns Frenesi Gates while a terrible thunderstorm rages outside. The scene is replete with apocalyptic imagery that complements the hellish deal being struck. The storm seems like "some first hard intelligence of an agent of rapture." It is also a "Beast" (212) that, unleashing "some nonliquid clattering on the roof that could only be insects of a plague" (215), "held the city down like prey, trying repeatedly to sting it into paralysis" (216). Vond, whose birth sign is Scorpio, seems to take cynical pleasure in the blathering evangelist on the television, a debased Saint John the Divine who declares: "Looks like we're in the hands of Jesus again" (213).

Pynchon conceives this scene ironically, as part of a more extensive eschatology. The irony differs from that of the other novels, especially *V.*, *Gravity's Rainbow*, and *Against the Day*, where the author treats apocalypse not as the "promised end" but as the secular cataclysm brought on by unbridled Faustian appetites. In *Vineland* the irony involves the triviality and abortiveness of apocalypse, which Pynchon imagines as the merest episode in a vaster and more splendid drama. The real denouement concerns the millennium, not its noisy and violent antecedents. In *Vineland* readers experience the first great *fin-de-millénaire* novel.

The millennium, again ironically, does not configure itself as the characters expect. Pynchon shows that the millennial expectations of Frenesi Gates and her would-be revolutionary colleagues lead to corruption as surely as the fascistic moral certainty of their antagonists in the Department of Justice. Strung out on this millennial dream, Frenesi is easily betrayed into a reenactment of the great mythic event with which history itself began. One discovers that millennial fictions, like ordinary apocalyptic ones, naturally invoke the Old Testament alpha as well as the New Testament omega: apocalypse, after all, completes something begun in the Garden of Eden. Thus one need not look far in this book to discover what Terrence Rafferty, in his perceptive *New Yorker* review, calls "the oldest story in the world—the original sin and the exile from Paradise."[13]

Frenesi does not err or lapse alone. Her co-optation is a general metaphor for what has become of sixties radicalism: it has been bought out, tamed, integrated, assimilated, turned. A major theme in this novel is that of "going over," being "turned" or co-opted by the immensely powerful system. DL, for example, recalls the moment when her father, Moody, "went over" (120), and the estrangement of Hubbell and Sasha Gates, apparently over his decision to go over to the studios' pet union ("I . . . made my shameful peace" [291]), provides another, more poignant example. Frenesi sells out, too—she joins "the snitch community" (74) and goes on the federal payroll, like her two successive husbands, Zoyd and Flash (Zoyd, at least, manages to earn his federal checks by feigning insanity, not playing Judas).

In Pynchon's other novels, including *Against the Day* and *Inherent Vice*, the psychological and social drama also involves conversion—sometimes reprehensible, sometimes otherwise. Oedipa Maas eventually sees that she must join the disaffected and disinherited—that she can no longer define herself simply as a member of the complacent American middle class. In *Gravity's Rainbow*, similarly, the Counterforce enlists those—Osbie Feel, Webley Silvernail, Pirate Prentice, Ensign Morituri, Roger Mexico, Katje Borgesius, Carroll Eventyr, even Brigadier Pudding—who decide to participate in a great "division" in "The Parliament of Life" (536).

Pynchon's first novel, on the other hand, focuses on negative conversion. In *V.* Pynchon construes as entirely monstrous the heroine's going over to—her embracing of—the forces of entropy and the inanimate. Yet entropy (etymologically "a turning") proves universal, and "going over" is revealed as a part of nature.

Thus is it also in *Vineland*, where the Eden of "green free America" becomes a "scabland garrison state" (314) through a series of betrayals that stem less from villainy than from something in the natural scheme of things. Here the Eve-like Frenesi—her name an anagram of *sin free*—betrays her cause and the Adamic Weed Atman by succumbing to the "serpent hypnosis" (376) of Brock Vond. The apple is a .38-caliber Chief's Special, and the murder of Weed Atman is the Fall. Vond is an amateur of physiognomic character study (he believes in the warmed-over phrenology of Cesare Lombroso), and ironically his own face is a kind of diabolical cliché: "high smooth forehead, the cheeks that still hadn't lost all their baby fat, the sleek and pointed ears, small chin, and slim little unbroken nose" (130). The other characters call him "the enemy," and he does not seem to age. As careless with truth as the Father of Lies himself, he tries to convince Frenesi that Weed Atman really was his creature all along. He tells Prairie that he, Brock, is her real father.

When he invites the hapless Frenesi to help him snare Weed Atman, he twice insists that his interest is the man's soul. "I want his spirit" (213), he says. "Anyone can deliver me his body" (215). Frenesi fulfills her part of the bargain with Vond at Rex Snuvvle's beach house in Las Nalgas. When Frenesi speaks of photographing the confrontation with the allegedly double-dealing Atman, Howie remarks, "It's takin' his soul" (236), and just before the fatal moment, as it is in fact recorded, one sees in Atman "a long, stunned cringe, a loss of spirit that could almost be seen on the film . . . some silvery effluent, vacating his image, the real moment of his passing" (246). Frenesi's bargain with the devil implicates her in the murder of a man whose Hindu surname, as noted previously, denotes the supreme spiritual essence. His first name, Weed, suggests more than the "Sacrament of the Sixties" (342). It is also the Anglo-Saxon word for garment, a familiar metaphor for the body. Frenesi, like the original Eve, has promoted the death of both the body and the soul.

Pynchon, developing this myth with great subtlety, does not indulge in superficial moral categorizing. He avoids the simplistic depiction of prelapsarian and blameless counterculture souls ensnared by emissaries from the Great Satan in Washington, D.C. The author recognizes Frenesi's complicity in her fate; he knows that the preterite connive at their preterition. He also recognizes that the Fall and other such myths—signifiers too likely to float, after all—are susceptible to deconstruction. Sister Rochelle, for example, subjects the myth of Eden to a feminist reading that complements the novel's larger subversion of the apocalyptic myth. The aporias in the Eden story, says Sister Rochelle, center on Eve's suppressed sibling, Lilith. "Back then, long ago, there were no men at all. Paradise was female. Eve and her sister, Lilith, were alone in the Garden. A character named Adam was put into the story later, to help make men look more legitimate, but in fact the first man was not Adam—it was the Serpent" (166).

Vineland, of course, is as much Sister Rochelle's version of the story as any other. Frenesi and DL are Eve and Lilith, innocents in the Edenic sixties. Their friendship in fact antedates Frenesi's fateful romantic encounters. With the advent of the ophidian Brock Vond, whom Frenesi meets in a courthouse in Oregon, innocence itself seems to contract a wasting disease. Subsequently, in California, Frenesi meets Weed Atman, the Adam "put into the story later."

Sister Rochelle's story is only one of a number of feminist strands in the narrative. Pynchon registers much female experience here, and this emphasis may have something to do with a perception that, of all the consciousness-raising programs of the radical sixties, only the women's movement retains anything like the old integrity. Thus he makes women—Prairie, DL, Frenesi—his central characters. Moreover, the author who began his career, in *V.*, with a parody of Robert Graves's myth of the White Goddess, is at pains in his fourth novel to develop a feminist genealogy. In all of his previous work only Paola Maijstral—whose father and grandfather figure more prominently in *V.* than their wives—has as much attention paid to her antecedents as do male characters like Herbert Stencil and Tyrone Slothrop. But here one encounters a genealogical plenitude that centers on women, a generational unfolding that proceeds matrilineally from Eula to Sasha to Frenesi to Prairie.

As Virginia Woolf says, "We think back through our mothers if we are women."[14]

Much of this novel's energy and pathos derives from the search for the mother that Prairie undertakes. As noted previously, this search reverses or reconfigures the conventional search for the father, for patriarchal authority, reason, and order. The search for the mother is a search for connectedness and feeling—for the familial and communal principle itself. As Salman Rushdie observes, "These are the values the Nixon-Reagan era stole from the 60s and warped, aiming them back at America as weapons of control. They are values that 'Vineland' seeks to recapture."[15] In the end Prairie finds her mother, and the success of her quest allows Pynchon to conclude *Vineland* with a fine evocation of an extended and diverse family spread out over a rich California landscape—fields strawberry and Elysian—that is a transparent symbol of America. This, after all, is the millennium: humanity as family.

And this is new. When has Pynchon ever given this much attention to family before? Like Nathanael West, this author generally provides little in the way of families for his characters (this will change, of course, with *Against the Day*). Of the stories, only the Salingeresque "Secret Integration" features familial detail. Aside from the Mendozas, the Bortzes, and perhaps the Maijstrals, there are virtually no families in the early novels. In *V.*, Benny Profane briefly visits his parents' apartment in their absence, and thus the reader never sees him interacting with them. Other characters have only one parent. The connection between Evan and Hugh Godolphin is merely sketched in to be sundered. Victoria Wren wastes no time estranging herself absolutely from her father and sister. She becomes in turn more myth than mother to Herbert Stencil. In *The Crying of Lot 49*, one encounters a host of isolates associated in one way or another with the Tristero, along with such solitaries as Roseman the lawyer, Genghis Cohen the philatelist, and Dr. Hilarius the psychiatrist. Once separated from her husband, Oedipa Maas has no family. There is no least hint of a family for Pierce Inverarity, either—only for Metzger, whose mother allegedly was out to "kasher" him. Roger Mexico, a character in *Gravity's Rainbow*, is not even that fortunate. "My mother is the War" (39), he observes. Pökler's family in that novel goes to pieces; Thanatz, Erdmann, and Bianca are a sick parody of a family. The lineage of Tyrone Slothrop may extend back to Puritan times, but his parents sell him to Dr. Jamf and that corporate monster, the "IG." His mother, Nadine, is imagined as hungry for the gold star that will signify a son sacrificed on the altar of war.

But *Vineland*, significantly dedicated to Pynchon's parents (of Pynchon's previous four volumes, only *Gravity's Rainbow* has a dedication, to his classmate at Cornell, Richard Fariña), demonstrates a strong new interest in the idea of family. Two decades later, reviewing *Inherent Vice*, Bernard Duyfhuizen will characterize "the primacy of a family unit, especially when children are involved," as "[t]he one unambiguous bit of morality in Pynchon's later fiction."[16] There was a hint of this interest in the *Slow Learner* introduction, a reference to the author's having in recent years learned something of "marriage or parenting" (10). And indeed, when Zoyd Wheeler proudly demonstrates his diaper-changing technique, one notes the kind of child-care detail that suggests experience: he "made sure his ex-mother-in-law noticed he was wiping in the right direction" (296). The novel's conclusion, at any rate, is a comedic vision of family wholeness, one that extends beyond the bounds of race and nationality, as Zoyd joins Prairie, Frenesi, Flash, Justin, and the others at the Traverse-Becker family reunion. Zoyd seems to be being healed by his immersion in family. Even those resentful ghosts the Thanatoids seem integrated, and Weed Atman and his murderer's daughter form a special bond. Takeshi and DL will become lovers, the Vomitones embrace Alexei, and Prairie's dog Desmond comes back to her.

Only Brock Vond, that banal Blicero, remains unassimilated to this vision, and his exclusion from any familial bond reveals the significance of his surname, an apocope of the Dutch word *vondeling*, a foundling. In the end, defeated, Vond crashes a more or less pirated helicopter and calls Vato and Blood to come for him. They answer a call from the dead, as they routinely do. But this is no Thanatoid, destined to take up residence in Shade Creek: Vond is last seen about to cross an astral river into hell itself, his spiritual home all along.

In the midst of what Zachary Leader calls "the pure-souled gathering or return which concludes the novel,"[17] Pynchon can introduce a patriarch to balance his otherwise wholly matriarchal vision. Jess Traverse addresses the issue, so central to this book, of "karmic imbalances — unanswered blows, unredeemed suffering, escapes by the guilty" (173), and through him Pynchon invokes an ultimate victory over at least the social forms of evil. The Traverse patriarch insists that justice holds its own, and his reading of those lines from Emerson in the closing pages augurs at once a personal and a millennial righting of ancient wrongs: "Secret retributions are always restoring the level, when disturbed, of the divine justice. It is impossible to tilt the beam. All the tyrants and proprietors and monopolists of the world in vain set their shoulders to heave the bar. Settles forever more the ponderous equator to its line, and man and mote, and star and sun, must range to it, or be pulverized by the recoil" (369).

But Pynchon is too honest to endorse Emerson's visionary affirmation uncritically or to overstate the validity and prospects of his own millennial dream. Many of the family faithful here will awaken on the morrow like the knight in "La Belle Dame Sans Merci"—on a cold hillside, with no birds singing. Zoyd will never be reunited with Frenesi, nor will he recover his house. His dream of torching that ramshackle edifice hints at a whole world of resentment on the part of those who cannot enter the house of American conformity and prosperity. Most problematic of all is Prairie's strange desire that Brock Vond return in his helicopter. She—and the generation she represents—is as susceptible as her mother to a dark temptation.

Whether or not Jess Traverse—or Emerson—speaks for Pynchon, visionary *Vineland* reveals considerable artistic growth on the part of an author whose first novel contains only the single meliorist hint: "Keep cool but care" (366). Even if one must admit that *Vineland* falls short of the extraordinary work of Pynchon's early career, it remains a remarkable achievement. Its prose is supple, its ideas compelling, its technique indicative of a resistance to calcification and mannerism. If a few of its "circus animals" prove superannuated, others can still roar and prance—and Pynchon introduces two or three new attractions. Few writers could advance beyond their first season of virtù as resourcefully as Pynchon, and in *Vineland* he affirms that, like the originator of the circus animals metaphor, he will continue to grow and remake himself, continue to delve into that foul rag-and-bone shop of the heart to produce imaginative work "made luminous, undeniably authentic," as he says in his introduction to *Slow Learner*, "by having been found and taken up, always at a cost, from deeper, more shared levels of the life we all really live" (21).

Attenuated Postmodernism

Creator of the most significant body of fiction in contemporary America, Pynchon may have spent some of the nearly twenty years between publication of his third and fourth novels discovering the limits of the postmodernist aesthetic. *Vineland*, the long-awaited fourth, appeared seventeen years after the publication in 1973 of the monumental *Gravity's Rainbow*, widely recognized now as the most important American novel published since World War II. Having asked, in the preceding section, whether those seventeen years saw this author's art develop, one can affirm that Pynchon does not stand still as a maker of fiction. In *Vineland*, which may represent a turning point for Pynchon, the author keeps his hand in, modifying some of his old tricks and trying out new ones. In a consideration of this novel's traditional and contemporary features, one encounters an evolutionary text, an experiment in literary hybridization. Perhaps testing the premise that the postures of literary exhaustion may themselves be exhausted, the author combines modernist concerns and postmodernist techniques with some of the features of two kinds of realism: social and magic. In this section, in addition to scrutinizing the vestiges of an aesthetic or style that Pynchon might seem to be outgrowing, I will glance at the Abish-like question "how postmodern is it?" in the course of gauging the traditional elements and fresh invention that compose this hybrid. The argument here, introduced in a brief comparison of Pynchon's career with that of Joyce, will focus on technique and the treatment given history and culture (including myth). The author of *Vineland* views these topics through a postmodern lens: they appear foreshortened, flattened, all surface. Yet the novel's title and its mythic extension of contemporary history hint at a broader view. Though Pynchon tends to deconstruct the myths he invokes, they complicate the rendering of an otherwise comprehensively ahistorical contemporaneity. Through a combination of this eccentric mythography with a moral earnestness expressed as a penchant for political didacticism, Pynchon produces, in *Vineland*, a fiction devoted less to indeterminate postmodernist "play" than to totalizing modernist "purpose."[18]

On the face of it, Pynchon's is the definitive postmodern career. In book after book, he has seemed to be Harold Bloom's "strong poet," creatively misreading his modernist forebears. Indeed, a comparison of his work with that of Joyce, a literary father to generate considerable anxiety, reveals some interesting parallels. With the exception of the late sport *Slow Learner*, Pynchon's 1984 collection of early stories, the fiction-publishing careers of these two writers match up, volume for volume, until the American, spared the untimely *Brennschluss* of the Irish master, began to pull ahead in terms of sheer productivity (*Mason & Dixon* appeared when Pynchon was 59—the age at which Joyce died). Joyce's first book-length fiction appeared in 1914, his fourth and last twenty-five years later, in 1939. Pynchon's first novel and his fourth span a nearly identical period: the twenty-six years from 1963 to 1989. In the space of exactly a quarter of a century, each of these writers gives his age its gold standard in fiction, the one defining modernism in the novel, the other postmodernism. Yet the two careers move toward an instructive divergence. The early volumes of Joyce appeared within two years of each other; those of Pynchon, within three. Joyce's first book, *Dubliners* (1914), is a meticulously structured set of linked fictions that anatomize a culture. Pynchon's *V.* (1963), a highly episodic and fragmented novel that at least one early reviewer (Meixner) took to be a congeries of cobbled together pieces from collegiate creative writing courses, is also meticulously structured, also a cultural anatomy. *Dubliners* moves toward a final vision of snowy paralysis, *V.* toward the triumph of the inanimate. *V.* was followed in 1966 by *The Crying of Lot 49*, in which the failure of American promise gradually manifests itself to a protagonist, Oedipa Maas, whose age (twenty-eight in 1964, the novel's present), education (Cornell), and places of travel and residence (Mexico and California) seem to make her a female Thomas Pynchon. A kind of oblique spiritual autobiography or conversion narrative, *Lot 49* is Pynchon's portrait of the artist in youth and, as such, corresponds to Joyce's autobiographical novel, *A Portrait of the Artist as a Young Man* (1916).

The seven-year period between *Lot 49* (1966) and *Gravity's Rainbow* (1973) corresponds to the six-year period between *Portrait* (1916) and

Ulysses (1922). *Gravity's Rainbow* and *Ulysses* are quests, "encyclopedic" fictions that, epic in scope, catalog whole cultures with broad attention to the literary and historical past. Each is, in its own way, a strange amalgam of family romance and Telemachiad: Stephen Dedalus discovers a father in Leopold Bloom, Tyrone Slothrop in the evil scientist Dr. Lazslo Jamf. Stephen, of course, is Joyce's autobiographical character, and perhaps one recognizes a further element of autobiography in the Pynchon novel, too, inasmuch as it concerns a person who, like the author, simply fades from sight after embarking on a quest that makes him the "Zone's newest celebrity" (377) and brings him face to face with the possibility that Western culture "might be in love, in sexual love" (738), with its own death.

As the years went by after *Gravity's Rainbow*, one wondered whether its successor would, unimaginably, sustain the Joycean parallel. What complex, Viconian meditation, its hour come round at last, slouched toward Little, Brown (or Penguin) to be born? In what idiom would it be written—would it be dense with Herero and Maltese portmanteau words? Pynchon's fourth novel was officially published early in 1990, but it was actually in the bookstores in late December 1989. In terms of the paradigm, both dates are significant. The earlier is the fiftieth anniversary of the publication, in 1939, of *Finnegans Wake*, which appeared seventeen years after Joyce's previous novel, *Ulysses*. The year 1990 marks the same seventeen-year period since the publication of Pynchon's last novel, *Gravity's Rainbow*.

But the parallel falters: *Vineland* is not the postmodern *Finnegans Wake*. At most one can say that Vineland County, California, is as mythic a landscape as "Howth Castle and Environs" and the River Liffey. One can note, too, that Leif Ericson, who gave America its first name and Pynchon his title, is among the innumerable strands in the weave of the Wake: "lief eurekason and his undishcovery of americle."[19] But these are frail and exiguous crossties for continuing the parallel rails laid thus far. The breakdown in the parallels suggests that the fate reserved for Pynchon's aesthetic differs radically from that reserved for Joyce's. Perhaps modernism was fated to end with a bang, postmodernism with a whimper.

Though *Finnegans Wake* announced a new aesthetic in its structure—that of a giant Möbius strip—and in its parodic features (it burlesques the medieval dream vision), it is, first and last, the supreme modernist text. Like its modernist predecessors, it exploits myth, probes consciousness and its mysterious subsurface, and outrages aesthetic sensibility in a prose and structure of consummate "difficulty" (how helpful, Eliot's unpretentious word). The parody, like that of *Ulysses*, is reconstructive rather than deconstructive. If like other modernist works it holds a mirror up to cultural fragmentation (it was published on the eve of World War II), it composes the fragments artistically, for the program of modernism, however iconoclastic, was always some kind of cultural reclamation.

But postmodernism has no such pretensions. It was always a holding action, a "literature of exhaustion," self-canceling in its most basic premises. Parody and replication in postmodern literature exist to underscore the death of the author and to allow an extra season or two to exhausted forms. In Jean-François Lyotard's formulation, as noted at the beginning of this chapter, postmodern literature "puts forward the unpresentable in presentation itself."[20] A literature largely about itself and its own strategies of re-presentation, it perennially enacts the universal semiotic law: there is no "transcendental signified" behind the arbitrary signifiers—presence is infinitely deferred. Perhaps, like signification itself, the postmodern aesthetic is a house of cards, and likely to exhaust itself at a faster rate than other literary movements. Thus the literary apotheosis toward which modernism moves (in a number of texts) is not available to postmodernism, and thus *Vineland* corresponds not to *Finnegans Wake* but to the new literary start Joyce did not live to undertake.

Vineland does not seem to be "reflexive" in the approved contemporary manner—a manner that, in all three of his previous novels, Pynchon has shown he can execute brilliantly. But it features at least a few of the quarterings of a postmodern pedigree. It relies heavily on parody, for example, and it favors (or seems to favor) historical surface over historical depth. It also resists the hierarchization of culture. This refusal to differentiate high culture from low, like the attention to surfaces, is a prominent feature of postmodernist aesthetics. The denial of authority, in all its senses, means the deconstructing of high culture's pretensions to that authority. Thus Pynchon can imagine Pee-wee Herman starring in *The Robert Musil Story* (370). Thus, too, in the multiple parody in *Vineland*—of ninja fictions, television soap operas, espionage novels, and detective thrillers—Pynchon tends to minimize the "critical distance" that, according to parody theorist Linda Hutcheon, commonly accompanies the specific type of "repetition" that is parodic.[21]

Where he does not parody popular culture, he catalogs it. What is remarkable is that, in contrast to his previous practice, he catalogs little else. He systematically denies himself the usual resources of allusion in its full range. In fact, he limits himself to one major literary allusion (one discounts the passing reference to Deleuze and Guattari) and a couple of musical allusions. Only the literary reference—to the Emerson quotation in William James—is presented seriously. Both musical allusions, on the other hand, are comically undercut. When Prairie starts to learn about her mother from Darryl Louise Chastain, she appropriately hears music from *Tosca,* for the tale she will hear concerns the suffering of her Tosca-like mother and the Scarpia-like Brock Vond. But the music is played by a pseudo-Italian band at a Mafia wedding. Similarly, in the novel's elegiac conclusion, an entire Thanatoid village awakens to the strains of Bach's "*Wachet Auf,*" evidently with the chorale's powerfully suggestive opening line intended to come to mind: "*Wachet auf, ruft uns die Stimme*" ["Awake, for the Voice calls us"]. The melody materializes as "piping, chiming music, synchronized, coming out of wristwatches, timers, and personal computers, engraved long ago, as if for this moment, on sound chips dumped once in an obscure skirmish of the silicon market wars . . . as part of a settlement with the ever-questionable trading company of Tokkata & Fuji" (324–25).

Normally this author peppers his fictions with references that establish historical depth as well as cultural breadth, and readers have marveled at his ability to evoke, in *V.,* turn-of-the-century Alexandria, Florence, or southwest Africa; the places and feel of much of Europe in 1944 and 1945 in *Gravity's Rainbow,* and great swaths of geographically metastatic history in *Against the Day.* These evocations of place and time have generally involved a considerable body of cultural allusion, both high and low. Even in *Lot 49,* where the rural California setting is not particularly congenial to evocations of high art, one finds painting, literature, music, and film to be important features of the fictional landscape. But through a kind of *askesis* (to "misread" a term of Bloom's), Pynchon here dispenses with the high-culture allusion almost entirely.

Meanwhile the density of reference to the ephemera of popular culture is almost numbing. Pynchon refers often to movies, as in *Gravity's Rainbow*, but here he neglects historic films and art cinema in favor of *Gidget, Dumbo, 20,000 Years in Sing Sing, The Hunchback of Notre Dame, Godzilla, King of the Monsters, Friday the 13th, Return of the Jedi*, and *Ghostbusters. Psycho* and *2001: A Space Odyssey* are the most substantial films mentioned. The author helpfully supplies dates for these films, parodying scholarly practice, and he invents a number of droll film biographies, including *The Frank Gorshin Story*, with Pat Sajak, and *Young Kissinger*, with Woody Allen. Even more insistently jejune are the allusions to the titles, characters, stars, and music of such television programs as *Star Trek, The Brady Bunch, Gilligan's Island, Jeopardy, Wheel of Fortune, I Love Lucy, Green Acres, Smurfs, CHiPs, Superman*, and *The Bionic Woman*. This depressing litany—the intellectual horizon of the American mass mind—subsumes less obvious manifestations of popular taste as well: mall culture, "roasts," video and computer games, new-wave hairstyles, breakfast cereals, even "'sensitivity' greeting cards" (38). Pynchon's intent here is not entirely satiric, for no doubt he is genuinely fond of much popular culture. In the introduction to *Slow Learner*, he declares that "rock 'n' roll will never die" (23), and the sentiment is shared by the founders of the People's Republic of Rock and Roll, who name their new state "after the one constant they knew they could count on never to die" (209). Perhaps, too, Pynchon wishes to eschew cultural elitism and demonstrate solidity with the masses. But the virtual absence of historical depth in this body of allusion makes a devastating statement about the shortness of the American cultural memory. This, ultimately, is the point of his constant allusion to the signs and texts of popular culture. Pynchon denies himself much of the cultural and historical dimension of the previous novels and commits himself to imagining the relentlessly ahistorical consciousness of contemporary American society. The implicit judgment of this shallowness, finally, reveals a moral dimension—always in fact an element in Pynchon's work—that distances this author from the moral neutrality or nihilism sometimes alleged to be the postmodern norm.

Unlike those who inhabit the world he describes, Pynchon himself has an acute sense of history that also leavens his brand of postmodernism. His historical consciousness reveals itself in the guise of that universal history called myth. If the myths invoked in *Vineland* coexist uneasily at the edge of a mutually deconstructive exclusivity, they nevertheless provide the story's action with a temporal depth: they render it "historical" in spite of itself. Thus Terrence Rafferty does not err when he observes that "American history plays itself out" in the bed of Brock Vond and Frenesi Gates.[22] The play of myth, then, circumvents the nominally ahistorical vision in *Vineland*. One can sometimes differentiate modernists from postmodernists in their treatment of myth—where modernists exploit myth as universal, instinctive truth, their successors either deconstruct it as an unreliable "metanarrative" (the breakdown of metanarratives, says Lyotard, is the ground for "the postmodern condition")[23] or examine it as a language that, like all language, speaks its speakers rather than the other way around. Pynchon, as Kathryn Hume demonstrates in *Pynchon's Mythography*, has never divorced himself entirely from the modernist position on myth; and in *Vineland* he has it both ways—privileging at least one myth, deconstructing at least two others. The Faust myth, for example, seems to function in a fairly conventional manner: the federal prosecutor is Mephistopheles; film-making Frenesi is Faust. Yet the myth and the mythical identities prove unstable. The Faust here is also an Eve in the American Eden who betrays her Adam, the hapless Weed Atman. The Mephisto figure, Brock Vond, is also the serpent who tempts them to a fall and a primal murder. These two myths, however, are not at odds, for Faust's passion merely updates that of Adam and Eve. The stories contain the same elements: a diabolical tempter and human souls reaching for forbidden knowledge. But Pynchon complicates matters by introducing, through Sister Rochelle, a mise en abyme: a subversive, feminist version of the Eden myth with Frenesi and DL as the primal Eve and Lilith in an Eden in which "the first man . . . was the serpent" (166, my ellipsis). This revision of the story seems a minor detail in the novel, and perhaps one at first disregards or discounts it in the desire for a totalizing version of a cherished American literary myth. But its seeming insignificance reveals the deconstructive point: it is one of the aporias around which at least one strand of meaning begins to unravel.

Feminism, by its very nature, is deconstructive—it locates the aporias in the "phallogocentric" discourse of patriarchy. In *Vineland*, the familiar myth undergoes a twofold feminist deconstruction: the patriarchal version of the myth is undercut once by Sister Rochelle's version—and again by the mythic action as Pynchon shapes it. For the mythic individual who makes the moral choice (traditionally an Adam in American fictions: Hawkeye, Huckleberry Finn, Isaac McCaslin) is the American Eve, Frenesi Gates. *Vineland*, then, is a surprisingly "writerly" text: it invites its reader to grapple with closure-resistant, open, multivalent myths that self-de(con)struct under the instruments of analysis.

Yet *Vineland* retains a myth that its author celebrates rather than deconstructs. Pynchon's setting is a representation of the American land, and he refuses to surrender the myth of American promise, which he seems to construe in terms of some continuing, provisional validity of a leftist political alternative to contemporaneous conservatism. The novel's title announces the mythic ground. It evokes more than the California setting and reputation for viniculture. The author situates the imaginary town that gives the novel its name up near the California border with Oregon, and he expects the reader to make the nominal connection with a town on the other side of the continent. The latitude of the real Vineland—Vineland, New Jersey—pretty much coincides with that of the imagined California "Vineland the Good" (322), haven for Zoyd Wheeler and other displaced persons. This implied spanning of the continent at the latitude of its greatest breadth jibes with the novel's symbolic detail to suggest that Pynchon's setting is really the whole vast tract that the Vikings discovered and named Vineland at the end of the first millennium. Thus the title of Pynchon's fourth novel, published at the end of the second millennium, reminds American readers that their land has been known to history now (in the West, at least) for exactly a thousand years.

The novel contains other miniaturized symbols of America. A central example is the People's Republic of Rock and Roll, symbolically the counterculture America of the sixties, delirious with freedom, under surveillance, doomed, the Richard Nixon monolith at oceanside casting its shadow, an obvious symbol of repression to come. Perhaps, too, Zoyd Wheeler's house, of which he has been forcibly dispossessed by unconscionable federal power, is another such symbol. At the end, he is flirting with the idea of putting it to the torch—which America's dispossessed may yet do to the house they are unable fully to enter. As in *Lot 49*, Pynchon contemplates the paradoxes of dispossession and preterition in the land of promise.

Vineland, then, is a meditation on the American social reality, a return to the ground Pynchon seems to think he did not cover adequately in *Lot 49* (he remarks in the introduction to *Slow Learner* that he thinks his second novel merely a long story, not technically accomplished). Though *Vineland* is not *Lot 49* redivivus, one notes points of contact—most obviously the California setting—between the two. In the earlier novel the heroine, Oedipa Maas, meets a member of the Paranoids, an aspiring rock group, and offers to give her DJ husband, Mucho, a tape to plug. Now the reader learns that Mucho, "after a divorce remarkable even in that more innocent time for its geniality" (309), has become a successful recording industry executive (like *V.*'s Rooney Winsome)—and that he has shepherded Miles, Dean, Serge, and Leonard to success.

But where in this later story is the Oedipa who realizes at the end of *Lot 49* that the only way she can go on being relevant to her country is "as an alien, unfurrowed, assumed full circle into some paranoia" (182). The heroine of *Vineland*, Frenesi Gates, may be a version of that new, desperate Oedipa—estranged from a man with a Dutch surname and living a furtive, underground existence. Oedipa seems a less flawed person than Frenesi, but both characters are symbols of the American conscience—radicalized in the sixties, co-opted in the eighties. The two novels also explore the significance of drug use. In *Lot 49*, Oedipa does not perceive Mucho's involvement with LSD as positive, but it does link him to the marginalized Americans she will come to embrace. In the later novel, the reader learns that Mucho proceeded to addict himself to cocaine before giving up drugs altogether. Mucho's addiction and the horrors, however comic, of the "Room of the Bottled Specimens" (310) are among the book's few concessions that there might be a downside to drug use. But Mucho becomes an entrepreneur as he goes straight—and his entrepreneurism makes him suspect in Pynchon's economy. Here

one glimpses the equation that partially accounts for Pynchon's somewhat disturbing refusal to depict drugs in a negative light: taking drugs
(as opposed, perhaps, to dealing them) remains a powerful metaphor
for the idea of an alternative to the rapacious capitalism and consumer-
ism that afflict American society.

One sees a more meaningful contrast between these books in their
handling of history. Oddly, it is the book with ostensibly the more shallow
historical draft — *Vineland*, with its foreshortened historical sense — that
reveals its author as truly concerned about the way the present evolves
out of the past. In *Lot 49*, several hundred years of history are the means
to make Oedipa's quest interesting and complicated, but this past is only
superficially imagined as accounting for her American present (Oedipa's
historical research serves the epistemological theme — the infinite reticulation of "paranoid" interconnectedness — rather than the sociological
one that links her story to Frenesi's). In *Vineland*, by contrast, Pynchon
again examines the American present, but with specific reference to a
recent — and radically different — past. This equipoise between sixties
and eighties keeps *Vineland* from being the simpleminded exercise in
nostalgia some have taken it for. Far from the sour grapes of some bitter
ex-hippie, it is a treatise on the direction history has taken, without our
having given it much thought. Moreover, his own implicit political orientation notwithstanding, Pynchon exposes the millenarian canker in the
flower children as rigorously as he diagnoses the reactionary carcinoma
of the next generation. *Lot 49*, set in 1964, is a story of consciousness
being raised — an allegory of 1960s America repudiating conformity,
racism, and militarism. It looks backward to the Eisenhower 1950s and
forward to the Summer of Love. *Vineland*, set a generation later in the
portentous year of 1984, looks backward to that summer — and forward
to some Republican version of the thousand-year Reich. It reveals how
the nation has allowed an earlier passion for justice to go dead, to be co-
opted by a conservative backlash and an attendant dissipation of liberal
energy.

In a single generation — from the midsixties to the mideighties,
America veered from a liberal to a conservative bias, from the New
Frontier and the Great Society to "Reaganomics," from hordes of stu-
dent demonstrators to whole undergraduate populations majoring in

business, from Yippies to yuppies. In *Vineland* Pynchon examines these societal extremes and the historical currents they ride or embody. Interestingly contemporaneous with David Lodge's *Nice Work*, a refitting of the nineteenth-century "condition-of-England" novel, *Vineland* would seem in its hybridization also to undertake such an old-fashioned assessment. It is a condition-of-America novel. That condition, as a result of the Reagan revolution and, before that, the "Nixonian Repression" (71) or "Nixonian Reaction" (239), is imagined as darkening, "a prefascist twilight" (371), if not the actual night. "Nixon had machinery for mass detention all in place and set to go," says a Pynchon character. "Reagan's got it for when he invades Nicaragua" (264). The "Reagan program" is to "dismantle the New Deal, reverse the effects of World War II, restore fascism at home and around the world" (265).

Pynchon makes his political sympathies plain enough. But the polemics have little to do with the novel's art, which one sees in the indirection and economy that deliver this and other Pynchon works from the realm of propaganda and didacticism. This author's art—an art far superior, it seems to me, to that of such novelists on the left as early Dos Passos or Steinbeck or Vonnegut—commands the aesthetic interest of readers who may find the politics somewhat overwrought. Pynchon contrives, by diving into the wreck of mythic metanarrative, to imbue with extraordinary historical resonance a story that ostensibly depicts the vitiation of the historical sense. He remains the only contemporary writer whose grasp of history's mythic dimensions merits comparison with that of Joyce—and the author of *Gravity's Rainbow*, *Mason & Dixon*, and *Against the Day* may yet present us with a fiction on the scale of that writer's last book.

Reports of Postmodernism's Death Exaggerated: *Inherent Vice*

In his California novels—*The Crying of Lot 49*, *Vineland*, and *Inherent Vice*—Pynchon presents varied and surprising allegories of America. Their antic features, however, have misled the occasional reader. Writing up the last for *Publishers Weekly*, reviewer David Kipen differentiates these fictions from their Brobdingnagian fellows: "Across five decades now," he

observes, Pynchon has "more or less alternated these West Coast chamber pieces with his more formidable symphonies (*V*; *Gravity's Rainbow*,
Mason & Dixon; *Against the Day*). Partisans of the latter may find this one
a tad slight."[24] Such partisans, however, would be confusing economy
with superficiality, Beethoven with Boccherini. Pynchon merely adds
anarchic humor to the originality, complexity, profundity, even tragic elevation of great chamber art, whether musical or literary. Even Haydn's
apocryphal Kazoo Quartet, described in *Gravity's Rainbow*, proves something considerably more than a Spike Jones gag (itself pretty complex,
as Pynchon observes in his liner notes for a 1994 collection of Jones material).[25] Performed at a dinner given by munitions magnates, the "subversive" Haydn composition disrupts the unsavory proceedings, its mannered silences intimating knowledge suppressed by military-industrial
entities busy changing their Nazi spots. "A-and wait'll those *kazoos* come
on!" (*GR* 713). One does not, then, accept the invidious distinction between chamber and large-orchestra works (indeed, obliged to choose,
one would rather take Beethoven's late quartets to the proverbial desert
island than the symphonies of a lesser composer). Pynchon's genius and
wit shine as brightly in the "chamber pieces" as in the compositions on
a nominally grander scale, and the critical geometer sees in *Inherent Vice*
an elegant secant to that "German symphonic arc, tonic to dominant,
back again to tonic" (*GR* 443).

Though thematically related, each of Pynchon's quartet-like California
novels has its own character, and each, whether wholly or partly set in
the 1960s, presents a different cautionary perspective on American
history and postwar culture. These fictions concern the frontier that
has figured so powerfully in America's conception of itself. In *Against
the Day*, the author mentions Frederick Jackson Turner (52), and the
famous historian may serve as presiding spirit for Pynchon's several
visions of the West Coast—at once the literal, geographical end of the
American frontier and, in *Inherent Vice*, the mythic "ark" (351, 352) of
deliverance for the survivors of that fanciful "Atlantis of the Pacific"
(101), sunken Lemuria. More than geographical or cartographic, a
frontier is also temporal: just as Turner once conceptualized the closing of the American frontier, so does Pynchon imagine a succession of
low dishonest decades, to paraphrase Auden, displacing one bright with

promise. In *Inherent Vice*, the author returns to this temporal frontier, focusing on a period five or six years after the action of *The Crying of Lot 49*. Present time in this latest of the California novels appears to be "[c]irca 1970" (172). The dust jacket mentions "the tail end of the psychedelic 60s." The narrator refers to a 1969 movie, *The Big Bounce* (318). At one point, the protagonist rents a "'69 Camaro" (218); at another, the trial of Charles Manson, which began in the early summer of 1970, is said to be imminent (280).[26] The final chapter begins with a reference to the Lakers' loss to the Knicks in game seven of the NBA finals—an event that took place on 8 May 1970—Pynchon's birthday. Whether or not the action extends back into some part of 1969, one has the sense of what the French call an *année charnière*, or hinge year.

In his Larry "Doc" Sportello, Pynchon teases the reader with the prospect of another Galahad, in pursuit of another grail. But the quest plot, as I have previously noted, undergoes a significant attenuation after *Gravity's Rainbow*. A devolution, then, another *askesis*: from Oedipa's sharply focused pursuit of the Tristero, through the multiple pursuits of *Vineland*'s characters, to the somewhat confused investigations undertaken by the protagonist in *Inherent Vice*. In his latest novel, in short, Pynchon pays relatively little attention to the conventions of quest narrative. As his vision matures, he seems to feel that too much linearity may misrepresent or betray or oversimplify what Žižek calls "the new world of dispersed multiple identities, or radical contingency, of an irreducible ludic plurality of struggles."[27]

In the culture at large and in Pynchon's *Inherent Vice*, however, the quest narrative survives as the detective story. This fiction challenges the reader, prompted by flyleaf language about the author's "working in an unaccustomed genre," to determine just what transformation of the familiar detective novel the author essays: how, for example, does this witty performance differ from similar efforts by Robert B. Parker, say, or Carl Hiaasen, or, as a number of reviewers and bloggers suggested, Elmore Leonard? Does Pynchon embrace the genre or parody it? To ask the question is to be reminded of the extent to which pastiche figures in—and enables—postmodernist storytelling. To paraphrase John Barth, *Inherent Vice* is a detective novel in quota-

tion marks. Its author deliberately blurs the boundary between genre
fiction and the art novel, both subject already to ironic postmodern
manipulation.

Every detective story concerns an encounter with vice, inherent or
otherwise. The more inherent the vice, the more noir the fiction. But
this is to moralize prematurely. Introduced late in the narrative by Doc's
lawyer friend Sauncho, the phrase that provides this novel's title signi-
fies, first, a simple principle in manufacturing, commerce, transport,
insurance, and law. Like William Gaddis in his 1994 novel *A Frolic of His
Own*, Pynchon builds his story around a phrase with an obscure legal significance. Yet anyone seeking a definition in one of the standard diction-
aries of legal terms will find few entries under *inherent vice*. The phrase
does turn up in lexicons of business terms—and in the online Society
of American Archivists' *Glossary of Archival and Records Terminology*. The
archivists define *inherent vice* or *inherent fault* as "the tendency of material to deteriorate due to the essential instability of the components or
interaction among components." An example: "nitrate film and highly
acidic paper suffer inherent vice because they are chemically unstable.
An object made of metal and leather suffers inherent vice because the
leather causes the metal to corrode."[28] But the inherent vice problem
chiefly exercises the insurance industry, which must, in writing policies
and dealing with "particular average claims" (359) and the like, differentiate naturally occurring deterioration from damage or spoilage involving negligence on the part of manufacturers or carriers. Inherent vice
would, then, be a concern of entities such as *Vineland*'s Wawazume Life
& Nonlife; in Pynchon's third California novel, the phrase has a particular meaning for "Sauncho's colleagues in marine insurance" (351).

A onetime sailor himself, the author of *Inherent Vice* displays considerable knowledge of nautical lore. Like Melville or Conrad or, indeed,
Patrick O'Brian, he understands those "[t]entacles of sin and desire"
that "crept through all areas of Pacific sailing culture." He knows naval history, too. Doc's attorney, Sauncho Smilax, works for the firm of
"Hardy, Gridley & Chatfield" (91), named for a waving of naval heroes: Thomas Masterman Hardy, Nelson's flag captain at the Battle of
Trafalgar; Charles Gridley, Commodore Dewey's flag captain at Manila
Bay in the Spanish-American War; and Ernle Chatfield, Admiral Sir John

Jellicoe's flag captain at the Battle of Jutland. Probably not easy to make partner at this firm.

More to the point, Pynchon also understands "that strange world-bound karma which is of the essence in maritime law" (91). Though he gives the nineteenth-century jurist Joseph Arnould the wrong first name (his own), he deploys with precision such specialized terms as *lagan* (goods sunk but marked for later retrieval) and *barratry* (fraud on the part of a ship's master). As for the phrase that supplies his title, *inherent vice* (not actually introduced until the penultimate chapter), he supplies a definition, through Sauncho, that makes it sound like entropy redux. Like Murphy's corollary to the laws of thermodynamics, inherent vice represents "what you can't avoid" (351). Hearing about it from Sauncho, Doc associates the legal doctrine with the idea of original sin, and in fact both concern slippage that is inevitable: not merely what can go wrong—what *must*, in the sublunary sphere, go wrong.

Doubled Docs

Pynchon, whose first name derives from the Hebrew for *twin*, has always engaged duality—commonly through odd instantiations. A pair of historically discrete yet complementary narratives, for example, structures both *V.* and *Vineland*, and *Gravity's Rainbow* abounds with two-person teams—Fuder and Fass, Crutchfield and Whappo, Höpmann and Kreuss, Wobb and Whoaton, Takeshi and Ichizo, etc. There, too, as in *Mason & Dixon* and *Against the Day*, Pynchon develops what he characterizes as gnostic shadow actions and shadow meanings, a whole realm of "knowing" from which various elites (or simply "They") exclude ordinary citizens. In *Against the Day*, he introduces, moreover, elaborate historical parallelism, plays on bilocation, and thoughts on the strange twinning of images in certain pieces of the calcareous crystal called Iceland spar. Charles Mason and Jeremiah Dixon, as will be seen in the next chapter, resemble more than one archetypal pair.

Hence, in *Inherent Vice*, the recurrent conceit of doubled Docs. His erstwhile girlfriend, Shasta Fay Hepworth, describes Doc and the tragically co-opted Coy Harlingen as "peas in a pod" (313). Doc shares with Harlingen "[a] gift . . . for projecting alternate personalities, infiltrating, remembering, reporting back" (299). In fact, nearly every other male character takes a turn as second Doc. His doppelgängers include the murdered Glen Charlock (320), the blacklisted film star John Garfield, and police detective Christian Bjornsen. "Bigfoot's not my brother," Doc protests at one point, "but he sure needs a keeper" (350). Characterized twice as Doc's shadow (207, 350), Bigfoot embodies Jung's powerful idea of a counterself with which one must, in the name of psychological health, come to terms.

A Jungian analyst would say that Doc is required to integrate—not to become—this shadow. Bigfoot may accuse him and his fellows of infantile behavior, but Doc legitimately refuses to abandon or outgrow his hippie identity. Like Hamlet, he cultivates an antic disposition that keeps the straight world, law enforcement, respectability, and (for the most part) violence at bay. Like Slothrop in *Gravity's Rainbow*, Doc frequently dons disguises: wigs, moustaches, straight-world clothes, Liberace's necktie, even the suit worn by John Garfield in *The Postman Always Rings Twice* (344). The fluid identity implied in all the disguises makes him a shapeshifter or trickster, Southern California's own Till Eulenspiegel.

"[T]here were," then, "these two Docs" (318)—and a ship with two names and, amid any "driveling of dopers" (131), at least two realities. The reader can connect all the doubling with any of several thematically relevant binaries: body/soul, feeling/thinking, master/servant, freedom/bondage, and the "[o]nes and zeroes" (365) of unity and nothingness. The increasingly troublesome gulf between political left and right, as will be seen, figures with particular prominence. In this novel, as in *Lot 49*, Pynchon gauges the great American duality of economic rapacity and the redemptive spirituality that secures our city on its hill.

One discerns in Doc a trace of Fitzgerald's Nick Carraway: each, after all, focalizes the story of a "sensitive tycoon" (ironic when applied to the sinister Crocker Fenway [348], this epithet actually suits Mickey Wolfmann, who has evidently tried to reverse his part of the capitalist juggernaut). Both Nick and Doc are good, if reluctant, listeners. Taught "to reserve all judgments," Nick finds himself "the victim of not a few veteran bores" who want a confidant. Similarly, Doc "wished he had a small aggravation fee for each time somebody had spilled more than they meant to." Doc's friend Sortilège "thought this was a form of grace" (224). Carraway listens because, as he remarks in his very first sentence, his father long ago told him to keep in mind "that all the people in this world haven't had the advantages that you've had." Within five sentences, repeating the precept, he makes a small but significant change:

> Reserving judgments is a matter of infinite hope. I am still a little afraid of missing something if I forget that, as my father snobbishly suggested, and I snobbishly repeat, a sense of the fundamental decencies is parceled out unequally at birth.[29]

"Advantages" becomes "decencies," and with that single shift, Fitzgerald sketches the American theme of *The Great Gatsby*. One word connotes the material or social, the other the moral. Doc, too, on the mean streets and chaotic freeways of Los Angeles, wrestles with the great conundrum of idealism and materialism in the national ethos. Pynchon, like Fitzgerald, knows how to moralize America, founded on a promise that eludes us still.

According to certain versions of the national myth, neither the legal principle (*inherent vice*) nor its theological congener (original sin) obtains on these shores. Yet Pynchon does not want simply to debunk American exceptionalism: he wants the nation to live up to its rhetoric, to *realize* the special destiny that Tyrone Slothrop's ancestor William would have heard invoked by John Winthrop aboard the *Arbella*. Sauncho imagines not destiny but its darker synonym when he speaks of a place "where the American fate . . . failed to transpire" (341). In this fatalism, he speaks for the author only in part. Gatsby-like, Pynchon wants, as it were, to change the past. Why not, the author asks in all of his novels, go back and embrace the destiny once embodied, in its most pure form, in the American myth of promise? But as the decade of the sixties retreats (borne back ceaselessly into the past), Pynchon imagines a boat against the current—now the *Preserved*, now the *Golden Fang*, now Gilligan's *Minnow*, even—that might still pass into better hands. *The Golden Fang*, on its way "into some safe receivership" (358) when last seen, may yet become the lawful prize of Doc's friend Sauncho, who has had the foresight, apparently, "to take out a policy" that will give him standing in any "litigation" to decide her fate (359).

But Pynchon grounds questions of moral direction here in a some-what fatalistic politics. *Inherent Vice* came out, significantly, in the same year that the Tea Party movement materialized out of widespread fears that the Democratic Party, energized after sweeping the 2008 elections, would promote a socialist agenda. In his earlier fictions, notably *Gravity's Rainbow* and *Mason & Dixon*, Pynchon historicizes the national divide between left and right by briefly (and sometimes proleptically) evok-ing the passions of Catholic vs. Protestant, Whigs vs. Tories, federalist vs. antifederalist, the agricultural interest against the industrial, North vs. South, and New Deal against those who, like Tyrone Slothrop's fa-ther Broderick, hated its architect, Roosevelt (*GR* 373). But *Inherent Vice*, though set in the sixties, addresses the antipathy of left and right in terms somewhat more conducive to prospect than to retrospect. America's mythic past receives considerable attention, but the political climate evoked seems frequently to mirror the appalling polarization ob-taining in the first decade of the twenty-first century—the polarization that, nasty enough in the Clinton years, manifested itself with particular virulence from 2004 (Bush's dubious victory over Gore) up to and after the election of Barack Obama.

One sees a progression among the sixties novels in the passion their author brings to depicting the forces of reaction. In *The Crying of Lot 49*, Pynchon represents as relatively harmless the posturing of the meta-Bircher Peter Pinguid Society, but in *Vineland* he expresses an abhor-rence verging on the Swiftian for the right's perennial flirtation with fascism. A character even asserts that Nixon's bag of tricks included con-centration camps for the unruly. A similar strain of outrage permeates *Inherent Vice*, in which Pynchon imagines a "private army of vigilantes" (207) tolerated, even assisted, by the Los Angeles police and less visible "agencies of command and control" (265, 268). The latter-day Brown Shirts of Vigilant California would like to set all the hippie liberal social-ist tax-raising "pinko fucks" (323) straight with a little touch of—if not the sjambok—then "the terminally illegal Gleichschaltung Model 33 Automatic Bazooka" (201). A typical piece of Pynchon erudition, the name of this imaginary but plausible-sounding weapon is not that of any real-world firearms manufacturer. If one takes it for some cousin of Glock, Heckler & Koch, Mauser, or Walther, however, all the better for the joke. The word in fact refers to the Nazi doctrine of "bringing into line," i.e., eradicating pockets of individuality and resistance to the complete control of the state. Pynchon suggests, in a number of ways, that some such process perpetually wears away the American will—and right—to be different. He means to identify and resist American *Gleichschaltung*.

Better Destinies

Hugh Kenner once remarked that in *Hamlet* "every scene and speech seems striving to be the definitive formulation of the play." By the same token, detail after detail in *Inherent Vice* offers itself up as either thematic capsule or embryonic allegory. Teeth, for example, or *Gilligan's Island*.

The many references to teeth, to start with a prominent feature, compose a bizarre dentistry theme that *Inherent Vice* shares with Pynchon's other novels. The toothlessness of heroin addicts, the prospect of "new choppers" (300) for Coy Harlingen and his wife, and a boat and a "high-rent loony bin" (111) named for a tooth, not to mention a "weird-ass building" shaped like one (office space for the creepy Dr. Blatnoyd and other "honky dentists" [293]), invite comparison with similar material in *V.* (Eigenvalue the "psychodontist," *V.*'s conjectural false teeth of titanium, Seaman Ploy's weaponized dentures), *Gravity's Rainbow* (Ensign Morituri's "bright set of teeth" and "polyhedral" [473] dentition), and *Vineland* (the strange business at the dental clinic of Dr. Elasmo). One understands these patterns in terms of the odontological hermeneutic laid out some years back by Theodore Ziolkowski. "When teeth occur in cultural contexts," he observes, "they tend to be characterized by one of three attributes: potency, beauty, or pain."[30] In his varied images of dental preterition, Pynchon participates in a tradition going back to the Bible and to classical antiquity. If sound teeth signify general health, then evocations of toothlessness and creepshow dentistry hint at some ghastly, progressive societal pathology. As for buccal bling—a golden fang, for example—it masks either the work of decay or the absence of sensible things on which to spend one's money.

Pynchon being Pynchon, however, thematic originality lurks in the unlikeliest of figures. As in *Vineland* (and, obliquely, in *Against the Day*), Pynchon invokes the *Gilligan's Island* television program as heteroclite index to or mirror of the American idea on the cusp between modernity and postmodernity. On one occasion, Doc and Sauncho treat plot developments in an episode of the program as "code" for the hapless private eye's situation vis-à-vis Shasta Fay and Mickey Wolfmann (89). Later Sauncho becomes the Skipper, and Doc reprises his role as Gilligan (354). The playful allusions to television and other popular culture have of course become a Pynchon signature—like the working in of Pig Bodine or one of his avatars in "Low-lands," *V.*, *Gravity's Rainbow*, *Mason & Dixon*, and *Against the Day* (one wonders, incidentally, at his absence in a story that revolves around a mysterious sailing vessel, *The Golden Fang*). Somewhat more seriously, Pynchon invites his reader to discern in the basic *Gilligan's Island* situation a piece of unconscious television allegory. Thus the marooned *Minnow* suggests the ship of state in sixties disarray. The seven castaways represent a little cross section of American society, like the seven passengers in John Ford's *Stagecoach* (or those in the French story it reconfigures—Guy de Maupassant's "*Boule de Suif*"). In this figuration, the Skipper becomes the president, Thurston Howell the plutocrat, the Professor the intellectual (or what passes for one on American television). In the three female characters, one sees the three faces of the American Eve: voluptuous entertainer, Kansas farm girl, rich matron. Gilligan is the bumbling everyman, the schlemiel. He arrives on the American scene in 1963—as does his spiritual twin, Benny Profane.

The dark, distended double of the *Minnow*, in fact, is the *Golden Fang*. Having originated as a Canadian vessel, it is not the great craft that figures in the patriotic poetry and rhetoric of the powerful state that occupies the middle latitudes of North America. Indeed, if the *Golden Fang* is a symbol, it must be some representation or embodiment of the continent as a whole, the grand bark of so many European dreams. Formerly an "honest old fishing vessel," the *Preserved* (the appellation artfully suggests both embalming fluid and the workings of divine deliverance) "had come to be inhabited—possessed—by an ancient and evil energy" (110). Its original name may have come to Pynchon from the nautical novels of Patrick O'Brian, whose characters include the colorful Preserved Killick, Captain Jack Aubrey's steward (Pynchon's naming a rock band Spotted Dick may also derive from O'Brian). But Pynchon is no stranger to the "virtue names" catalogued in Charles Bardsley's *Curiosities of Puritan Nomenclature*. In addition to *Preserved*, these include *Patience, Temperance,* and *Constant*[31] (among the ancestors of Tyrone Slothrop, Pynchon includes a Constant and, unable to resist, a Variable).

Now the *Preserved*, now the *Golden Fang*, the vessel that sails in and out of *Inherent Vice* seems to represent two versions of a meta-America, the one *Arbella-* or *Mayflower*-like, the other the ship pirated by and prostituted to dark interests. Toward the end, "as if . . . handling a case," Sauncho strikes an elegiac note:

> there is no avoiding time, the sea of time, the sea of memory and forget-
> fulness, the years of promise, gone and unrecoverable, of the land almost
> allowed to claim its better destiny, only to have the claim jumped by evildo-
> ers known all too well, and taken instead and held hostage to the future
> we must live in now forever. May we trust that this blessed ship is bound for
> some better shore, some undrowned Lemuria, risen and redeemed, where
> the American fate, mercifully, failed to transpire. (341)

This little peroration abounds in echoes of Pynchon's own prior work and that of others. From Auden's "As I Walked Out One Evening"—

> O let not Time deceive you,
> You cannot conquer Time.

—to the rhetoric of Robert Frost ("the land was ours before we were the land's") and Barack Obama ("As Americans, we have demanded, strived for, and shaped a better destiny"), these words resonate and command attention.[32] Pynchon's readers will think, here, of claim-jumpers in *Against the Day* (121), and of Oedipa Maas's doleful reflections on the American legacy diverted into the wrong hands. The phrase "years of promise" turns up in many contexts—from accounts of the Cuban Revolution to a life of Paul Robeson. But perhaps one does not go far wrong in hearing a deliberate echo of the sonnet John Quincy Adams wrote on the birthday of his father, the old president:

> Who but shall learn that freedom is the prize
> Man still is bound to rescue or maintain;
> That nature's God commands the slave to rise,

And on the oppressor's head to break the chain.

Roll, years of promise, rapidly roll round,

Till not a slave shall on this earth be found.[33]

Making its way in "the sea of time," Pynchon's troubled bark sails the ocean of history, and the author of *Inherent Vice* logs its passage through the straits of one American decade. Those who post o'er land and ocean are often charged with mapping and charting, but "[b]ack in junior college, professors had pointed out to Doc the useful notion that the word is not the thing, the map is not the territory" (194). This precept, famously articulated by the linguist Alfred Korzybski,[34] distills much that theorists have said about the gap between signifier and signified. Pynchon observes the principle in his remark, in *Lot 49*, about "the word, or whatever it is the word is there, buffering, to protect us from" (129). But books are also sign systems, maps to territories, and those who write them rightly resist reductive assertions about the validity of mimesis, the legitimacy of artistic representation. Thus the narrator characterizes the map-territory dichotomy as only a "useful notion," not some Saussurean absolute. One measure of literary achievement, after all, lies in the precision and resourcefulness with which an artist confounds the Korzybskian principle, pulls real rabbits out of stage-prop hats, depicts imaginary gardens with, as poet Marianne Moore says, real toads in them, and devises charts somehow coextensive with the great territory of reality itself. More than any other contemporary novelist, Pynchon undertakes this magical cartography, this faithful "mapping" of the American territory.

Thus he includes in *Inherent Vice* a version of Plato's cave, that powerful, ancient parable of perceptual estrangement from reality. Plato's self-referential figure is a map of mapping. The dancing shadows on the walls of the cave "map," as it were, an illusory "territory," but Plato's parable maps the territory of perception itself. Pynchon's novels, like all great representative art, marry the Platonic idealism to the Aristotelian real. Like Professor Glimpf, who commandeers the "Mittel-werk Ex-press" (*GR* 310) to deliver Slothrop from the cave where Marvy's Mothers carouse, casting their antic shadows on the walls like so many Brocken specters, Pynchon conducts his readers to the daylight (and sometimes to the

Kirghiz Light, or to a "heavenwide blast of light" in Siberia [*ATD* 779], or, prophetically, to "the Light that hath brought the Towers low" [*GR* 760]). In the Southern California of *Inherent Vice*, which harbors survivors of a lost continent like the Atlantis Plato speaks of in the *Timaeus* and *Critias*, fog and smog function as walls of the American cave:

> As Doc approached downtown L.A., the smog grew thicker till he couldn't see to the end of the block. Everybody had their headlights on . . . He thought about Sortilège's sunken continent, returning, surfacing . . . in the lost heart of L.A., and wondered who'd notice it if it did. People in this town saw only what they'd all agreed to see, they believed what was on the tube or in the morning papers half of them read while they were driving to work on the freeway, and it was all their dream about being wised up, about the truth setting them free. What good was Lemuria to them? Especially when it turned out to be a place they'd been exiled from too long ago to remember. (315)

As Pierce Inverarity would say, it may be time the people of this American city "had a little visit from the Shadow" (*Lot 49* 11), personification of the agency that occasionally brings home to the complacent that, as Weird Al Yankovic sings, "everything you know is wrong." The Shadow lurks, too, in the silences of the Haydn Kazoo Quartet.

A different traffic situation figures in *Inherent Vice*'s closing paragraphs, set in dense fog in which motorists on the Santa Monica Freeway form a "convoy," each following the taillights ahead. "[L]ike a caravan in a desert of perception" (368), all make their way through an eerie dreamscape that may call to mind the nocturnal land evoked in the conclusion of Cormac McCarthy's 2005 novel *No Country for Old Men*, in which the defeated sheriff dreams of a horseman, his long-dead father, riding before him in dark, mountainous country, bearing live coals in a horn that glows dimly in the distance. One generation carries the fire (the ideas, the values, the cultural capital) that warms the next—unless the coals go out or the belated followers fall too far behind. At the end of Pynchon's novel, Doc will "wait," the narrator observes, "[f]or the fog to burn away, and for something else this time, somehow, to be there instead" (369). Pynchon's image, like McCarthy's, is tender yet far from sanguine. In the fog of national memory, the decades retreat like taillights, disappearing, one after another, into history or myth. Thus is it with the decade in which, Pynchon suggests, the country tragically failed to find some oasis in its desert of perception.

The Golden State occupies a special place in the imagination of the author: he ends both *Gravity's Rainbow* and *Against the Day* in Los Angeles. Sprawled at what was once the frontier terminus, California distills—then and now—some American essence. Disneyland, star worship, Valley Girls, psychopaths, pockets of time-warp hippies—they are all part of a picture that European pundits from Jean Baudrillard to Bernard-Henri Lévy have tried to explain, along with Orange County politics, the City Lights Bookstore and the Beat ethos it memorializes, the Austrian bodybuilder, the shrines to Nixon and Reagan, the lattes and "lifestyle," and the freak-filled Santa Monica Freeway, where "[t]hey come gibbering in at you from all sides, swarming in, rolling their eyes through the side windows, playing harmonicas and even *kazoos*, in full disrespect for the Prohibitions" (*GR* 755–56). Among those detained for harmonica playing, one recalls, is the obscure "Kabbalist spokesman Steve Edelman" (753). The surname means *nobleman*, and he comes to mind because, in the end, California is a mise en abyme in the original, heraldic sense. It occupies a corner of the escutcheon, the map-like shield of *Edelmann* identity, that it reproduces in miniature.

Early in *Inherent Vice*, one encounters a mise en abyme in its newer, literary-theoretical sense in Doc Sportello's black velvet painting, which depicts "a Southern California beach that never was—palms, bikini babes, surfboards, the works" (6). In much the same way, Pynchon contrives to enlarge the already supersized myth of California in the sixties. He derives his picture of the place and the decade from personal experience as augmented by a host of popular culture sources—everything from Beach Boys lyrics to *Gidget* movies to television programs such as *Gilligan's Island, Scooby-Doo!, The Jetsons, Dark Shadows, The Brady Bunch, The Flintstones,* and *CHiPS* (Frenesi, in *Vineland*, masturbates to reruns of the last). Pynchon thinks of the sixties as a crossroads of American history, a place where the nation revisits the earliest of its moral choices. Here a vestigial innocence vies again with every dark propensity in the human heart. In *Lot 49* (the only sixties novel actually published in that decade), this struggle remains undecided. In the later novels (including those set at a considerable remove from the sixties), Pynchon recurs to this theme with more and more fine-grained attention to historical circumstance and antecedent. Thus in *Vineland*, the struggle between American innocence and the temptation to "go over" or "sell out" (to capitulate, that is, to a statist imperative) survives largely as a memory made bitter by the political tenor of the Reagan era ("present time" in the frame narrative, as noted before, is the portentous year 1984, but most of the story concerns events two decades earlier). In later fictions, the author traces the etiology of the struggle: in *Mason & Dixon*, he reviews the energies and choices at play on the eve of a revolution that would deliver a long-gravid Enlightenment of its *grösste Säugling*, the United States of America. In *Against the Day*, Pynchon depicts this archetypal agon—whereby, after all, the nation will or will not realize its moral destiny—as it meshes with the global conflict of capital and labor at the end of the nineteenth century and beginning of the twentieth. That novel's foregrounded images of light, day, electrification, and supernal effulgence recur at low wattage in its successor, *Inherent Vice*, whose hero perceives "the Psychedelic Sixties" as a "little parenthesis of light" that "might close after all, and all be lost, taken back into the darkness" (254). Writing from the vantage of the twenty-first century, Pynchon invites recognition of a prophetic element in Doc's thoughts: it did, it was.

Locke sank into a swoon;
The Garden died;
God took the spinning-jenny
Out of his side.
                    —WILLIAM BUTLER YEATS, "Fragments"

CHAPTER FIVE

The Luddite Vision

Mason & Dixon

Early reviewers and critics, praising Pynchon for his confidence with scientific, technological, and mathematical subjects, may have over-estimated his commitment to such material.[1] His allusions to *Scientific American* notwithstanding, the author's intentions seem always to have involved more than didactic exhortation of readers to become scientifically knowledgeable. He has suggested, to be sure, that humanists who ignore science can do little more than defer to—or rail against—the ascendancy of technologues. He has sought, too, to deny science the power that mystery tends to wield over ignorance. Yet beyond these arguments, in one novel after another, Pynchon has devoted his formidable powers of subversion and satire to exposing the false premises behind the technocratic syllogism. Thus in *V.* a woman seeks to transform herself into a machine. In *The Crying of Lot 49* a nutty inventor invites volunteers to communicate with Maxwell's demon. In *Gravity's*

Rainbow various characters seek, as technological grail, the Rocket that will complete the abortive Armageddon of World War II. In *Vineland*, the villainous federal agent Brock Vond perishes in one of the "dead-black Huey slicks" (375) he favors in his private, highly mechanized war against pot-growing former hippies like Zoyd Wheeler. In *Against the Day*, chronicling advances in electrical technologies early in the twentieth century, Pynchon hints at their evolution toward some scarcely imaginable event horizon of photovoltaic weaponry. In *Mason & Dixon*, finally, an astronomer and a surveyor violate the American wilderness in the name of cutting-edge cartography. Here Pynchon scrutinizes the age in which technology began to come into its own — and with it the modern world's spiritual desperation. He exposes the fallacy of scientific rationalism at the moment of its great effloration in the eighteenth century.

If the seventeenth century saw an explosion of true science (Kepler's formulation of planetary orbits, Newton's optics and laws of motion, Boyle's chemistry, Leibniz's calculus), the eighteenth century saw science expanded and applied. Pure science (Buffon in zoology, Linnaeus in taxonomy, Priestley and Lavoisier in chemistry) vied with practical applications, as Watt patented the steam engine, Arkwright the spinning jenny, and Cartwright the power loom. Adam Smith demonstrated the logic of markets; astronomers strove to determine a practical method for determining longitude at sea. Diderot published the monumental *Encylopédie* (focused less on philosophy and great ideas, one may recall, than on mechanical and technological processes), and Benjamin Franklin, that paragon of canny pragmatism, invented the lightning rod, bifocals, and a new stove while demonstrating the rational principles of economic success. Meanwhile faith in human perfectibility grew as philosophy sought, in human affairs, some equivalent to the laws of physics. Surely civilized humanity could return to the natural nobility still visible, as Rousseau suggested, among savages. Surely human institutions, studied carefully enough, could be made answerable to reason. The century reached its apogee, some would say, with realization of a great experiment in self-government founded on rational principles: the American nation.

In *Mason & Dixon* Pynchon anatomizes this nation on the eve of its founding. Like other novelists and historians, he identifies a strange mix of philosophical rationalism, spiritual yearning, and economic rapacity in the American salmagundi. But uniquely he settles on the surveying of the Mason-Dixon Line as symbol of and index to the forces that would become America. Like the kabbalists at the tavern called the Rabbi of Prague, he sees that the handiwork of Mason and Dixon may be read, in its cartographic westering, "much as a Line of Text upon a Page of the sacred Torah,—a Tellurian Scripture" (487). As kabbalists seek mystical significance beneath surface meanings, so does Pynchon descry in the line arrowing its way into the continent a host of portentous intimations regarding the future of the nation whose birth, as the surveyors take their sightings, looms on the historical horizon.

Pynchon's views of the American eighteenth century incline, predictably, to the iconoclastic. Certainly the portraits here of George Washington or Benjamin Franklin bear little resemblance to the lovable figures depicted in older American histories. Franklin, his eyes hidden by spectacles that change color as often as the skin of a Vheissuvian spider monkey, represents mercantile forces that will elbow aside a host of spiritual and cultural alternatives in the New World. Washington, too, has his eye on emerging markets, and he dreams of an Ohio Company as rich as New York, Pennsylvania, or Massachusetts. The kabbalists may speak for the idea of a different America—now lost—when like Melville in *Israel Potter* they inveigh against "Projectors, Brokers of Capital, Insurancers, Peddlers upon the global Scale, Enterprisers and Quacks . . . The coming Rebellion is theirs,—Franklin and that Lot,—and Heaven help the rest of us, if they prevail" (487–88).

American Subjunctive

Piety and weaponry hand in hand. At once spiritual and materialistic, idealistic and brutal, America has always displayed the instinct for contradiction and paradox that Fitzgerald, an early literary hero of Pynchon's, probes with such subtlety and economy in *The Great Gatsby*. Pynchon, too, studies the American paradox, which shows to peculiar advantage, he suggests, in the years immediately preceding the Revolution. Subject to a fundamental duality, the United States seemed to exemplify the triumph of reason and faith in human potential, yet without sacrificing its identity as a place of spiritual distinction—a city on a hill. Pynchon intimates, indeed, that the Europeans who crossed the Atlantic in growing numbers were fleeing not religious coercion so much as the Old World's crescive secularism. America, to them, represented "one more hope in the realm of the Subjunctive, one more grasp at the last radiant whispers of the last bights of Robe-hem, billowing Æther-driven at the back of an ever-departing Deity" (543, cf. 480). Home to "the poor fragments of a Magic irreparably broken" (612), America was, absurdly, "this object of hope that Miracles might yet occur, that God might yet return to Human affairs, that all the wistful Fictions necessary to the childhood of a species might yet come true, . . . a third Testament" (353, Pynchon's ellipsis).

The language here reveals the attenuation, perhaps tragic, of religious faith, absurdly committed to hope, broken magic, "wistful Fictions," an absconding deity, and "the realm of the Subjunctive" (the imagined-as-true). Indeed, as one knows from studying the founders of the American state, the secularizing ideals of the Enlightenment— notably deism—also found a home on these shores. Thus Pynchon lays considerable emphasis on the secularism of the age. He characterizes the "times" as "unfriendly toward Worlds alternative to this one. Royal Society Members and French Encyclopaedists are in the Chariot, availing themselves whilst they may of any occasion to preach the Gospels of Reason, denouncing all that once was Magic, though too often in smirking tropes upon the Church of Rome . . . One may be allowed an occasional Cock Lane Ghost,—otherwise, for any more in that Article, one must turn to Gothick Fictions" (359, my ellipsis) like the stories serialized in *The Ghastly Fop*.

In a number of ways *Mason & Dixon* represents an expansion of sentiments previously articulated in Pynchon's 1984 article "Is It O.K. to Be a Luddite?" Noting in this essay a "clear identification between the first Luddites and our own revolutionary origins," Pynchon expresses an interest in the struggle between scientific rationalism and the perennial yearning for mystical possibility.[2] In the novel, similarly, the author characterizes America as a crossroads for the energies of the eighteenth century, and here the Mason-Dixon Line becomes a powerful symbol of rationalism's putting its mark on a land once consecrated to multiple perspectives. For those unsure after *V.*, *The Crying of Lot 49*, *Gravity's*

Rainbow, Slow Learner, and *Vineland, Mason & Dixon* allows a glimpse of just what kind of Luddite Pynchon himself is.

In the article Pynchon looks at the Luddite phenomenon of the late eighteenth and early nineteenth centuries for what it reveals of popular resistance to the materialism and incremental godlessness of Enlightenment thinking. "[F]olks in the 18th century believed that once upon a time all kinds of things had been possible which were no longer so. Giants, dragons, spells. The laws of nature had not been so strictly formulated back then" (40). At a time when science and the Industrial Revolution seemed to advance without check, Pynchon observes, "religion was being more and more secularized into Deism and nonbelief." But an "abiding human hunger for evidence of God and afterlife, for salvation—bodily resurrection, if possible—remained" (41). Describing this hunger as a disruptive presence within the Age of Reason, he recognizes in Gothicism and Romanticism, as many before him have noted, manifestations of resistance to an untrammeled Enlightenment narrative. He draws his examples from both European and American culture, with particular reference to Methodism, the Great Awakening, Freemasonry, and such fictions as Walpole's *The Castle of Otranto* and Shelley's *Frankenstein.*

This last, characterized as a "Luddite novel," an "attempt . . . to *deny the machine*" (40), begins and ends amid the same polar wastes—frequently invoked in Pynchon's previous work—that Jeremiah Dixon claims, late in his story, to have traversed in the "small Sledge of Caribou Hide" (739) of a mysterious emissary, a kind of Hermes Psychopompus of the Arctic. Dixon's experience resembles that of Shelley's Robert Walton, the arctic explorer who beholds, in Frankenstein's hideous creature, a ghastly precipitate in the beaker of Enlightenment rationalism. As Walton perpends the lesson embodied in the dying Victor Frankenstein, victim of a Faustian dream of scientific mastery, so must Dixon be brought into imagined contact with what his own science threatens with extinction. Poised between two historical paradigms, Dixon visits one of those "holes at the poles" theorized by John Cleve Symmes (and certain characters in *V.*). Entering the hollow earth, "the World beneath the World" (498), he encounters the race those above call "Gnomes, Elves, smaller folk" and, in a reversal of Swift's Academy of Lagado (itself an inspired meditation on intellectual hubris in the Age of Reason), visits "the local Academy of Sciences" (740) to learn the toll that researches such as his will have on this fabulous realm: "'Once the solar parallax is known,' they told me, 'once the necessary Degrees are measur'd, and the size and weight and shape of the Earth are calculated inescapably at last, all this will vanish. We will have to seek another Space'" (741). Dixon's parable, told to Mason, his fellow measurer of the earth, recapitulates and expands a conceit introduced over a hundred pages earlier by the lumberjack Stig. In both instances, Dixon defends the fantasy by alluding to the Book of Job, specifically to those passages in which an angry deity chastens human intellectual presumption.

Dixon's visit to the "*Terra Concava*" (740) makes retroactively clear the novel's many references to the subterranean realm. These include the "Islands in Earth's Magnetic Field" (442) and the perfectly spherical lead deposits (547) described by the crystal scryer, Jonas Everybeet; the cavern Mason and Dixon visit near South Mountain (497); and "Capt. Shelby's 'Mound'" (598), which seems to inspire Mason's yarning when, searching for Schiehallion, the Scottish mountain "too regular to be natural" (748), he has a conversation, in 1773, with Samuel Johnson. On this occasion, evidently imagined by Wicks Cherrycoke, Dr. Johnson cautions Mason against deism, which represents the attenuation of miraculous possibility in the world. Much earlier, in one of her visitations on St. Helena, the dead Rebekah urges Mason to "[l]ook to the Earth" and hearken to "Tellurick secrets" (172) still capable, perhaps, of chastening rationalism untempered by spirit. Like Dr. Johnson, she implies that modern science threatens more than gnomes and elves. It denies that consciousness or spirit might survive annihilation of the body and thereby threatens the dead with an oblivion yet more absolute.

Pynchon suggests that the subterranean realm represents a vital, if dangerous, alternative to Enlightenment self-delusion. The darkness of this realm figures the something tenebrous at the human heart—and at the heart of history, too. The resisters of rationalist excess—Pynchon joins Blake, Yeats, D. H. Lawrence—have always construed this darkness, when acknowledged, as fecund. When repressed, it engenders reptiles of the mind. Nor do the reptiles scatter when exposed to light; indeed, *The Crying of Lot 49*'s Dr. Hilarius is driven mad by, among other things, the realization that psychoanalysis, whose inventor discovered repression in one of the supreme achievements of Enlightenment thinking, cannot finally banish the demons of the human spirit. The letting-in of light, efficacious at first, eventually effects a different kind of repression, blighting the growth of any spiritual mushrooms in those once-dark cellars of the psyche.

Pynchon also gauges political repression, targeting the colonialism that notoriously justifies itself as a bringing of light to the benighted (one thinks of Kurtz's painting in *Heart of Darkness*). The author subverts this tendentious symbolism in repeated references to the infamous 1756 incident in which the "Peevish Wazir" (562) of Calcutta plunged a selection of Europeans into a dreadful oubliette, a "black hole" in which the reader recognizes a complex metaphor for all that an age of reason might seek to deny. Pynchon limns the terrible political meaning of that cornerstone of Freudian doctrine, the return of the repressed. Of the "146 Europeans . . . oblig'd to spend the night of 20–21 June 1756" (152, my ellipsis) in the nawab's airless dungeon, only 26 survived. Those to whom evil is done, says the poet, do evil in return.

Modern astronomy contributes further to the symbolism of the black hole. The star that has collapsed and created a gravitational pull so powerful as to preclude the escape of light is yet another metaphor that pronounces on the Enlightenment pretension to knowledge. Just as light can be swallowed in a black hole, so must the Age of Reason be schooled to its own limitations. All totalizing systems—colonialism, for example, or capitalism, or logocentrism, or language, or, for that matter, Ptolemaic astronomy—may be described as subject to the creation of black holes. Each defines itself in such a way as to seem all-subsuming—yet sooner or later each reveals inward collapse. Each is, in the Althusserian sense, "ideological," in that a false consciousness is promulgated that allows, as it were, only the thinking of certain thoughts. As with Orwell's Newspeak, the counterideological thought is precisely that which cannot escape the ideological gravity. Orwell imagined Newspeak as the invention of especially resourceful totalitarians, but its true horror lies in the recognition that it was always already there, a metastasizing cancer of discourse.

Some such dynamic explains the frequently conflicted terms in which Pynchon's title characters express themselves. Dixon, a surveyor with an above-average education, and Mason, a sensitive scientist of the second rank, attempt to be good eighteenth-century empiricists, men of reason, but neither can stop seeking evidence of magic and the supernatural. Mason, in particular, will eviscerate the hollow-earth theory one moment and dream of messages from Rebekah, his dead wife, the next. In the midst of the New World's bare-knuckle politics and brutal hustling for lucre, both characters evince a variety of humanistic perceptions and sympathies, from an abhorrence of slavery and genocide to a powerful hunger for miracle. Amphibii of the age, Mason and Dixon enact within their own intellects the increasingly unequal struggle between reason and magic.

Though Pynchon avoids simplistic representations of the mighty forces he charts, he plays, as always, with comically exaggerated characterization. If Wicks Cherrycoke, the artist-storyteller and heteroclite man of the cloth, defines one pole of sensibility, Wade LeSpark, the arms merchant brother-in-law who reluctantly provides shelter and listens to his story, defines the other. Even more antithetical are Padre Zarpazo, the arch-Jesuit, and Captain Zhang, the "mystic Chinaman" (543) who represents an idea of magical possibility at odds with European rationalism. Zarpazo, a character who defends every proposed atrocity in the language of reason, a character ostensibly religious to the point of superstition (especially regarding feng shui, Zhang's magic), confounds such opposed categories as *rational* and *fideistic*. The Wolf of Jesus pursues control, speaking of "walls," "right lines," and "imprisonment." He embraces carceral imagery in language that betrays him (language that Foucault has taught us how to read). In that "the Impurity of this Earth keeps him driven in a holy Rage," he resembles Moldweorp, the spy disgusted by human *sozzura* (filth) in "Under the Rose." One recognizes, too, an affinity with Captain Blicero, the character in *Gravity's Rainbow* who orients himself toward the north and death. Zhang calls Zarpazo "Lord of the Zero" and observes that "his Vows include one sworn to Zero Degrees, Zero Minutes, Zero Seconds, or perfect North." Zarpazo is the story's least sympathetic geometer, the extreme embodiment of what Mason and Dixon undertake. "'[T]is his Destiny to inflict these Tellurick Injuries," Zhang declares, "as 'tis mine to resist them" (544).

As chief spokesman against the Line, Zhang strives to articulate its enormity in terms that mix the mystical with the historical. A "Geomancer," he practices what cartographic historian John B. Henderson characterizes as "an art concerned primarily with siting of . . . structures in places where they would harmonize with and draw upon the flow of the energetic pneuma (*qi*) that circulates through such features of the terrain as mountains and streams."[3] Zhang's remarks about the occult properties of terrain, along with his prophecy regarding the retribution that must follow the marking of the earth with right lines, lie at the heart of the book. The Visto, he avers, "acts as a Conduit for . . . *Sha*" or "Bad Energy," and he describes "a Wind, a truly ill wind, bringing failure, poverty, disgrace, betrayal, — every kind of bad luck there is, — all blowing through, night and day, with many times the force of the worst storm." Boundaries, says Zhang, should follow nature, should honor the *shan* or dragon within. "To mark a right Line upon the Earth is to inflict upon the Dragon's very Flesh, a sword-slash, a long, perfect scar" (542, my ellipsis; cf. 547). "Bad History," Zhang subsequently observes, will follow "Bad Energy": "Nothing will produce Bad History more directly nor brutally, than drawing a Line, in particular a Right Line, the very Shape of Contempt, through the midst of a People, — to create thus a Distinction betwixt 'em, — 'tis the first stroke. — All else will follow as if predestin'd, unto War and Devastation" (615). With characteristic indirection, Pynchon hints here at what the Mason-Dixon Line would become in the moral economy of another century. Zhang prophesies the Civil War.

Upon completing their task, Mason and Dixon "understand . . . that the Line is exactly what Capt. Zhang and a number of others have been styling it all along—a conduit for Evil" (701, my ellipsis). But internecine conflict is for Mason and Dixon a remote evil, the nation it will divide not having been founded yet. Pynchon, by the same token, devotes his attention to the more proximate ills of the century in which his surveyors carry out their fated commission. The blazing of the Visto due west, for example, enacts in miniature the expansion on that compass bearing of white civilization. The Line defines a trajectory that will intersect, at right angles, its natural antitype: the ancient north-south "Warrior Path" of Native American cultures.

Chief among Pynchon's concerns, then, are the eighteenth-century contexts within which the Line drawn by Charles Mason and Jeremiah Dixon came into being—came to be, half a century after its completion, a notorious demarcator between South and North, slave and free. Yet one of the lessons of *Mason & Dixon* is that neither the North nor the South ever had any kind of monopoly on shortsightedness, brutality, or folly. When Dixon suggests to Captain Zhang that "Negro Slavery" exists "upon one side . . . and not the other," Zhang rejoins that "Slavery is very old upon these shores,—and there is no Innocence upon the Practice anywhere, neither among the Indians nor the Spanish nor in the behavior of the rest of Christendom, if it come to that" (615–16, my ellipsis). Thus Pynchon, creator of such unsympathetic Southerners as the offstage Twinkletoes Dugan in "The Small Rain" and Major Duane Marvy in *Gravity's Rainbow* (Roony Winsome, in *V.*, is more problematic), declines the opportunity for simplistic moralizing—for what Mason calls the "Inexpensive Salvo" (302).

As such droll circumlocutions on a later century's colloquialisms reveal, the author's fidelity to eighteenth-century actuality does not prove constrictive. Indeed, one recognizes in *Mason & Dixon* a book that contextualizes its meditation on spatial phenomena (the Line and its orientation to the heavens) by a remarkably exhaustive attention to the temporal—to time, that is, in all its manifestations. Thus Pynchon imagines astronomers' clocks talking to each other and surveys the contrasting cultural attitudes to time among Maryland Catholics and Pennsylvania Protestants. To chasten his former student, William Emerson sends Dixon, a "Newtonian" who "wants all Loans of Energy paid back" (318), a perpetual-motion timepiece. Elsewhere Pynchon refers to the Virginia Resolutions of 1769 as "that Dividing Ridge beyond which all the Streams of American Time must fall unmappable" (395). From consciousness to history to eternity, "the cruel flow of Time" (605) figures here as spatial parallax.

"Time is but the stream I go a-fishing in," says Thoreau in one of the more memorable passages of *Walden*. It is, moreover, a passage that defies logic, shifting as it does from temporal to spatial exemplification, then inverting both coordinates. Time is at once the stream that is "shallow" and the streambed that is eternal. He fishes in and drinks from the temporal stream, which he then, heart-stoppingly, reveals as an image of "the sky, whose bottom is pebbly with stars."[4] I suspect that Thoreau is in the back of Pynchon's mind in some of the conceits about sky-fishing in *Mason & Dixon*, but more apropos here is the conflation—peculiarly American, perhaps—of spatial and temporal. It is a conflation that manages to be supremely and elegantly congenial to the intellect at the same time that it frustrates logic in its less imaginative forms, and some such mental high-wire act is, Pynchon implies, necessary to intellectual balance in any time congratulating itself as an Age of Reason.

How easy, for example, to lose one's mental balance in attempting to comprehend, with Pynchon's characters, what becomes of the five and one-quarter degrees—Captain Zhang calls them "that Slice of Azimuth" (629)—removed by the Jesuits from the Chinese circle (which thereby loses both its non-European character and its graceful congruence with the annual round of 365 and one-quarter days). As Zhang notes, this act of spatial adjustment complements an even more confusing act of temporal adjustment: England's conversion, in September 1752, to the Gregorian calendar. What becomes of the eleven days that disappeared when, almost two hundred years after it was first promulgated, the English accepted the reform introduced by Pope Gregory? The conversion strikes many, of course, as a capitulation to papist interests. As Mason's father observes, "if the Popish gain advantage in Time's Reckoning, they may easily carry the day" (190). The attention to calendar reform serves a number of thematic strands. Most simply it contributes to the general dread of "Jesuit" machinations. Pynchon contrives, too, to make the time-change paranoia suggest new variations on a colonialist theme as Mason, tiring of the endless task of explaining sensible if mind-frustrating science to lay doubters, concocts fantasies worthy of Cyrano de Bergerac with which to regale those who persist in badgering him about the supposedly lost days. On one occasion he suggests that a race of strange, Asiatic pygmies has colonized the eleven days; on another he claims that when "the rest of England" (556) made its instantaneous transition from 2 September to 14 September 1752, he for some reason lurched into 3 September and went on to experience, in its entirety, the interim unknown to all others. Stumbling into a depopulated Oxford, "this Metropolis of British Reason," he finds it "abandon'd to the Occupancy of all that Reason would deny" (559). He experiences, as it were, the colonization by unreason of reason itself. Mason's fantasies, like the calendar reform they pretend to rationalize, have a disorienting effect—even on Mason himself, for he is not altogether immune to wonderment regarding the supposedly lost days. Whether or not he would agree with the Franklin who calls time "our greatest problem" (287), he knows himself time's prisoner.

If "Time is the Space that may not be seen," as William Emerson writes to Dixon, humanity should, the Reverend Cherrycoke explains, be thankful: "out of Mercy, we are blind as to Time,—for we could not bear to contemplate what lies at its heart" (326). What lies there, as longtime Pynchon readers know, is an absence of any rationale, a nothingness, an emptiness, the triumph of death and entropic principle. Mason would like to think that "[t]his Life . . . is like the eleven days,—a finite Period at whose end" (561, my ellipsis) he will be reunited with his dead wife, Rebekah. But it is in an altogether less sanguine sense that this life resembles the eleven days: it is an anomaly, untransfigured by some imagined exemption from the mortal state. A remark of Wicks Cherrycoke's about the eleven days lost to calendar reform carries portentous overtones: "We think of 'our' Time, being held, in whatever Time's equivalent to 'a Place' is, like Eurydice, somehow to be redeem'd" (555). But of course Eurydice's redemption is a failure.

Thus Mason's remark about Franklin—"By Reputation, he is a man entirely at ease with the inner structures of Time itself" (271)—says more than is at first evident. Those "inner structures" are merely the inexorable cogs and wheels of oblivion: Franklin, as a hero of the Enlightenment, is in league with forces hostile to the vital principle. Indeed, in one of the novel's more unsettling tableaux, Franklin leads a serpentine dance out of a tavern and into the street—an eloquent representation of the idea that rationalism leads its followers a merry dance indeed. Two centuries later, Americans continue snaking along in the wake of this Philadelphia philosophe, not recognizing the Conga line as a Dance of Death.

Simple discrimination between space and time as they figure in *Mason & Dixon* can present challenges to the reader, who is occasionally hard-pressed even to identify the entity under review. What is one to make, for example, of the reverie into which Wicks Cherrycoke sinks after a fatiguing day of carriage travel? Having been along on such carriage-rides before (in Cervantes, in Fielding, in Smollett, in de Maupassant, in a John Ford film, even), the reader is attentive to allegorical suggestion: the ride will presently reveal itself as life-journey, the carriage passengers as societal cross section. But here the symbolic dimension emerges only when, at Mr. Knockwood's new inn on Octarara Creek, the reverend retires on a curious reverie:

> "What Machine is it," young Cherrycoke later bade himself goodnight, "that bears us along so relentlessly? We go rattling thro' another Day,—another Year,—as thro' an empty Town without a Name, in the Midnight . . . we have but Memories of some Pause at the Pleasure-Spas of our younger Day, the Maidens, the Cards, the Claret,—we seek to extend our stay, but now a silent Functionary in dark Livery indicates it is time to re-board the Coach, and resume the Journey. Long before the Destination, moreover, shall this Machine come abruptly to a Stop . . . gather'd dense with Fear, shall we open the Door to confer with the Driver, to discover that there is no Driver, . . . no Horses, . . . only the Machine, fading as we stand, and a Prairie of desperate Immensity. . . ." (Pynchon's ellipses, 361)

Pynchon here refines a memorable figure, in *Gravity's Rainbow*, of ecological folly in a European setting: "Living inside the System is like riding across the country in a bus driven by a maniac bent on suicide" (412). Cherrycoke's, however, is an "American" dream, as unanchored and illogical as the fading consciousness from which it emerges. One cannot extend one's stay when one has not yet stopped—though perhaps, in memory, one can remain at some recollected place. But the coach, which is bound to time, must be reboarded—time cannot be arrested, even in fantasy visits to the past. Like the carriage in the Emily Dickinson poem, this vehicle carries its passengers towards eternity. The destination not reached is, more concretely, the heavenly city toward which

Western humanity once thought itself en route. As religious certainty wanes, however, the carriage reveals itself as driverless and horseless. "Fading as we stand," it has become some such contraption as H. G. Wells's Time Machine, a device that carries one forward toward a vision of the entropic heat death—or, in the present, American instance, toward "a Prairie of desperate Immensity." This is at once the prairie into which the as yet embryonic republic will expand and the vast vacancy of a godless, rationalistic dispensation. American time, American space.

Mending Wall

From Benny Profane and Oedipa Maas to Tyrone Slothrop and Zoyd Wheeler, Pynchon's characters struggle impotently against enormous forces. The twin protagonists of *Mason & Dixon* do not violate the expectations of readers schooled in Kute Korrespondences. In their timorous surmises after the *Seahorse* fiasco, Charles Mason and Jeremiah Dixon discover themselves minor players in a larger political, cultural, and scientific drama, "Lodgers inside someone else's Fate, whilst belonging quite someplace else" (75). When Policeman Bonk presents himself to them in Capetown, he seems a mildly silly figure of authority, but later, recognizing his own pawnlike standing, he admits to the confusion, the vulnerability, and the feelings of inadequacy that reveal a curious bond between himself—sometime fascist bully—and the humble and increasingly paranoid servants of the Royal Society. Subsequently, in America, Captain Zhang characterizes Mason and Dixon as "Bystanders. Background. Stage-Managers of that perilous Flux" he calls *Sha*. He further characterizes the Line on which they expend their spirit as merely a "Stage-Setting, dark and fearful as the Battlements of Elsinore, for the struggle" (545) between himself and the monomaniacal Jesuit Zarpazo. The reference to *Hamlet* invites the reader to recognize in Mason and Dixon the Rosencrantz and Guildenstern of the eighteenth century.

Like Pynchon's other paranoids, however, Mason and Dixon are victims not of a plot but of certain constraints on the imagination. Their paranoia functions as an index to or metaphor for their struggle to think independently—to think in terms divorced from their age and the conditions of knowing therein. Thus defined, paranoia constitutes a form of resistance to the Enlightenment episteme, an attempt to escape what Blake calls "mind-forg'd" manacles and Pynchon the "mental Cilice" (230) or chastity belt of the mind. The implied struggle for perceptual freedom moves, in *Mason & Dixon*, through a spectrum from the personal to the geopolitical to the cosmic. That is, the protagonists' concern about the supposed ire of the Royal Society over the letter of protest they write after the *Seahorse* affair, along with their iterations of Dixon's query as he reflects on the massacre of peaceful Indians at Lancaster, Pennsylvania ("[w]hom are we working for, Mason?" [347]), swiftly modulates toward engagement with the more historical dimensions of paranoia. Those with whom they come in contact, for example, suspect them as spies in the endless wrangling between interests characterized alternately as those of Maryland vs. Pennsylvania, Catholic vs. Protestant, or, in terms suited to the coming rebellion, Tory vs. Whig. The very times, in other words, are plot obsessed, and the rearguard actions of faith against the triumphant armies of reason compound the sense that one's least gesture may have cosmic consequences.

The Society of Jesus, for centuries the bête noire of English Protestantism, provides the chief target of Anglo-American paranoia in the novel. Though Pynchon's Jesuits no doubt owe something to Monty Python, historical perceptions in fact require little embroidering: from the death of Queen Mary to the defeat of Bonny Prince Charlie, from the Gunpowder Plot to the Glorious Revolution and the French and Indian Wars, the Protestant, English-speaking world struggled with real and imagined "Popish" or "Jesuitical" enemies.[5] The colonies were not spared. An early, pre-Revolutionary struggle took place in the New World between a largely Catholic (and Jesuit) French interest and a largely Protestant British interest. Too, the Crown had granted one of the earliest American charters (1632) to George Calvert, Baron Baltimore, whose Maryland colony became a haven for his fellow Catholics, often at odds with colonists of the opposing persuasion. In 1691 Maryland became a royal province, and in 1692—and again in 1702—attempts were made to establish the Church of England as its official faith. Through much of the eighteenth century in Maryland, Catholic services could be performed only in private homes. The other colonies saw even more virulent distrust, hatred, and persecution of non-Protestants. In 1696 the

South Carolina Legislative Assembly guaranteed religious freedom to all Christians—except Roman Catholics. In 1700 Catholic priests were banned from Massachusetts and New York.

Again, an important measure of Pynchon's accomplishment here lies in the extent to which he successfully reconstructs contemporaneous perceptions of the boundary established by Mason and Dixon. The notoriety of that Line as symbol of the divisions between the agrarian, slave-holding South and the industrial, abolitionist North was a development of the century succeeding the one in which it came into officially sanctioned cartographic existence. In the century of its laying out, the Line was perceived as dividing Calverts from Penns, Maryland from Pennsylvania, locally Protestant from locally Catholic ("locally" because farther north, in former French Canada, were more Catholics, and farther south, in Virginia and the Carolinas, were more Protestants). At the same time, however, Pynchon represents the Line as archetypal, emblematic of divisions the Christian West has always construed as essential. The drawing of lines—in division, differentiation, discrimination, and other such boundary-making—is as old, it seems, as creation itself. According to the Genesis presumably read by Catholic and Protestant alike, acts of demarcation were among the first items of divine business. They commence a mere four verses into the Old Testament as the deity divides light from dark and ordains the firmament to divide the primordial waters. Mr. Edgewise, on the coach to Philadelphia, describes all land and boundary disputes as mere "Sub-Division" (361) of those first, divinely executed demarcations.

In human hands, however, boundaries become occasions of discord. Thus the reader may notice a certain picking-up of lawsuits as the Line inches towards completion, offering fresh opportunities "among the most litigious people on Earth,—Pennsylvanians of all faiths" (324). Rhodie Beck, for example, whose husband Zepho metamorphoses into a were-beaver at the full moon, threatens a lawsuit against the hapless surveyors when, to the considerable embarrassment of several parties, they neglect to predict a lunar eclipse. More and more, boundary disputes and litigation follow the Line, which takes the hapless surveyors through the territory of Frau Redzinger, who has been paying taxes to Pennsylvania but may have thereby allowed her property to fall into escheat in Maryland (360), and of the mad Captain Shelby, who "exhibits signs of mania upon the topic of Land-Disputes . . . , with Boundary issues a particular Passion" (585, my ellipsis). Shelby seems, nonetheless, instinctively to recognize a certain kind of boundary drawing as work requiring the assistance, as "Third Surveyor" (604), of the devil himself. Small wonder that no answer is imagined for the "fatal" question the Mohawks may ask: "Why are you doing this?" (641).

That question—asked in a variety of ways throughout the novel—concerns something more basic than the surveying feat of Mason and Dixon. It reminds readers that Pynchon's story concerns the drawing of a boundary line that has built-in aesthetic, metaphysical, spiritual, and epistemic dimensions. Blazing the Visto with their little army of assistants, Mason and Dixon resemble Enzian and the *Schwarzkommando*, riding another "interface" between scientific paradigms and phases of history. But the author does not limit himself to either the Mason-Dixon Line or to the lines and boundaries of private property. Thus he characterizes the "grimly patroll'd Line" between life and death as the "very essence of Division" (703). Early in the story Mason, Dixon, and the Reverend Wicks Cherrycoke, sailing to South Africa, cross the Equator—Uncle Ives calls it "some Geometers' Abstraction that cannot even be seen"—and undergo the traditional ceremonies. With the sun directly overhead, they cross, without incident, the line dividing the northern hemisphere from the southern, pass "thro' the Gate of the single shadowless Moment" (56).

Yet "in the world that is to come, all boundaries shall be eras'd" (406). The pronouncement applies, first, to the Apocalypse and to the American Revolution, but it also invites recognition of other boundaries that, late in the twentieth century, function *sous rature* if at all. Like other postmodernists, that is, Pynchon problematizes the lines supposedly differentiating history and fiction. When the unimaginative weapons merchant, Wade LeSpark, complains of "too much . . . failing to mark the Boundaries between Reality and Representation" (429), one wonders who else fails to mark them—indeed, whether such boundaries can be said to exist in *Mason & Dixon*.

The fluid, unfixed line between history and romance, between the real and the imagined, indicts the very logic of rationalism. Any attempt to firm up this line leads not to objectivity but to the imposition, more or less fascistic, of a single official perspective. Not by accident, then, does Mason, chary of "betraying" his dead wife, tell Dixon a story apparently unconstrained by fact when asked to speak "of how Rebekah and he first met" (167). Captain Zhang is described as "yet another damn'd Fabulator, such as ever haunt encampments" (552). Most interestingly, the Reverend Wicks Cherrycoke, joking about his "Authorial Authority" (354) in one place and calling himself an "untrustworthy Remembrancer" (8) in another, draws the reader/audience's attention to his own possible unreliability as narrator. By the same token, he allows his tale to subsume, at points, a story or stories from *The Ghastly Fop*, Pynchon's imaginary Gothic periodical. Read by characters at disparate narratological levels (Mason and Dixon on the one hand, Tenebræ and Ethelmer on the other), this periodical bleeds into—indeed, discourages the privileging of—the narrative of Wicks Cherrycoke in ways that resist our desire for distinctions between the real and the fanciful. As Gothic troubles the smooth eighteenth-century sea of rationalism, so does this particular example of Gothic militate against one's desire for a readerly, unambiguous narrative.

The narratological point suggests that one must recognize as fictional the boundaries between fiction itself and the reality or history naively taken to occupy a separate epistemological category. "If the traditional historical novel attempts to replicate a way of life, speech and costume," observes T. Coraghessan Boyle, "the post-modernist version seeks only to be just that, a version."[6] Historical fiction—and *Mason & Dixon* is no exception—seeks always to remind its readers that the semantic distinction between the words *story* and *history* will not stand scrutiny. The word *history* originally meant "a narrative either veracious or imagined," as in the full title of the celebrated novel by Fielding: *The History of Tom Jones, a Foundling*. Through the process linguists call aphaeresis, the dropping of an initial syllable, *history* became *story*—but without the original form's disappearing. Seeming to vie with each other semantically, the two words afford a convenient but misleading distinction, largely absent in other languages related to or influenced by Latin (these retain only one ambiguous form: either the original, as Russian *istorya*, or the shortened form, as Italian *storia*).

Pynchon suggests that the most valuable history recognizes its own fictive underpinnings to achieve imaginative insight into the human condition. In John Barth's *The Sot-Weed Factor*, a novel with which *Mason & Dixon* has numerous affinities, a character affirms the ancient superiority of the poet to the historian—indeed, to the whole tribe of traffickers in the narrowly factual. "Men think he hath a passkey to Dame Truth's bedchamber and smiles at the scholars building ladders in the court."[7] Both Pynchon and Barth remind the reader that truly disinterested discourse does not exist—least of all for historians. Thus Pynchon recurs to the idea that history is never simply a matter of accurate facts one can recover, objectively marshal, and present in a narrative form immune to the fictive undertow. Like any other discourse, history is always constructed, always subject to subjectivity. For historians, as for anyone else, "[*p*] *randium gratis non est*" (317)—there's no such thing as a free lunch. Wicks Cherrycoke, chief spokesman for this recognition, plays with his auditors (not to mention the reader) when he earnestly notes what appears to be the odd recurrence of eleven-day units in the field journals left by Mason and Dixon. Any such mensuration, he invites his auditors to object (and they do—"Poh, Sir!" [555]), derives from the conscious or unconscious projection of the researcher. Like Herbert Stencil or Oedipa Maas, in other words, the traditional historian pursues an ultimately chimerical objectivity, a spurious grail.

Hence, in chapter 35, the debate regarding distinctions between history and romance. Wicks speaks here for the metahistorical perspective, as his listeners articulate the commonsense objections. Mr. LeSpark, for example, quotes the Great Lexicographer: "Dr. Johnson says that all History unsupported by contemporary Evidence is Romance" (351). When his brother, the bibulous Ives, delivers himself of a tirade against novels, the new form that outromances the romance, one recognizes an inchoate syllogism that seeks to disparage the historical novel—*Mason & Dixon*, for example—as little more than an oxymoron. Wicks, however, dismisses the earnest pursuit of unitary truth and mischievously suggests that the greater the element of romance, the better the history. He rejects the sober fact-mongering of a Gibbon in favor of the richer, paradoxically less deluded homages to Clio that Herodotus wrote—and in later ages Sir John Mandeville, Captain John Smith, and Baron Münchhausen. Wicks, like Aristotle, values history only insofar as it allies itself to the insights of poetry or, more broadly, of literature. "Who claims Truth, Truth abandons" (350), he declares, articulating a kind of parallax view of history. By implication, Truth creeps in where the imagination reigns—especially imagination of multiple perspectives. At its best, historical fiction allies itself to that search for the miraculous so inimical to the logocentric pretensions of the Enlightenment. If this is history as carnival, history constantly threatening to "converge to Opera in the Italian Style" (706), it is also the history that Wicks can characterize as a record of humanity's "Hunt for Christ" (75).

This last phrase has a sting in its tail. Far from the dancelike quest for salvation Wicks momentarily imagines, the hunt also involves, as the freethinking Aethelmer hastens to point out, "ev'ry Crusade, Inquisition, Sectarian War, the millions of lives, the seas of blood" (76). The original "hunt for Christ," one recalls, was undertaken by the soldiery of King Herod, desperate to forestall the new dispensation. The slaughter of the innocents was preceded by an augury that inspired, in the flight into Egypt, the common era's first embrace of preterition ("I am passed over"). It was also the Holy Family's introduction to a paranoia that, in both the short term and the long, proved wholly justified.

Yet Pynchon's career-long emphasis on paranoia, often taken to be little more than a holding of the mirror up to a characteristic psychopathology of the age, reveals itself in his fifth novel as potentially transformative. Pynchon sees paranoia as *pharmakon*—at once the poison and its remedy. Thus the paranoia of Mason and Dixon, at first the measure of their inconsequence, becomes the gauge of their sensitive resistance to rationalist excess. They come to see that their Line does a great deal more than signify where Pennsylvania ends and Maryland begins. They recognize in the Line an epistemic watershed, a boundary between dispensations.

By the same token, the Line becomes for Pynchon, in the end, an unusual emblem of his own art and his own philosophical outlook. As boundary and as literary subject, the Line resembles the wall in a well-known Frost poem. In "Mending Wall," one recalls, the speaker tells a whimsical story of meeting a neighbor periodically to walk the wall that divides their property, repairing it as they go. "Something there is," the speaker twice observes, "that doesn't love a wall."[8] This something would seem to be nature itself, the earth, what Captain Zhang calls the *shan*. It is also, more simply, winter, and winter's subversive agent, frost. Perhaps the poet whose name derives from this climatological condition also "doesn't love a wall." Certainly the spectacle of the neighbor making for the wall with a stone in each hand prompts the speaker to see him, momentarily, as "an old-stone savage armed" who "moves in darkness." The poem, with this image, becomes a meditation on the territorial imperative, the atavistic instinct that insists on boundaries between self and other, mine and thine. If there is something in nature that does not love walls, there is something else—in the human heart, also ruled by nature—that insists on them.

Frost, as in so many of his poems, invites recognition of a startling analogy between his callings as farmer and poet. He describes the activity shared with the farmer on the other side of the fence as "just another kind of outdoor game, / One on a side." The reader who recalls Frost's remark about free verse (he likened it to playing tennis without a net) will recognize wall mending as the symbol of that other game, poetry, in which, perhaps, one "wins" by writing iambic pentameter that, never violating the rhythms of speech, deceives all but the most vigilant eye, all but the most acute ear. Frost reflects here on the relationship between poet and audience. The poet wants the walls down, wants to communicate—but knows full well that meaningful communication depends, in some paradoxical way, on those very walls. It is the poet-speaker, after all—the one who seems to disapprove of the activity—who initiates the wall mending.

A similar element figures in Pynchon's meditation on the larger meanings of the Mason-Dixon Line. Commonly credited with no small postmodernist refinement and extension of the reflexive gesture that Frost and his contemporaries made a signature of modernist literary practice, Pynchon seeks to subvert or restructure the old mix of adversarial and collaborative between author and reader—he radically reimagines Frost's wall or net, along with the rest of the literary "game." Though winning the game remains problematic, one knows that the surest way

to lose is to track down a meaning that pretends to account for all elements of the text—as, in fact, one was invited to do by the modernists
(at least as read by the New Critics they called into existence). The binary of winning or losing—like Pynchon's manifold variations on the
seductive logic of either/or ("either Oedipa in the orbiting ecstasy of a
true paranoia, or a real Tristero" [*Lot 49* 182])—constantly teases with
the prospect of resolution or closure. Thus Pynchon seduces his readers
into actions that mirror those of his questing protagonists. As Herbert
Stencil, or Oedipa Maas, or Tyrone Slothrop, or Prairie Wheeler seeks
V., or the Tristero, or the Rocket, or Frenesi Gates, so do readers pursue
a grail-like textual wholeness that constantly retreats before them. Just
another kind of indoor game, one to a side.

A necessary corrective to certain forms of totalizing thought, such
play is not necessarily at odds with the transcendental signified. In *Mason
& Dixon*, as in his previous novels and stories, Pynchon plays with myth
making and the signifying loop—but not in any cynical spirit of iconoclasm. As a serious artist, Pynchon strives to do full justice to the complexity of the world and history, language and the human mind. Thus
he does not reject the possibility that spiritual realities have been obscured by centuries of what Derrida calls "logocentric metaphysics." One
can argue, I think, the mounting evidence of Pynchon's spiritual and
metaphysical (even religious) seriousness, his disinclination to privilege
either the scientific and technological message or the endless lesson of
textuality.

Which is not to say that Pynchon is, as the Hemingway character says,
croyant. Pynchon insists only that undiluted rationalism makes impossible the apprehension of such spiritual reality as may exist. By the same
token, though much exercised by the Line, Pynchon may not agree with
those of his characters who construe it as irredeemably evil. He might
differ, that is, with the reviewer who sees in *Mason & Dixon* "an indict-
ment of private property, arguably man's most pernicious invention."[9]
Pynchon surely recognizes in the surveying of the Line a legitimate activity of human beings who must pay attention to boundaries or lapse,
as Frost hints, into vastly more primitive forms of territorialism. On this
score one errs, I should think, to take either the fulminations of Zhang
or the conclusions of Mason and Dixon as definitive formulations of

authorial views. Pynchon's real attitude to his subject matter might best be characterized as Faulknerian: he reveals the built-in, programmed elements of tragedy in the human struggle with landscape and history. If he sees the seeds of tragedy in the totalizing assurance of Enlightenment discourse, Pynchon is not, in the end, the perfect Luddite. In the latter days of the rationalist dispensation he must make especially cogent the antirationalist case, but he does so less as mystic than as apologist for balance.

Life, like a dome of many-coloured glass,
Stains the white radiance of eternity.
—PERCY BYSSHE SHELLEY, *Adonais*

. . . the ancient spacious booms of a
detonating sky.
—DON DELILLO, *Mao II*

CHAPTER SIX

Pynchon, Genealogy, History

Against the Day

One cannot overstate the centrality of historical questions and issues in the work of Thomas Pynchon. What makes his fictions so compelling—more, perhaps, than any other quality—is the variety and complexity of historical rethinking they invite and perform. Tiina Käkelä-Puumala, in a recent study, locates "Pynchon's historic interest" in "the era of modernization we have been living in since the 17th century . . . Puritanism, the Enlightenment, industrialism, scientific revolutions, global economy, information explosion, simulation—throughout his fiction Pynchon is very much a writer of modernization, of its historical preconditions, aims, and limits."[1] Shawn Smith characterizes Pynchon as "the pre-eminent American postmodernist writer" and "an innovative and profound historical novelist as well."[2] One may wince at such a bald assertion: this author the practitioner of a form "condemned," as Henry James said, "to a fatal cheapness"?[3] But in fact, risking such obloquy as may still attach to the label, Pynchon has candidly applied it to himself. Replying to critics of Ian McEwan in a letter to the *Daily Telegraph* in 2006, he casually affirms that, whatever the license creative artists enjoy, "most of us who write historical fiction . . . feel some obligation to accuracy."[4] Accuracy, however, may vizard itself in curious ways, and Pynchon proves, as one might expect, something of an unconventional historian. He reinvents and reconceptualizes history as what a Nietzsche or a Foucault would call genealogy. Foucault characterizes this strain of historiography as "gray, meticulous, and patiently documentary."[5] Stripping away the layers of ideological legitimation, the genealogist-historian lays bare the play of power that so swiftly seeks to disguise its workings. Of course, a novelist working in this vein risks fatiguing and alienating readers. John Dugdale, reviewing *Against the Day* for the *Sunday Times* of London, called it *Moby-Dick* without Ahab or the whale.[6] But readers who find the overall point of *Against the Day* elusive may better tolerate the *longueurs* of Pynchon's sixth novel if they recognize the technique as that of the genealogist. Only incidentally interested in routine historical iconoclasm, Pynchon undertakes a radical reframing of the essential questions and answers about the past. Bernard Duyfhuizen, characterizing "[p]ower and the movement of history" as "a pervasive theme in Pynchon's writing," notes a reversal here. Where "[u]sually he shrouds the sources of power in many layers of governmental or corporate bureaucracy so that its effects are mainly felt while its origins remain hidden," Pynchon now represents power as something more than the faceless bête noire of paranoids everywhere.[7] The author means to effect a turning inside-out of the way his readers think about and understand power, its manifestations in discourse, and its workings over historical time. Recognizing what in "Truth and Power" is called "the essential political problem of the intellectual," Pynchon explores "the possibility"—as Foucault put it—"of constituting a new politics of truth."[8] Only the "patiently documentary" approach will do here.

In the opening chapter of *Discipline and Punish*, Foucault describes the protracted torture and execution of a would-be regicide, then interprets the spectacle as a "political ritual," a discourse of royal power.

Such spectacles, he observes, served the same purpose in the eighteenth century as a well-staffed constabulary and an elaborate penal apparatus in modern times. But in every historical period power seeks its own perpetuation. It seeks control. Less barbaric now but every bit as spirit crushing, power constantly fosters and adapts to the means of its own legitimization. Foucault ends a subsequent chapter with a disturbing rhetorical question: "Is it surprising that prisons resemble factories, schools, barracks, hospitals, which all resemble prisons?"[9]

Lamenting the "functional disease" of "American architecture," Norman Mailer makes a similar observation: "one could not tell the new colleges from the new prisons from the new hospitals from the new factories from the new airports."[10] But philosopher and novelist differ in their emphases, the one enthralled by the articulation and reticulation of power, the other appalled by its brutality. In the subtle scholasticism of his observations about tendentious architecture or the penal code, Foucault blunts the edge of what he intends as a political critique. For real engagement and effective polemic, by contrast, one turns to a Mailer or a Pynchon. If either seeks to reveal power's insidious — or blatant — workings, it is always, still, with an eye to imagining a world in which various oppressive forces can be countered, dismantled, resisted. Pynchon in particular, from the beginning of his career, has looked for ways to expose and subvert the Faustian imperative, the drive towards more knowledge and more power that characterizes a world order shaped and sustained by what in *Against the Day* he calls the "capitalist/ Christer gridwork" (1075).

Heteroclite Historiography

In *Against the Day*, observes Henry Veggian, Pynchon seizes upon and transforms "the genealogical authority of the modern historical novel."[11] The postmodern critic of historical fiction needs, first, to repudiate the contumely of Henry James and the special pleading of Georg Lukács. Rather than argue, with Lukács, against the very existence of the historical novel as a separate genre (he asserts that history naturally breathes through the work of any respectable novelist), one must make distinctions among historical fictions, between the historical novel (often maligned, though its practitioners include Tolstoy and Faulkner) and the historical romance (as written by authors as different as Scott, Hawthorne, and Frank Yerby), or between both and the postmodern hybrid that Linda Hutcheon characterizes as "historiographic metafiction."[12] By turns realistic and idealized, the first two traffic in versions of what supposedly was, but the more compelling form emerges out of postmodern uncertainty about the relations between *story* and *history*—words whose shared etymology, as I have noted before, undermines discrimination. Foregrounding its own artifice, such metafiction impugns or at least resists the very idea of a more objective historiography. It exposes the fictive undercurrent in every historical narrative.

As a genre, metafiction invites perceptions of ludic nonseriousness, but attentive readers have always recognized the perspicacity behind the playfulness. More than feckless fabulators, Pynchon and other accomplished writers of such fiction—including John Barth, Ishmael Reed, and, in *Kindred*, at least, Octavia Butler—reframe history in surprising ways. They insist that her susceptibility to a good story makes Clio the most complex—and generous—of muses. They also insist, with the ancients, that history belongs among the arts, not the sciences. But writers of historical metafiction always ask thoroughly serious questions about the past and, *pace* the postmodern episteme's supposed amorality, its shaping of the ethical present.

Pynchon learned his heteroclite historiography in a good school. Readers of *Against the Day* should recall the long-standing affinity between its author, born in 1937, and Henry Adams, born almost exactly a hundred years earlier, in 1838. One discovers in *The Education of Henry Adams* a remarkable amalgam of three or four genres: at once cultural history and spiritual autobiography, it reverses the premise of such classic or imaginary educational programs as Rousseau's *Emile* and Walter Shandy's Tristrapedia. Instead of describing, in prospect, an ideal education, it chronicles an ironically belated schooling that continually miscarries. Adams's thesis emerges only gradually. He argues, ultimately, that no education can prepare modern humanity for what has begun to transpire all about: the acceleration of a scientific, materialistic, relentlessly empirical age in which the raw power of the dynamo (and all the force-focusing technology it announces) displaces the spiritualized biological forces of former times, forces embodied in pagan deities—notably Venus—and in Christianity's idealized woman, the Virgin Mary.

Unduly deferential to the historicist pose (not to mention the eighteenth-century pedigree), critics seem seldom to emphasize or even notice Adams's credentials as modernist: surely, they imply, the *Education*'s author belongs intellectually and rhetorically in the nineteenth century. But Adams transcends the decades he passes in review. Invariably referring to himself in the third person, Adams hints at the furcation of consciousness and the self that would become a hallmark of modern alienation (not to mention what post-Freudian psychoanalysis would call decentering of the subject). Long before the twentieth century's distrust of any and all attempts at a rhetoric of sincerity, moreover, Adams had learned to frame his every observation with an irony that goes beyond even that of the classic exemplars of a modernist style. Observing that cultural unity gives way to chaotic multiplicity, moreover, he anticipates the Yeats who discovers that things fall apart, the Eliot who shores fragments, the Pound who sees a once-robust civilization as "two gross of broken statues" and "a few thousand battered books." Indeed, insofar as Adams may not subscribe, with them, to metanarratives of history (or at least "tradition"), he anticipates the postmodern episteme as well.

Thus Pynchon, beginning his career with artful echoes of Adams, has only to deploy a somewhat cooler irony, more incredulity towards metanarratives, more tolerance of truths multiple and mutually contradictory. In his first novel, *V.*, he introduces a major character who refers to himself in the third person and seeks, through ultimately autobiographical investigations, to understand his violent century in terms of its relation to a latter-day Virgin or Venus, a female entity at once terrible and infinitely seductive. In the varied avatars of the mysterious woman known as V., Herbert Stencil thinks he has discovered the twentieth-century equivalent of the divine female principle that had manifested itself, from antiquity into the Christian era, as fertility. But V. proves an intellectual chimera, the belated embodiment of the mythic thought that constantly falsifies historical reality in the name of a specious supernaturalism. In fact, she embodies a relentlessly entropic, unspiritual decay, a Spenglerian decline.

The reader of *Against the Day* may, then, discern a renewed relationship between its author and Henry Adams. Here Pynchon scrutinizes, more exhaustively than in *V.*, the period that Adams reviews in the latter part of the *Education*: the end of the nineteenth century and the beginning of the twentieth. Adams, in his closing chapters, chronicles contemporaneity, analyzing events and experiences little removed in time from his own present. Like a character in Samuel Richardson, he virtually writes to the moment. In *V.*, Pynchon does the same, bringing the action up to 1956, a scant seven years before its publication. In *Against the Day*, from a greater remove in time, Pynchon takes up the historical questions he inherits from Adams with some significant shifts of strategy and perspective. Again, as in *Mason & Dixon*, the author grapples resourcefully with the challenges of historiography. Not that he aspires to some narrow idea of "objectivity." Leaving to Adams the self-designation as historian, Pynchon rather aspires to the calling of fictive genealogist, the most historically meticulous of storytellers.

Postmodern historiographers recognize that, in accounts of the past, facticity swallows fact and objectivity remains elusive, chimerical. Echoing familiar pronouncements by Fredric Jameson, Andreas Huyssen observes: "The problem with postmodernism is that it relegates history to the dustbin of an obsolete episteme, arguing gleefully that history does not exist except as text, i.e., historiography" (172). No historical narrative fully escapes the tidal pull of storytelling, whose tendency to shapeliness and coherence inevitably misrepresents the disorder at the heart of history. Conversely, great storytelling can and does achieve, when it sets out to do so, extraordinary insight into the past. Certainly it has the power to memorialize. Thus Byron, shaking his head in *Don Juan* over the "[b]rave men" who "shone not on the poet's page, / And so have been forgotten" (1.33, 35–37), reminds his readers that history began as poetry and still owes a debt to literature. From Virgil, by the same token, one learns that all history strives to hang flesh on a single, skeletal verb. "*Fuit Ilium*," he writes: Troy *has been*. Nor does the historiographical factitiousness of the *Aeneid*—that elaborate faux genealogy for the Roman state—detract from the seriousness with which its author meditates on the manifold ways the present realizes the past.

But where Virgil's historiography coalesces in a vision of empire, Pynchon's parses imperial illegitimacy. Throughout his career, in fact, Pynchon scrutinizes history as what in *Against the Day* he calls "Time's pathology" (828). Whether he writes story or history, what hybridizes Pynchon's work is his contempt for objective distance, his passion for justice-based chronicle. From *V.* to *Vineland,* from *The Crying of Lot 49* to *Gravity's Rainbow,* and from *Mason & Dixon* to *Against the Day* and *Inherent Vice,* Pynchon insists on writing the history of the marginalized or, as he calls them, the preterite—those on whose backs an older idea of history unfolded. Like Foucault or the Guy Debord of *Society of the Spectacle* ("[e]xamining history amounts to *examining the nature of power*"),[13] Pynchon understands instinctively that a different history emerges if the investigator asks different questions—questions regarding just where and how power reveals itself in institutional structures, in socially conditioned habits of thought and speech, and in the rhetoric of science, politics, and the penal code. From this vantage, one can turn even popular entertainments inside out, making them disclose their complicity in the sanctioned distribution of power. In his foreword to the centennial reissue of Orwell's *1984,* for example, Pynchon characterizes "'crime dramas'" as "themselves forms of social control."[14]

In many ways, then, Pynchon's career unfolds as a deepening commitment to the preterite in history, "a progressive knotting into" (*GR* 3) the problematics of historiography. However perdurable and unchanging his convictions, his thinking and his art have evolved, and one cannot resist saying that, in his sixth novel, as in his third, readers "aren't in Kansas anymore." But what do readers see as Pynchon's books follow each other? In the course of their careers, some authors mature and change, each succeeding book marking some fresh moral discovery, some advance in technique, some new set of ideas. One sees positive examples of this career trajectory in the novels of E. M. Forster, say, or Don DeLillo (those of John Dos Passos belie the paradigm). Other writers—the unfortunate John Gardner comes to mind—seem always to have known their minds and their powers. Nothing in a later book contradicts anything in an earlier book. Though it can represent artistic calcification (one thinks of the Pat Conroys and even the Walker Percys who seem to write the same book over and over), such intellectual consistency ideally testifies to a mind seasoned and anchored early on. Thus is it with the author of *Against the Day*: one reads the Pynchon oeuvre as an ideational *roman fleuve*.

What a challenge, though, to deploy all that constitutes one's "voice" without actually repeating oneself. Great artists and lesser artists alike develop stylistic and thematic signatures. Those who read, listen to, or view a given writer's work can discern characteristic features that function as building blocks from which she or he constructs, first, a grammar, then the sentences that frame thought. One thinks of Yeats's gyres and cycles of history, of participle-loving Whitman's epic cataloguing, of the unfolding personal mythologies of Blake and Lawrence, of the creeping orthodoxy of a T. S. Eliot or a John Updike. Ideally, the emphases never betray mere obsession or degenerate (one thinks of Hemingway) into self-parody.

Pynchon's first critics thought they discerned such characteristic concerns in themes of entropy, paranoia, and conspiracy. But Pynchon himself, in his occasional nonfiction pieces over the years, has discounted the centrality of such concepts. Thus prompted, later criticism discerns less schematicism in Pynchon's storytelling. But the author still freights certain favored conceits with thematic immanence. These elements or motifs configure something like the rich polyphony of a career, and just as, in his early story "Entropy," Pynchon characterizes a spell of rapidly alternating February weather as "a *stretto* passage in the year's fugue" (*SL* 83), so may his readers think of *Against the Day* as a kind of fugal recapitulation (though hardly *stretto*, which in a musical score means "shortened" and "accelerated"). Readers familiar with Pynchon will recognize tropes familiar to them from previous novels—from *timbres fictifs* (548), philatelic "inverts" (978), and a stamp auction (1081) to *Achphänomen* (616) or Brocken Specters (632), ukulele virtuosity (15, 551–52), hollow-earth theories (115), Irrendentism (254, 761), Cesare Lombroso (172, 606), the gnostic Gospel of Thomas (579–80), labor history, the tarot, the rapture of souls (55, 787), the Shekhinah (960), "Sentient Rocksters" (133), a modest *Star Trek* joke (23), and a seaman named Bodine (517, 519). At one point, Pynchon even reintroduces La Jarretière, the dancer who perishes horribly in *V.*'s parody of *The Rite of Spring* (here the reader learns that in fact she survived). A randomized census unfolds, something only a Stith Thompson (author of the six-volume *Motif-Index of Folk-Literature*) might sort out or analyze.

But to what end or ends does Pynchon, in *Against the Day*, reframe and refine his former subject matter and themes? Does an order emerge? Does this feature's overdetermination signal some special meaning or meanings—or merely correct for undue coherence of such motific elements in the earlier fictions? The answer, I think, is that Pynchon has always been engaged—again one raids the lexicon of Foucault—in something like an "archaeology" of his historical moment. One fiction complements its fellows, and all coalesce as a post-Faulknerian exercise: a Yoknapatawpha of American and Western civilization.

Saeva Indignatio

Great comic geniuses often yield, over time, to a fierce, Juvenalian impatience with all that they have exposed to laughter. Philip Roth, once savagely funny, eventually surrenders to curmudgeonhood. Likewise Woody Allen. How amusing would Swift have been at the end, even without Ménière's disease? Shakespeare turns from merriment to the merely comedic, from all the world smiling, as in *A Midsummer Night's Dream* or *Twelfth Night*, to the ending that is merely not unhappy: perfunctory nuptials and revels ended. But Thomas Pynchon manages still, on the eve of his seventieth birthday, to leaven anger (based on his contempt for economic predation, his disgust at racism, his abhorrence of colonialism) with wit that delivers him, over and over, from the artistic error of tendentiousness. Pynchon knows better, in other words, than to waste energy on argumentation, or, rather, he argues enthymematically (i.e., with an unstated but widely accepted premise), inviting readers to extend their general sympathy for the downtrodden to workers treated, at the turn of the century, with little consideration, if not with outright injustice, by such powerful and rich employers as the fictional Scarsdale Vibe, who disguises rapacity with unctuousness, invoking "our Economy's long struggle to evolve up out of the fish-market anarchy of all battling all to the rational systems of control whose blessings we enjoy at present" (34). *Control*—the word figures as a Pynchon signature: he characterizes it in negative terms in all of his novels (it figures most memorably, perhaps, as

the obsession of the bizarre Padre Zarpazo in *Mason & Dixon*), and Vibe
presently articulates a more comprehensive vision — a plutocrat's creed.
Speaking to "the Las Animas-Huerfano Delegation of the Industrial
Defense Alliance (L.A.H.D.I.D.A.)," he delivers some candid remarks
about the workers that he and his kind blithely consign to the embrace
of that many-tentacled cephalopod described by Frank Norris (another
of Pynchon's nineteenth-century counterparts, along with Adams and
Emerson). Another, more rapacious Octopus Grigori (conditioned by
sinister Pavlovians in *Gravity's Rainbow*), capitalism gives its two-legged
prey little quarter. Completely untrammeled by "euphemism," Vibe's
orgy of self-congratulation represents — even for Pynchon — something
of a rhetorical high point:

> So of course we use them . . . we harness and sodomize them, photograph
> their degradation, send them up onto the high iron and down into mines
> and sewers and killing floors, we set them beneath inhuman loads, we
> harvest from them their muscle and eyesight and health, leaving them in
> our kindness a few miserable years of broken gleanings. (1000, Pynchon's
> ellipsis)

Vibe's gloating, complacency, and trenchant locutions — they run on for
another thirty-five lines or so — place him with *Lot 49*'s Pierce Inverarity,
who revels in his role of "rich, obnoxious gringo" (119); with the munitions magnates who convene towards the end of *Gravity's Rainbow*, and
with Wade LeSpark, the arms merchant of *Mason & Dixon*. All participate in enterprises directing human energies only into channels that fill
private coffers and enlarge the satanic kingdom of capital. In its violence,
Vibe's discourse constantly threatens to slip the bonds of metaphor. In
"harness," workers become little more than sentient draft animals, labor-
ing under "inhuman loads." One discerns in the diction here ("harvest,"
"gleanings") ironic reminders that industry has co-opted an older, agricultural order less given to the dehumanizing of toil. Characterizing
the exploitation of labor as a pleasurable perversion, Vibe represents
the body of the worker as subject to the gratification of appalling appetites, among them the voyeurism served when "we . . . photograph their
degradation." Referring, presumably, to photojournalism, which ostensibly documents horrific working conditions and moves others to sym-

pathy and outrage, Vibe expects his fellow plutocrats to remember that they own the media and employ those who take the pictures. Shocking photographs of sweatshop conditions sell newspapers. Throughout this apologia, Vibe pays less attention to the delights of lucre than to the perverse baronial pleasures that an attention-arresting figure like "sodomize" can only approximate. It suggests the vast catalog of violation suffered in the benighted Sodom of our factories and mines. *Bend over,* orders the master, the foreman, the boss, the owner: *here it comes. Again.*

In such rhetorical set pieces, Pynchon makes no effort to temper the expression of his disgust. He knows, however, that "[w]ise satirical practice requires the sensitivity and skill of a *fugu* chef at controlling toxicity, that is, knowing how long to suffer, and how gladly, and when to give in to rage, and the pleasure of assaulting at last the fools in question" (introduction to *The Teachings of Don B.*, xviii). Thus the reader would err to think that this author dispenses with artistic discretion. Rather, he alternates between the blunt instrument of satire, as seen above, and the extreme subtlety of his more nuanced historical themes. These he teases out with the patience, the instinct for indirection, of a postmodern Henry James. In scenes like the L.A.H.D.I.D.A. address, the author makes his political views clear, but such extravagance is balanced and framed by incremental intimations of other ideas the more powerful for their oblique presentation. The reader who would uncover these ideas must, like Shakespeare's Polonius, peel the onion of appearances. However tiresome and pedantic, Denmark's royal counselor gets a few things right. "We of wisdom and of reach," he says, "With windlasses and with assays of bias, / By indirections find directions out" (*Hamlet* II.i.64–66). The point requires an elaborate pair of figures, themselves examples of the obliqueness in question. Indeed, predicated on the principle of insight-fostering indirection, metaphor appeals to a universal delight in cogent analogy. But beyond simple metaphor lies the more generalized law observed by thoughtful literati (and their critics) in every age. Emily Dickinson affirms this precept in a couple of famous lines: "Tell all the Truth but tell it slant—/ Success in Circuit lies." Nor does the poet suspend the principle to make her point. Though semantically straightforward, the statement depends for its effectiveness on a kind of grammatical indirection. The word *slant* will serve equally well as noun, verb, or adjective, but it resists deployment as adverb. The sentiment, that is, calls for some such formulation as "tell all the truth, but slant it," or, more clumsily, "tell all the truth, but tell it in an off-kilter way." Opting in this famous pronouncement for the more strained, adverbial form, Dickinson "slants" usage itself and so delivers the line (and the poem) from aesthetic lese-majesty.

Pynchon seems to have sprung from the artistic matrix fully aware that effective literary representation cannot dispense with this principle. It dictates the obliqueness with which, in his first novel, *V.*, he treats his subject matter, the endless, accelerating violence of the twentieth century. He presents decidedly out-of-the way incidents leading up to and away from the Great War. By the same token, the reader encounters the greater war that followed only from the vantage of a Maltese non-combatant (or, rather, from his journals). When, in *Gravity's Rainbow*, Pynchon makes World War II and its aftermath his immediate setting, he contrives to speak only glancingly of the camps, the great battles, the atomic detonations. Pynchon leaves the full-frontal chronicling to the Herseys, the Wouks, the Styrons, for early and late he takes what a Salinger character calls "the long view." That is, he wants to see, as only a novelist can, the working-through of history's great themes and problems (a working-through that, in the last two centuries, has taken the form of coming to terms with the raveling of Kantian telos, the deflation of Hegelian *Geist*).

In many ways — the point bears repeating — one learns to read *Against the Day* by rereading *V.* Both fictions treat the Great War, that fulcrum of the twentieth century, with artful indirection. In a single paragraph of the earlier novel Pynchon presents a catalog of disasters to illustrate the workings of accident, but here the catalogue, spread through the text, eventually signals the imminence of a specific global catastrophe. At first, pure accident disguises the gathering malevolence, but presently the disasters begin to seem decidedly portentous: the Krakatoa eruptions of 1883 (506), the Adair County, Missouri, cyclone of 1899 (309), the great Galveston flood of 1900 (188), a train leaping the tracks at Frankfurt Bahnhof in 1902 (662), the 1905 collapse of the Charing Cross Station roof (662), and, recurrently, the 1902 toppling of the campanile in Venice (256, 662, 860, etc.), so evocative of the tarot card depicting a tower struck by lightning (which inspired certain images in *The Waste Land*). References to assassinations (of King Umberto I by Gaetano Bresci in 1900 [1011], of President McKinley by Leon Czolgosz in 1901 [372, 978], of Serbia's Alexander and Draga Obrenovich by their own guards in 1903 [228], of Russia's Grand Duke Sergei Alexandrovich in 1905 [595]) and attempted assassinations (of Queen Victoria by Edward Oxford in 1840 [230], of Henry Clay Frick by Alexander Berkmann in 1892 [737], of the Prince of Wales by Jean Baptiste Victor Sipido in 1900 [528]) recur with increasing fatality—though Pynchon elides the incendiary act of Gavrilo Princip in 1914. Instead of the assassination of Franz Ferdinand (which figures in "Under the Rose" and, more obliquely, in *V.*), Pynchon presents a droll account of the archduke's 1893 visit to America, where the fated heir to the Austro-Hungarian throne occupies himself in giving the jive idiom a Teutonic twist: "'*s los, Hund?* Boogie-boogie, *ja?*" (48). More seriously, Pynchon sketches the spasms of the dying Austro-Hungarian Empire—the incidents and conflicts that preceded the catastrophe of 1914, notably the annexation of Bosnia and Herzegovina by Austria in 1908, the Turkish and Albanian revolutions (1908 and 1912, respectively), the Italo Turkish War of 1911–12, and the First Balkan War of 1912.

Pynchon similarly suggests that in the decade or two before World War I the grand narratives of Victorian exploration gave way to more purposive scouting. Beginning with the Vormance expedition, nominally disinterested explorers devote themselves to spying out rail lines (or "the railworthiness of the terrain" [130]) that will be of crucial importance to the movement of troops when the balloon goes up. The narrator pays considerable attention to the "'Bagdad' railway concession" (228–29, 567), the Trans-Siberian Railroad (259, 567, 789), Chinese Turkestan railway shares (503), the Karawankenbahn (652), and the proposed rail links from Tuva, in southern Siberia, to the Taklamakan Desert in the far west of China (788–89) and from "the Bosnian border . . . to the Turkish railhead at Kossovska Mitrovitsa" (841–42). Everywhere, the vast "continental system" (567) of railroads represents the tentacles of spreading capital, the grid of future war.

Pynchon deploys other, more mystical auguries as well. Ryder Thorn, a "Trespasser" from the future, tells the sensitive Miles Blundell: "Flanders will be the mass grave of History" (554). The painter Hunter Penhallow dreams of "the mass-grave-to-be of Europe" and its portal, "an iron gateway" through which "an incalculable crowd" will make its way (578). The vision jells as a painting, described almost three hundred pages later: a "meditation on the fate of Europe, *The Iron Gateway*, in which shadowy multitudes trooped toward a vanishing line over which broke a hellish radiance" (867). The explicitness of these evocations waxes and wanes. Pynchon characterizes the mysterious cataclysm that visited Siberia in 1908, devastating miles and miles of forest and tundra, as, among other things, a foreshadowing of 1914–18. Thus he likens "what was nearly upon them" (778) in the Tunguska region to "the general war which Europe this summer and autumn would stand at the threshold of, collapsed into a single event" (797). Repeatedly, he invokes "the Great War everyone expects imminently to sweep over us" (903), the "general European war" (809, 871, 937, 938) that seems to have been augured by one event after another: "As if what towered above them out there in the dark, across the lines, were not exactly a new and terrible weapon but the spiritual equivalent of one. A desire in the mass co-conscious for death and destruction" (720). (Pynchon favors Georg Groddeck's term, "co-conscious," over its more familiar Freudian analogue.)

But these observations, though numerous, do not gather to a narrative climax. They fall as solitary pebbles in history's great, echoing bucket. Towards the end of the novel, Pynchon speaks of the trenches and treats the Great War in curiously subdued tones, touching on "one night in the early autumn of 1914" (1022) and characterizing Flanders as "a poisoned sea brought still" (1023). The "great influenza epidemic" of 1918 (1024) takes its horrific toll even as, "[o]ut in Europe, the great Tragedy went rushing on" (1026).

This calculated refusal fully to represent that "great Tragedy" may explain the insistent references to doubling and bilocation. As Käkelä-Puumala has observed, Pynchon often recurs to "the exaggerated display of binary pairs" that signal themes of "mythical, Manichaean dualism."[15] But the point here is not the binaries, per se, nor their putative hierarchalizing tendencies. The novel's pervasive play on "the unyielding doubleness of everything" (957) rather supports an idea of *Erwartung* (that pregnant word from *Gravity's Rainbow*) as a beleaguered postmillennial humanity awaits an "end of history" unlikely to resemble the Fukuyama paradigm in any way. Marx famously observed (in *The Eighteenth Brumaire of Louis Bonaparte*) that history transpires twice, "the first time as tragedy, the second as farce." But in fact, Pynchon suggests, it repeats itself as yet greater tragedy. As an historical novelist, then, Pynchon contrives in *Against the Day* to refine the old idea of the past as what Barbara W. Tuchman famously called a "distant mirror" of the present. The past actually mirrors the *trajectory* of the present.

The witty description of the novel that appears in its jacket copy (evidently penned by Pynchon himself—his name appears after the similar text that appears on Amazon.com) affirms precisely such a meaning: "As an era of uncertainty comes crashing down around their ears," the characters must negotiate "an unpredictable future." A century later, readers contemplate a similar situation. In the era of *Against the Day*, that is, readers may well recognize the not-so-distant image of their own day: "With a worldwide disaster looming just a few years ahead, it is a time of unrestrained corporate greed, false religiosity, moronic fecklessness, and evil intent in high places." In the Amazon.com version of this description, an ironic disclaimer follows: "No reference to the present day is intended or should be inferred." Here the fin de siècle thematics is characterized—via the rhetorical strategy of a denial that invites denial—as bearing some resemblance to the slightly postmillennial moment of the novel's appearance. "Events that happen in narrated time," observes Heinz Ickstadt, "resound in the narrating time that is the reader's present."[16]

Thus overdetermined, the repeated imagining of doubleness—the two Asias (249), the two Venices (136), the "[t]wo Agadirs," "the Two-*Stupendica* problem" (521), the many characters said to have or be doubles (Yashmeen Halfcourt [750], her father [759–60], Professor Edward Morley and Charles "Blinky" Morgan [62], Professors Renfrew and Werfner ["the Tiresome Twins" (230)], Scarsdale Vibe and Foley Walker [724, 742], Prince Rinpungpa and the Yogi [750, 766])—contributes to the perception that a shadow novel exists behind or to the side of the one we read. Indeed, the Iceland spar effect seen in the printing of the title on the dust jacket would seem to announce the existence of some such biblioganger. "[S]ome invisible narrative occupying . . . the passage of the day" (418), this shadow novel is the one writing itself early in the twenty-first century: as one *Against the Day* sketches the genealogy of the world conflict that set its stamp on the twentieth century, so do events in its phantom companion lurch toward another, more terrible conflagration. If Pynchon did not invent the apocalyptic novel (that honor goes to Mary Shelley, author of *The Last Man*), he remains one of its most terrifying practitioners.

Flying Toward Grace

In his early novels Pynchon depicts a figure not unlike the questing knight of the grail legend (as in *The Waste Land*) or an Adams-like character in pursuit of an elusive "education," but in the later ones — *Mason & Dixon* and *Against the Day* — the questers become multiple, the quest itself splintered and divided. All of Pynchon's protagonists, however, pursue a postmodern grail: not education but episteme, not knowledge but *gnosis* (a term fraught, as will be seen, with energy subversive of various kinds of orthodoxy). Readers, meanwhile, find themselves engaged in knight errantry of their own. Periodically, they join their peers for a conclave at, often as not, a large, round table. Occasionally, some Galahad or Perceval among them will learn to ask the right questions when shown, in the Chapel Perilous, the sword, cup, lance, and dish. The reader's quest, like that of an Arthurian knight, requires great perseverance, mastery of recondite lore, and a protracted struggle with illusion, for the text, as readers of Nabokov know, is the work of an enchanter who inveigles the unwary into confident identification with a protagonist who may, after all, be a highly unreliable center of consciousness. The quest requires, in other words, that the reader first identify with, then see through Pynchon's paranoid protagonist. However edifying one may find the obsession of a Herbert Stencil, an Oedipa Maas, or a Tyrone Slothrop, it must be transcended if meaning's true grail is to be won. In the end, the reader must discern the factitiousness of what draws Oedipa Maas into its web in *The Crying of Lot 49*, must recognize the parodic spirit with which Pynchon, in *V.*, invokes or echoes the ideas of Henry Adams and Robert Graves. The challenge to understanding becomes tougher in *Vineland*, with its now-midrashic, now subversively feminist readings of Genesis, and in *Gravity's Rainbow*, where the textual labyrinth includes teasing intimations of meanings that range from the gnostic to the kabbalistic and from the Orphic to the Masonic (that last signals an awareness, I think, of just where such doctrines—whatever their appeal to Mozart and the American founding fathers—edge over into silliness, where someone has, as it were, taken to "sneaking Whoopee Cushions into the Siege Perilous, under the very descending arse of the grailseeker" [*GR* 321]). In *Mason & Dixon*, a variety of magical lore, from kabbalah and Gematria to the "scrying" of crystals, anomalous mountains, and sundry "Tellurick Secrets" (172), complicates an Enlightenment parable about the emergence of the American nation. Clearly, Pynchon likes ancient, multivalent theologies and demonologies. They figure prominently again in *Against the Day*.

In all of his novels, Pynchon charts what critic John A. McClure would call a "postsecular" course between the godless Enlightenment juggernaut and old-time religion, cringing in its path. In his magisterial *Partial Faiths: Postsecular Fiction in the Age of Pynchon and Morrison*, McClure argues "that a body of contemporary North American fiction contributes vigorously to the more general cultural debate over the place of the religious in postmodern life and society and that it does so in ways that distinguish it sharply both from defenses of philosophical secularism and from the most salient forms of religious revival." Thus he undertakes to elucidate "some of this fiction's most characteristic strategies and claims: its plots of partial conversion, its project of ontological disruption, its efforts at once to reassert and to weaken religious conceptions of reality, and its attempts to imagine a new, religiously inflected form of progressive politics."[17] McClure makes a strong case for including Pynchon among the novelists who reaffirm spiritual possibility.

Thus in *Against the Day* "it seemed some revelation would emerge from the tensely luminous sky" (377). The language of belief—and belief thwarted—is ubiquitous, constantly invoked to characterize attempts on the part of various characters to seek religion in politics or science or mathematics.[18] They embrace capitalism, anarchism, aetherism, and other flawed models of transcendence. Studying electricity and electromagnetic currents, Kit Traverse thinks vectorism "could have been a religion, for all he knew—here was the god of Current, bearing light, promising death to the falsely observant, here were Scripture and commandments and liturgy, all in this priestly Vectorial language" (98). Kit's fellow student at Göttingen, Yashmeen Halfcourt, embraces mathematics, which some might think the very yardstick of rationalism, out of "her old need for some kind of transcendence—the fourth dimension, the Riemann problem, complex analysis, all had presented themselves as routes of escape from a world whose terms she could not accept" (942). From David Hilbert and Sofia Kovalevskaia to Hermann Minkowski and G. F. B. Riemann, from Gauss, Ramanujan, Weierstrass, and Ferdinand Georg Frobenius to Kronecker, Cantor, Sir William Rowan Hamilton, and Bertrand Russell, Pynchon catalogues mathematicians almost as exhaustively as Don DeLillo in *Ratner's Star*, a novel that scrutinizes the idea of mathematics as "what the world is when we subtract our own perceptions."[19] Pynchon suggests, more romantically, that all the great mathematicians "had chosen to submit to the possibility of reaching that terrible ecstasy known to result from unmediated observation of the beautiful" (635).

Elsewhere one reads of "mill hands with little patience for extreme forms of belief, unless it was Anarchism of course" (60). "At first," wandering into "a small variety theater" full of fervent anarchists, Lew Basnight, the reluctant security operative, "took it for a church" (49). Merle Rideout's scientific curiosity is also characterized in quasi-religious terms: he embraces "a small Ætherist community, maybe as close as Merle ever came to joining a church" (60). In an especially engaging passage, Merle recounts, in his own irreverent idiom, "a story . . . from the Infancy Gospel of Thomas, one of many pieces of Scripture that early church politics had kept from being included in the New Testament" (579). These "reachings after the transfinite," as Pynchon calls them in an homage to Donald Barthelme, reach one high point as Cyprian Latewood takes the veil in a strange religious order, the Brides of Night (961).[20]

But one cannot read about the Brides of Night without thinking of *Las Viudas de Cristo*, the convent brothel of *Mason & Dixon*, not to mention *Vineland*'s "Harleyite Order, a male motorcycle club who for tax purposes had been reconstituted as a group of nuns" (358). Certainly the author has little sympathy for the traditional "Christer" outlook (though the evensong scene in *Gravity's Rainbow* is replete with powerful sentiment). Especially problematic in this regard are his boys' book aeronauts, the Chums of Chance, who seek continually "to transcend 'the secular,'" with which they "must ever strive to minimize contamination" (113). They aspire, always, "to glimpse . . . some expression of the truth beyond the secular" (126). But a "secular" pun qualifies every such locution: as aeronauts, they largely avoid contact with the world—*seculum*—below their ship, the *Inconvenience*. As characters in boys' tales, moreover, they remain immortal, untouched by the secular in its root sense of "generation, age." Their "unquestioning faith that none of them, barring misadventure, would ever simply grow old and die" (418) is set back a bit when the Tunguska event, which reveals to them a sacred city, seems to strip away their fictive status and expel them into real time, the real world (793). Before and after this Siberian experience, however, they periodically interact with the "real" characters (this lability of diegetic levels, one recalls, figures also in *Mason & Dixon*, which embeds a serial fiction, *The Ghastly Fop*, whose characters occasionally wander into the frame narrative). In the closing pages of *Against the Day*, their airship grown *Laputa*-sized, the Chums remain firmly fictive, and that status must color one's reading of the novel's already famous last line: "They fly toward grace" (1085). Only characters in a boys' adventure serial can, in their new century or ours, set course for such a fantastic destination. In the end, one best understands the Chums and their adventures as some pure distillate of fiction itself. What flies toward grace is storytelling, with its perennial admixture of the subjunctive. Indeed, far from what an unfriendly reviewer called "a giant bag of imaginative hot air," the one-thousand-plus-page piece of storytelling we hold in our hands is recognizably figured in the *Inconvenience* itself, "now . . . grown as large as a small city" (1084).[21]

The Greek word for knowledge, *gnosis*, provides the etymological underpinning for the most prominent of the out-of-the-way religious ideas here. Gnosticism, while highly varied across great tracts of history, tends to something like coherence in the imagery with which it characterizes the esoteric "knowing" that is its spiritual goal. According to gnostic doctrine, the material world, along with our physical bodies, exists only to imprison or corrupt the pure light of divine being. The Gnostic strives, supremely, to free what Pynchon calls the "light that history would be blind to" (1016), but prodigies of human (the doctrinaire would say demonic) energy go towards its perpetual perversion or imprisonment.

Beyond invoking the "mysterious shamanic power" (143) of bilocation, Pynchon recurs often to gnosticism's dualistic ontology, a doctrine encouraging the perception that a pregnant doubleness—now sinister, now transcendent—dogs all that humanity knows of the world. Moreover, he refers repeatedly to—and names one of the sections of the novel for—"the doubly-refracting calcite known as Iceland spar" (114), characterized now as "the sub-structure of reality," now as "the doubling of the Creation, each image clear and believable" (133). If the refraction of light suggests its gnostic betrayal by matter, a *double* refraction might restore to eternity its white radiance. Through Iceland spar, in other words, the gnostic may glimpse creation untrammeled. Unless (always, the dual possibility) double refraction merely compounds light's primal corruption.

Given the hints in *Gravity's Rainbow* and *Mason & Dixon*, gnosticism may seem, in the present text, to offer itself as ideal hermeneutic. But gnosticism presents no straightforward, historically focused set of ideas. A tremendously varied tradition with roots in Manichaeanism and Zoroastrianism, as well as affinities with kabbalah and Orphism, it resists differentiation from its many antecedents and allied doctrines. Whether warped by the persecutions of orthodoxy (as notably embodied in the 325 Council of Nicaea, that notorious steamroller of religious variety and spiritual difference) or simply splintered by its own anarchic theology, gnosticism eventually proves limited as master mythos. On this score alone, the novel reaffirms its postmodern credentials. One can invoke no totalizing philosophy of history or culture to make sense of the past.

Though one errs to attempt to make any single doctrine the key to all the mythologies here, readers might well expect to encounter in *Mason & Dixon* and *Against the Day* more of what prompts Dwight Eddins to title his important 1990 study *The Gnostic Pynchon*. As Eddins observes, Pynchon alternates between the vision of an empty and meaningless universe and that of a universe rife with conspiracy that rises to the very clouds. Thus "the complex religious dialectic of Pynchon's fiction" involves, among other things, "the fluctuating tension between the notion of a neutral, structureless universe and that of a universe infiltrated by insidious structures of Control."[22] These structures represent the dark side of gnosticism, whose ancient adherents believed that an evil demiurge at once creates humanity and the world and completely traduces the true divinity that manifests itself as light. This gnostic premise, which works quite well to describe the universe of Pynchon's earlier novels (especially *Gravity's Rainbow*), figures more loosely in the later fictions.

One would not, that is, mistake the gnosticism of *Against the Day* for the near-absolutist doctrine of spiritual pessimism laid out in older histories of religion. The references to this esoteric doctrine in *Gravity's Rainbow*, incidentally, precede the work of Elaine Pagels by a number of years. Pagels's representations of gnosticism—and especially its suppression as the result of early Christian canon politics—would appeal to an author opposed, as Pynchon is, to social, religious, and political conformity. Though I am not aware of Pynchon's ever having said anything in print about Pagels, I rather think that, given his prior interest in gnosticism, he might well have allowed his thinking about it to be influenced by the sympathetic account that emerges in her 1979 study *The Gnostic Gospels*. Describing a gnosticism less given to convictions about human inadequacy before the blind demiurge, Pagels emphasizes its positive features, notably its empowerment of women and its arguments for a life devoted to realization of an inner light that is legitimately divine—a light obscured or quenched by the world's fallen state, by priestly betrayals of true spirituality, and by secular subordination to Caesar.

A religious philosophy that has survived fitfully from antiquity into the present, gnosticism effectively destabilizes hegemonic ideologies; it lends itself to a variety of guerilla campaigns against the excesses of empirical or logocentric thinking. Gnostic allusion, gnostic gestures, gnostic distrust of spiritual and other forms of coercion, gnostic resistance to straitjacketed orthodoxy: all serve to develop Pynchon's vision—Blakean or Lawrentian in its fierceness—of American promise and its betrayal. Lew Basnight thinks with melancholy sympathy of the "prophesiers who had seen America as it might be in visions America's wardens could not tolerate" (51). He echoes *Lot 49*'s Oedipa Maas: "how had it ever happened here," she wonders, "with the chances once so good for diversity?" (181).

Pynchon invokes gnosticism to frame his perspective on the historical problem of evil in the world—especially the evil of modern times, in which humanity strives endlessly to devise new ways to violate the earth, take life, wage war, and accumulate wealth. Often cloaked in one kind of piety or another, this corruption perpetually undermines any and all attempts to achieve political and economic justice, ecological balance, equity among nations, and the peace such equity might sustain. Some such larger thematic program seems to lie behind the novel's truly global vision. A geographical tour de force, it spans the United States, Mexico, Italy, Austria, Germany, the Balkans, England, Canada, Iceland, and great tracts of "inner Asia," including Siberia and a vast area subsuming parts of China, Kazakhstan, Tajikistan, Uzbekistan, and Kyrgyzstan. As he once re-created Alexandria and Florence at the turn of the century and Paris in 1913, Pynchon now conjures Venice, Guanajuato, Göttingen, Vienna, London, New York, Chicago, St. Louis, Los Angeles, and the mining towns of the Rocky Mountains. Reading this globe-spanning narrative, in fact, one thinks at times of that Remedios Varo vision of *el manto terrestre*, the great tapestry of the world that so entrances and moves *The Crying of Lot 49*'s Oedipa Maas.

The reader of *Against the Day* may also recall the "Holy-Center-Approaching" that, in *Gravity's Rainbow*, becomes a favorite "pastime" (508) in what Pynchon calls the Zone—nominally Hitler's Germany, prostrate at the end of World War II, but actually suggestive of a whole civilization reduced to Hobbesian essentials. The holy centers of that earlier novel run from the decidedly dubious to the sublime, from Peenemünde's Test Stand VII to the sublime "Kirghiz Light," presented as some powerful, blinding, highly spiritualized experience in the depths of central Asia. More powerful than, say, Shelley's "white radiance of eternity" and other such models of transcendence, the Kirghiz Light hints at less benign illuminations, hints as much at the fate of Hiroshima and Nagasaki as at anything more numinous. Indeed, holy centers themselves stand little chance of survival in a world largely incapable of spiritual vision.

In *Against the Day*, Pynchon returns to the conceit of holy centers and

the "single great episode of light" that brings something like a spiritually enabling annihilation. It occurs "always" in "a hidden place, the way
into it is not obvious, the geography is as much spiritual as physical. If
you should happen upon it, your strongest certainty is not that you have
discovered it but returned to it" (165). Thus the light manifests itself
fitfully, and for the most part ambiguously. Does the Tunguska event of
1908 (that "heavenwide blast of light" [779]) approximate revelation?
Does it model what is elsewhere, more generically, a powerful spiritual
experience that awaits pilgrims in Shambhala, the mythical holy city of
Buddhism; in Tannu Tuva; in "Aztlán, the mythic ancestral home of the
Mexican people" (277); or in another remote and forgotten corner
of Asia or Meso-America? Or does it merely announce secular apocalypse—a version of what visits those two small cities in Japan toward midcentury, or that Ukrainian power plant in 1986? How ironic, Pynchon
suggests, that a notorious nuclear disaster should occur at a place whose
name—Tchernobyl—puns on the Russian/Ukrainian word for "the
destroying star known as Wormwood in the book of Revelation" (784,
cf. 797). Pynchon adds to these intimations an elaborate, mysterious
account of the cataclysm visited on "a great northern city" upon the return of the fictional Vormance expedition. Like the toppled campanile
of Venice, the "charred trees still quietly smoking" and "flanged steel-
work fallen or leaning perilously" (150) proleptically figure what would
within a century (just as one millennium ended and another began)
befall the Twin Towers. By the same token, the civilization that in many
ways centers in New York breathlessly awaits the full realization of what
the destruction of the towers portended.

These examples reveal light under opposing aspects. It can illuminate, it can annihilate. But the historical reality principle dictates that
the darker side figure here with particular prominence. Etymology conspires to underscore the point that, wrongly conceived or valued, light
can betray. Phosgene, the poison gas, is named for light (953). The word
photography, designating the process by which Vibe and his minions can
document the degradation of workers, is derived from the Greek for
"light writing." Much partners, then, with the strikebreaking "Colorado
militia . . . in . . . giving light a bad name" (1008). By the same token,
enlightenment may take the form of the scarcely imaginable, and "the

terrible trans-horizontic light of what approached" (542) announces an apotheosis of ordnance, lighting up the Western Front and taking the lives, between 1914 and 1918, of ten million combatants. No ordinary crepuscular turning, "what looms in the twilight of the European future" (543) is the darkness that will follow the going out of lamps all over Europe.

One discerns the spirit behind *Against the Day*'s most important thematic feature—not to mention its title. Thematically, the "day" is that of gnosis, knowledge, truly enlightened thinking, the knot of ignorance untied. But this day, which might seem to find its nemesis in darkness and night, shifts its identity and its character as endlessly as Proteus himself. At Yz-les-Bains, an "Anarchist spa" (931), Yashmeen Halfcourt remarks, "We make our journeys out there in the low light of the future, and return to the bourgeois day and its mass delusion of safety, to report on what we've seen. What are these 'utopian dreams' of ours but defective forms of time-travel?" (942). To unpack this sibylline utterance, one must recall Wells's Time Traveler, who journeys on one occasion far into the future and there beholds the moribund sun on the very eve of the entropic heat death. By implication, the "day" familiar to the middle classes would seem to be little more than what the prisoners in Plato's Cave know of light. But what is supremely "against the day" is less ambiguous: it is "that dark fourth-dimensional Atlantic known as Time" (415), "[t]he one force no one knows how to defeat, resist, or reverse" (558). At once Wordsworthian and Wellsian, the light fades as the world moves into the future. Miles Blundell reflects that "somehow, the earlier, the great, light had departed" (551).

Thus Pynchon's vast novel is, among other things, a philippic, an inventory of all that is arrayed, in modern times, against the light. But in *Against the Day*, as in *Mason & Dixon*, the light is not the exclusive province of the Enlightenment, which has too often served to advance the coercive logocentrism, not to mention the rapacious self-justification, of "capitalists and Christers." Though he invests much energy in indicting that collective rapacity, the author also strives to affirm the legitimate, if fitful, striving of certain benign ideological forces in history. These include tentative, blind, but incremental steps towards what one might characterize as a greening of its *Geist*. The humble pursuit of political and economic justice, the restraint of colonial and capitalistic appetites—these promise a new and better dawn. A struggle, then, between light and dark, with much attention to reactionary politics, misguided science, and other forces ranged "against the day."

One flags this thematic feature with a certain caution—who would want to fall back into the tiresome cataloging of "dark-and-light imagery" that once passed for critical analysis? But never mind "imagery" (a word that caused one to cringe even before Simon Gray's 1971 play *Butley*)—what compels the reader here is the powerfully realized idea that the forces of darkness (darkness intellectual, spiritual, emotional) strive with considerable success, throughout history, *against the day*, the day of insight and knowledge, the day of an enlightenment in which the spiritual is not at odds with the intellectual. Meanwhile, light struggles to make its way against darkness. According to one formulation, "[t]he soul itself is a memory we carry of having once moved at the speed and density of light" (688).

The phrase that gives this novel its title acquires considerable resonance from its eightfold recurrence, notably in apocalyptic contexts, in the King James Bible. One encounters it most memorably in 2 Peter 3:7 ("against the day of judgment and perdition of ungodly men") and Romans 2:5 ("against the day of wrath and revelation of the righteous judgment of God"). But Pynchon intends no routine piety here. Such biblical echoes merely confer the stamp of ancient spiritual repugnance for any and all worship of Mammon, any and all laying up of merely material treasures. As noted previously, Pynchon discovers much in religious lore to exploit and even endorse. He comes at such thinking, however, by decidedly circuitous routes; nor should we, absent some pronouncement in propria persona, make too much of his gesturing towards assorted spiritual nostrums. Rather, Pynchon eclecticizes to disarm, destabilize, and subvert certain unimaginative forms of rationalism. "A mind all logic is like a knife all blade," observes Rabindranath Tagore. "It makes the hand bleed that uses it."[23]

If Pynchon subscribes to any kind of millenarian belief system, it may be the one represented as the modest credo of anarchists who believe in "certain hidden geometries of History" (373), geometries perhaps approximating the Emersonian faith that Jesse, the appealing, just-minded son of Reef Traverse and his sometime paramour Estrella ("Stray") Briggs, will as an old man articulate in the closing pages of *Vineland*. Stirring words, and worth quoting again: "Secret retributions are always restoring the level, when disturbed, of the divine justice. It is impossible to tilt the beam. All the tyrants and proprietors and monopolists of the world in vain set their shoulders to heave the bar. Settles forever more the ponderous equator to its line, and man and mote, and star and sun, must range to it, or be pulverized by the recoil" (*VL* 369). Not that Pynchon really recommends such sentiments to faith. Even as he affirms an old working man's vision of a just cosmos, the author expects his readers to hear Emerson's words,[24] stirring as they are, with skepticism. One must, that is, resist taking in anything more than the most broadly "subjunctive" spirit the Laodicean piety of a Transcendentalist pundit striving to affirm, with the previous century, that whatever is, is right. Thus the problematic adjective here—"divine"—ought perhaps to be understood only as a colloquial flourish, something Pynchon echoes without announcing any theistic conviction on his own part. But Emerson knew something of Eastern theology, and Pynchon would appreciate the trace of karmic doctrine in that figure of cosmic justice as self-leveling beam.

In his introduction to Jim Dodge's *Stone Junction*, Pynchon characterizes larceny and, more importantly, literary art as a species of such "karmic adjustment."[25] In *Vineland*'s Takeshi Fumimoto (possibly the same Takeshi who appears in *Gravity's Rainbow* as a wacky kamikaze), Pynchon elaborates the conceit: as a "karmic adjuster," Takeshi is, among other things, a figure of the artist. Thus the author of *Against the Day*, invoking something like the old idea of poetic deserts, conceptualizes fiction as literary *lex talionis*, a medium in which one may shape graceless reality—and even history—along lines more congenial to the deep and abiding human appetite for justice. This is the Pynchon who has saluted Ruskin's idea of the imagination as "a capacity responsive to the claims of fact, but unoppressed by them."[26] In the Amazon.com precis of *Against the Day* (a slightly different version of the novel's jacket copy, as noted before), Pynchon flags its "[c]ontrary to the fact occurrences" that represent "not the world" but "what the world might be with a minor adjustment or two. According to some, this is one of the main purposes of fiction."

Commodius Vicus

That phrase quoted at the beginning of this chapter—"most of us who write historical fiction"—represents more than "guild solidarity" (as he calls it in the introduction to *The Teachings of Don B.*) with an embattled fellow artist.[27] One may take Pynchon at his word, especially insofar as the historical range of *Against the Day*, 1893–1923, covers the thirty years that saw, as it were, modernity's birth and coming of age. The author chronicles the struggle between capital and labor, the competition for colonies, the deep pull of anarchy both philosophical and political, the wars, and the fluidity of international borders that could never accommodate all the nationalisms splintering and proliferating. "Lemberg, Léopol, Lvov, Lviv, and Lwów," recites a character: "all different names for the same city" (1079). Again, as in his first novel, *V.*, Pynchon makes World War I the crypto-fulcrum of recent history, but he pointedly declines to allow *Against the Day* to become a yet more Spenglerian version of Barker's *Regeneration* trilogy. He means to invite reflection on just what—comparable to World War I—might be on our *present* horizon. As Shawn Smith observes, "Pynchon's fiction reunites the present with the genealogy of destruction that spawned it."[28] The twenty-first-century analogue to the Great War has not yet come about, but even the most casual parallels drawn between the brushfire wars of the late nineteenth and early twentieth centuries and those of our own millennial era (the civil war among the states formerly part of Yugoslavia, the travail of Rwanda-Burundi and Darfur, the drawn-out agonies of Afghanistan and Iraq, the looming Armageddon in the Middle East, beaconed by Gulf Wars I and II) suggest a terrible prospect—something even more horrific than what overtook civilization in 1914–18.

Although he refers repeatedly to the approach (and, eventually, the fighting) of the Great War, Pynchon declines to characterize it as either narrative climax or historical climacteric—what William Pfaff once called "the most important event of contemporary Western history, one whose effects are still not exhausted. It closed doors opened by the Enlightenment and the French Revolution, and opened new ones, which led to cemeteries, torture chambers, and death camps."[29] The author's refusal to make the fulfillment of war auguries truly climactic poses one of this text's most interesting questions: why does a chronicle largely focused on the decades preceding 1914 not avail itself of a culmination as convenient to narrative as to history? Fought offpage, the Great War detains the reader only briefly as the novel reaches its conclusion. Pynchon brings his great airship into port in a short final section, "Rue du Départ," which runs to only twenty pages. Set in 1923 Paris (the popularity of Hahn's operetta *Ciboulette* indicates the year), with flashbacks to wartime Torino, Italy, this section offers little in the way of denouement. Kit Traverse and his wife, Dally, seem unable to restore their marriage; Kit's brother Reef and his family pass through Torino on their way back to America, where they end up in Vineland country and points north (they are last seen in Montana, Oregon, and Washington, hooking up with another Traverse brother, Frank, his wife or companion Stray, and Jesse, her son by Reef).

But Pynchon, true to the closure-resistant postmodern aesthetic, does not care to be limited to a single ending. In *V.*, for example, as "[a]ll things gathered to farewell" (379), he provides two conclusions, both set in Malta—but one in 1956, the other in 1919. In *Against the Day*, in which the endings are close to each other in time but far apart in space, "Rue du Départ" functions only as coda to the more elaborate conclusion of the long preceding section, which shares a title with the novel itself. Here Pynchon takes leave of a number of his characters in what appears to be 1921 Los Angeles—the date is implied by aeronaut Chick Counterfly's remarking that he and his father have not seen each other in "[n]early thirty years," not "since 1892 or thereabouts" (1034). (Nor has the reader heard anything about this "Dick" Counterfly, evidently a latter-day Pap Finn, in over a thousand pages.) Readers who recall the stunning, frame-violating climax staged in the same city at the end of *Gravity's Rainbow* may wonder at the largely bangless Los Angeles valedictory here. Why, indeed, the American West Coast, rather than some likelier European locale, for a conclusion on the eve of the very annus mirabilis of modernism—the 1922 that saw completion of Rilke's *Duino*

Elegies and publication of *Ulysses, The Waste Land,* and Wittgenstein's *Tractatus?*

If in fact the author has deliberately elided the year 1922 from his chronicle, it may be that he means to suggest a postmodern worm in the modernist apple, one episteme born at the very moment of another's perfect ripeness. In view of the more outré features of his 1920s Los Angeles, Pynchon may also intend, along with a kind of "genealogical" connection to that ICBM falling towards Los Angeles on the last page of *Gravity's Rainbow,* to echo the idea of the closing of the American frontier. He mentions Frederick Jackson Turner early in the narrative (52), and now he depicts characters modulating from their nineteenth-century identities into figures more familiar to twentieth-century story-telling. Lew Basnight becomes the West-Coast private eye (that tarnished American Adam) of later romance; Deuce Kindred, the classic Western villain, becomes a proto-Manson likely to receive "a death sentence" when picked up for "a string of orgy-type homicides" (1059). Merle Rideout and Roswell Bounce become figures out of the *Back to the Future* films.

The last two figure in the author's fanciful sketching of emergent technologies of the moving picture. In his 1984 essay "Is It O.K. to Be a Luddite," Pynchon invites consideration of the day "when the curves of research and development in artificial intelligence, molecular biology and robotics all converge."[30] One discerns in such observations hints of what this author, who in his essays occasionally signals future projects, will presently come to grapple with in his fiction. In his 2003 introduction to the centennial edition of *1984,* Pynchon notes that Orwell, too, in the letters and articles written concurrently with that novel, reveals the directions of his thinking. Pausing briefly over the question of just what Orwell "did and didn't 'get right'" about the future, Pynchon notes the burgeoning "technology . . . of surveillance" that represents only a slight modification of Orwell's imagined televisual panopticon. The author of "Tube"-saturated *Vineland* (Pynchon's own treatment of 1984) also salutes Orwell's accuracy with regard to "the ubiquity of television itself."[31]

In the closing pages of *Against the Day,* some kind of early television apparatus picks up—some fifty years early—what appears to be an episode of *Gilligan's Island* (1034), a childhood favorite of *Vineland* character Prairie Wheeler, great-great-great granddaughter of *Against the Day*'s Webb Traverse. Replete with understated intimations of the media storm and paradigm-shifting technologies to come, *Against the Day*'s California valedictory looks forward, as it were, to *The Crying of Lot 49*, *Gravity's Rainbow*, and *Vineland*—and on, perhaps, to some fictive meditation on what America may yet undergo in the new millennium. Readers curious about the larger vision of this greatest of contemporary novelists may expect further installments in a kind of postmodern *Comédie humaine*. Unlike Norman Mailer, who ends his turgid CIA novel *Harlot's Ghost* with "To Be Continued?," Pynchon offers only such continuation, such *retour de personnages*, as history—still unfolding—will allow. One suspects, however, that the next major fiction will treat the hundred or so years after 1922, an era that may yet culminate in some nastiness comparable, mutatis mutandis, to that Great War at the beginning of the twentieth century. With or without global conflagration, it will be depicted as the era dominated by what in the introduction to Jim Dodge's *Stone Junction* Pynchon calls "the grim, simplex desire for more information, more control, lying at the heart of most exertions of power, whether governmental or corporate (if that's a distinction you believe in)."[32]

CHAPTER SEVEN

The Historiographer Historicized

Pynchon and Literary History

Critical reading of Pynchon goes back half a century now—he published his first stories (not counting juvenilia) in 1959 and 1960. Upon the publication of *V.*, in 1963, he awoke, like Byron, to find himself famous. With the publication of *Gravity's Rainbow* in 1973, he became officially an eagle in the literary dovecote. Even relatively early in his career critics compared him to the likes of Rabelais, Swift, and Melville. Like Cervantes or Sterne or Joyce (who died only four years after Pynchon's birth), Pynchon takes naturally to grand, comedic visions of the culture that has shaped his imagination and sensibility. He has affinities with the great epic poets as well. His catalogues—of disasters, of trash in a used car, of stamp anomalies, of prewar British candies—link him to Homer, to Spenser, to his countryman Walt Whitman. Like Milton, he can recount a creation story fraught with sexual politics (Eve, Lilith, and Adam become, in *Vineland*, Frenesi, DL, and Brock Vond) or imagine history's omega (the descending Rocket in the closing pages of *Gravity's Rainbow*). As Virgil chronicles the mythic genesis of *patria*, so does Pynchon, in *Mason & Dixon*, imagine the moment at which the disparate ingredients of the American nation first coalesced, like amino acids in the primordial soup. Like Swift, Pynchon can imagine a flying island (the tumescent airship of the Chums of Chance in *Against the Day*). Like Dante, he can evoke hellish abjection (Brigadier Pudding) and even conduct readers on a tour of the infernal regions, as announced by an epigraph purporting to come from the doubly apocryphal Gospel of Thomas ("Oxyrhynchus papyrus number classified"): "Dear Mom, I put a couple of people in Hell today" (*GR* 537). Unless the correspondent quoted here is "Thomas" himself (beating the Apostle Paul to the first-person punch, not to mention the epistolary form), the personage addressed would appear to be the Holy Mother, another of the numinous female entities that, as Henry Adams and Robert Graves famously affirm, stalk through the Western imagination, from the fertility figure found at Willendorf forward to the Greco-Roman Venus and thence to the Virgin venerated by Christians (this ancient conceit, which figures also in Greta Erdmann's impersonation of the Shekhinah, is elaborated exhaustively in the eponymous heroine of *V.*).

Any artist of great ambition or great gifts invites a crucial question: does she or he effect change or merely consolidate some inherited aesthetic? William Butler Yeats, in "Easter, 1916," imagined the political ideologue as a stone in the river of life. But artists, too, aspire to lithic permanence—whether for their work or for its subject matter ("so long lives this," runs the sonnet refrain, "and this gives life to thee"). One way or another, they strive to discern or create some momentary stay of the circumambient flux. Literary history itself resembles a river that great boulders cause to churn and boil—and sometimes to take a different course.

Properly to gauge the achievement of a Thomas Pynchon, one must go back to the earliest phase of his career, back to the moment at which this "individual talent," as Eliot would say, contemplated the "tradition" of which he aspired to become a part. "[O]ur culture," the great sociologist Karl Mannheim remarks, "is developed by individuals who come into contact with the accumulated heritage."[1] For Pynchon, a proxi-

mate part of that heritage would have been the work of the modernists, whose pervasive influence and authority he and his contemporaries
could hardly have avoided. But for serious writers of fiction coming
of age at midcentury, modernism was no longer a complete ecosys-
tem of letters, self-sustaining and inviolable. Many in that generation
had begun the work of reframing its premises, setting the stage for a
displacement less tentative than what either the belated naturalism of
Wright (*Native Son*) and Mailer (*The Naked and the Dead*) or the briefly
robust Beat movement had accomplished. With the aging of Faulkner,
Hemingway, Ellison, and Eliot, Pynchon and company—the generation born in the 1920s and 1930s—sought a theme answerable to
late-fifties *Erwartung*.

Pynchon himself seems early on to have viewed the modernist aesthetic as overdue for some creative subversion. Long before he would
reflect (in the *Slow Learner* introduction) that T. S. Eliot had not been a
particularly benign presence in his apprentice prose, Fausto Maijstral, in
V., can be heard waxing wry about the dubious influence of that poet on
his literary confreres (he quotes a deft parody of "Ash Wednesday"). In
the introduction to a reissue of *Been Down So Long It Looks Like Up to Me*,
by the same token, Pynchon recalls his and Richard Fariña's attending
a party at Cornell dressed up as Fitzgerald and Hemingway, respectively.
Indeed, such icons may have supplied only postures to imitate with varying degrees of irony.

But what, exactly, had Pynchon read? Did he view his predecessors
with respect? Did he level at displacing them—or merely at becoming
their peer? Did he know, early on, that he was not alone in recognizing
a new episteme and crafting a new aesthetic? One begins to answer these
questions by considering some of the allusive practices of this author, as
well as statements, in propria persona, about his early reading. These
include his remarks on a 1959 grant application and his self-disclosure
in the 1984 *Slow Learner* introduction.

Shortly after graduating from Cornell, Pynchon applied (unsuccessfully) for a Ford Foundation fellowship. The application, as summarized
by Steven Weisenburger, provides glimpses of the literature Pynchon
himself saw, early on, as formative. He tips his hat to the occasional
parental or grandparental presence (Voltaire, Byron, Henry James), but

most of the authors he names figure as older literary brothers or uncles (writers still active during Pynchon's formative years). In addition to T. S. Eliot and a couple of science fiction authors (Ray Bradbury and Alfred Bester), he mentions William Faulkner, Thomas Wolfe, F. Scott Fitzgerald, Nelson Algren, and the Beats (from whom he claims, at this early stage, to have distanced himself).[2] These names provide a first census of the company he has since joined.

Twenty-five years later, in the *Slow Learner* introduction, he waxes somewhat more nostalgic about the Beats. As noted previously in this study, he mentions Kerouac and Burroughs, emphasizing the impact their fictions had in a decade as buttoned down as the 1950s. He calls Kerouac's *On the Road* "one of the great American novels." Such work, he notes, provides one context for his own early efforts, notably "Entropy" ("as close to a Beat story as anything I was writing then"), which strikes the mature writer as an attempt at "sophisticating the Beat spirit with second-hand science" (7, 14).

He also lists Henry Adams, certain nineteenth-century scientists, Norbert Wiener, Edmund Wilson, Machiavelli, Helen Waddell, John le Carré, Shakespeare, Graham Greene, and Spike Jones (for whose posthumous CD *Spiked* Pynchon would, years later, write liner notes). Briefly mentioning Philip Roth and Herbert Gold, he salutes for *The Adventures of Augie March* and Norman Mailer for "The White Negro." He notes, too, the impact of *Howl, Lolita,* and *Tropic of Cancer,* along with such periodicals as the *Chicago Review,* the short-lived *Big Table* (only five issues), *Evergreen Review,* and *Playboy.* He invokes, finally, a number of popular writers (John Buchan, E. Phillips Oppenheim, Helen MacInnes, Geoffrey Household), and one would err to think of his having, as it were, outgrown them. Much of his originality—and much of what makes him postmodern—reveals itself in his ironic appropriation of tropes endemic to formula fiction. His pastiche style embraces such "low" material as much as it does high art. Thus he makes of pastiche something wonderfully original, something his followers and imitators would in many forms make the formal and stylistic touchstones of postmodern narrative art.

For the most part, the statements in the *Slow Learner* introduction correlate with the evidence of the allusions, which extend across all of

American letters, not to mention great tracts of British and world literature. Ranging from Machiavelli to Mary Shelley, from Jacobean tragedy
to Emerson, from Rilke to the Argentine poet José Hernández (author
of *Martín Fierro*), and from Charles Dodgson to Federico García Lorca,
Pynchon's allusions reveal a remarkably wide breadth of reading, as well
as a global sensibility and literary ambition. Of course it is one thing to
mention a writer, another really to embrace that writer's aesthetic or
moral vision. Thus one discerns only a casual connection to, say, the
Emily Dickinson quoted in *Gravity's Rainbow*, but real affinities with the
Transcendentalists (especially Emerson, whom he quotes in *Vineland*),
with Melville, and, later in his career, with the American realists and nat-
uralists who described the great octopus of American capital (Pynchon
recapitulates their anatomy in *Against the Day*). Another kind of literary relationship exists with the Puritans, among them the author's own
seventeenth-century ancestor William Pynchon, author of a heterodox
1650 treatise, *The Meritorious Price of Our Redemption*. Thus a "sect of most
pure Puritans" figures in *Lot 49* (155), and Roger Mexico, in *Gravity's
Rainbow*, deplores "the damned Calvinist insanity" (57). More importantly, Pynchon adapts and subverts certain Puritan doctrines: election,
preterition, and what (again, in *Gravity's Rainbow*) he calls "orders behind the visible" (188).

Pynchon refers, too, to a number of works that do not actually exist:
the journals of Father Fairing, *The Courier's Tragedy, Cashiered, Alpdrücken,
The Ghastly Fop*, the various adventures of the Chums of Chance. Insofar
as these faux texts, however outrageous or bizarre, commend themselves
to at least nonce credulity, they resemble the imaginary works that figure
so often in the fictions of the Argentine master Jorge Luis Borges. They
reveal, too, the erudition that Pynchon brings to pastiche. Each of these
imaginary works distills some textual essence—often with a discernible
model. Thus *Alpdrücken* (in *Gravity's Rainbow*) contains, as it were, the
whole of German expressionist film, and Diocletian Blobb's *Peregrinations*
(in *Lot 49*) condenses the seventeenth-century travel writings of Thomas
Coryat, Fynes Moryson, and Peter Mundy. The Chums of Chance parody
Tom Swift, identified at one point as their "colleague" (*ATD* 794), and
his predecessors The Rover Boys. *The Courier's Tragedy* compiles plot elements and stylistic features favored by Webster, Heywood, Marston, Ford,

and Massinger—the Jacobean playwrights anagrammatized in the name Wharfinger.

Not that Pynchon invokes only literary texts. He peppers his fictions with references to film, TV, cartoons, and music of every stripe—from all those "German symphonies" sporting "both a number and a nickname" (*Lot 49* 18) to Dion, Frank Zappa, and the many others who convince him, as he declares in the *Slow Learner* introduction, that "rock 'n' roll will never die" (23). One of the running jokes in *Vineland* involves imagined biopics in which a film or television personality takes the role of some famous personage to whom she or he bears an uncanny resemblance: like the twinned image in a piece of Iceland spar ("the doubly-refracting calcite" frequently invoked in *Against the Day* [114]), Pia Zadora stars in *The Clara Bow Story*, Sean Connery in *The G. Gordon Liddy Story*, and so on.

A curiosity: applying for that Ford Foundation grant, Pynchon stated a desire to write opera libretti, which, so far as one knows, he never did (though he alludes often, especially in the early work, to famous operas: *Don Giovanni, Madama Butterfly, Tosca, Manon Lescaut*). This abortive vocation, however, represents a haunting parallel with one of those seemingly inconsequential facts about Lee Harvey Oswald, as gathered in appendix 13 of the Warren Report. The future assassin once listed, on an application, "writing short stories 'on contemporary American life' as his vocational interest."[3] DeLillo, who refers to this application in his 1988 novel *Libra*, calls Oswald "Jack Kennedy's secret sharer."[4] Only two years Pynchon's junior, Oswald is something of a secret sharer of his great literary contemporaries as well. Although heads of state had been assassinated before (as Pynchon repeatedly shows in *Against the Day*), Oswald augured things to come, and some would say he ushered in postmodernity itself. If artists have a prophetic function, one credits a remarkable prescience in the author of *V.*, who put his finger, early in 1963, on a pulse that had scarcely begun to throb.

Culture Wars Redux

The quarrel between the ancients and the moderns survives today as a nagging doubt, on the part of some critics, regarding the legitimacy of a politicized standard of literary achievement. That is, some judge writers by their sensitivity to issues of race, gender, and class, while others persist in preferring Oscar Wilde's simple criterion for excellence: "Books are well written, or badly written. That is all."[5] To determine a writer's place in literary history, in any event, one must consider the validity of current criteria for literary achievement and compare them to an older and perhaps more durable aesthetic chastened—where not elbowed aside altogether—by perspectivist thinking about canonicity. One can, as it happens, make the case for Pynchon either way.

Certainly he can lay claim to the traditional prerequisites of permanence: he writes beautifully and creates humane, insightful fictions that grapple resourcefully with history and the passions that make it. Shapely, sublime, and verbally rich, his imagined worlds vie for legitimacy with what Tyrone Slothrop, in *Gravity's Rainbow*, calls "the authentic item" (184). Dispensing, early on, with traditional handling of character and plot, Pynchon eventually came to engage what in the introduction to *Slow Learner* he calls the "deeper, more shared levels of the life we all really live" (21). Early and late, however, his fictions merit the praise famously uttered by the Jane Austen heroine who defends the novel as a "work in which the greatest powers of the mind are displayed, in which the most thorough knowledge of human nature, the happiest delineation of its varieties, the liveliest effusions of wit and humour are conveyed to the world in the best-chosen language."[6] Happily, current criticism—for example, Elaine Scarry's 1999 book *On Beauty and Being Just*—has begun to feel its way back into aesthetic categories that Austen's Catherine Morland would have recognized. Indeed, as a connoisseur of the Gothic, Catherine Morland would share Pynchon's appreciation of "beauty as Rilke defined it, the onset of terror just able to be borne."[7] The beautiful becomes intrinsic again to evaluation and judgment and merit.

At the same time, Pynchon's readers discern as much sensitivity to questions of race, gender, class, and the colonial or postcolonial fate of "pigmented populations" (*V.* 245) as the politicized criticism of the age could wish. To his credit, Pynchon represents ethnicity with great compassion, wit, subtlety—and a saving irreverence. In *Vineland* particularly, as noted in a previous chapter, Pynchon charms readers with clever experiments in the representation of ethnic accents in English and even of foreign speech as if it were English. The explosive, exclamatory statements of the Japanese characters capture the quality of their language as experienced by Western patrons of art cinema. More common is the effect of foreign-language typography, spelling, diacritical marks, and punctuation imported into English. Deft and aurally precise, this technique never becomes tendentious or patronizing. That is, even as Pynchon captures the locutions of Chicano/as by writing *i* as *í* (or with Spanish-style bracketing quotation marks and exclamation points), he never descends to the Speedy Gonzalez/José Jiménez stereotype. That said, Hector or Vato is, in his way, every bit as comic as that travesty of Gallic naughtiness, the Marquis de Sod (the lawn entrepreneur of local TV commercials).

Always sympathetic to the struggle of the colonized (as the reader sees in the Egyptian and southwest African chapters of *V.*), Pynchon can take credit for insisting that the world remember what the Herero suffered in German southwest Africa in 1904. His strategy, incidentally, bears a superficial resemblance to the technique seen in early films about the Vietnam War. Sometimes criticized for their one-sided account of the experience (one never saw the face of the Asian foe), they were defensible as exercises in cinematic point of view: American soldiers, thrust into an unconventional war, fought faceless shadows. Pynchon is at once more exercised and more subtle. The reader witnesses atrocity (the gratuitous shooting of an old woman, other deaths by clubbing and whipping, the gang rape and murder of a teenage Herero girl), but victims remain nameless and in effect faceless — until, that is, the hapless "Sarah," whose individualized suffering somehow brings fully into focus — and to devastating effect — the agony of multitudes.

Depicting African Americans, on the other hand, Pynchon blends irreverence with warmth and sensitivity. Readers encounter Cleveland "Blood" Bonnefoy (another *Vineland* character); McClintic Sphere in *V.*; Carl Barrington, the imaginary friend, and McAfee, the musician, in "The Secret Integration"; and Gershom, George Washington's resourcefully impertinent slave in *Mason & Dixon* (at one point in that novel Jeremiah Dixon relieves a slave driver of both whip and human property). Elsewhere, the author exposes stereotype and the subconscious dread behind it. Under the influence of sodium pentothal, Tyrone Slothrop, in *Gravity's Rainbow*, becomes a self-disclosing tabula of bizarre racial fears: "'Good golly he sure is *all* asshole ain't he?' . . . 'Grab him 'fo' he gets away!' . . . 'Yowzah!'" (64, my ellipses). In the same novel, Pynchon's sympathy for the oppressed or marginalized (he calls them the preterite, those passed over) leads him to an elaborate counter-Freudian play on the blackness of Enzian and his fellow *Schwarzkommando*. Erecting the great 00001 rocket just after V-E Day, the black rocket troops reassert, among other things, the manhood compromised by their colonial history.

In all of his fictions, Pynchon scrutinizes history's omissions and misrepresentations. Nor does he neglect the history of letters. One can make what may seem an extravagant or hyperbolical case for Pynchon's importance by arguing that the ontogeny of his career recapitulates the phylogeny of literary history. In his immense ambition and in the encyclopedic or Menippean energies that he deploys, Pynchon performs the very idea of literature—from its primitive beginnings through the capillary branchings of postmodern and post-postmodern practice. By turns comic, satiric, ironic, and romantic, he effortlessly shifts, too, between lyric and epic expression. *The Courier's Tragedy*, in *Lot 49*, reveals his grasp, even, of dramaturgy. A burlesque of Jacobean revenge drama, it is an especially assured performance, its language, its double couplets, its archaic diction, its assemblage of plot elements across a wide spectrum all conspiring to reveal an iceberg's worth of highly specialized literary knowledge. It also prompts consideration of whether Pynchon engages the possibilities of tragedy in a less antic vein. He seems in fact to defy the pundits who think the conditions of modern life inimical to real tragic elevation (not that any amount of literary genius is likely to deliver the term *tragic* from its progressive journalistic degradation). To be sure, one discerns nothing so splendid as tragedy in the unheroic fate of a Leni Pökler, who probably does not survive the Dora slave labor camp's liberation, or a Brigadier Pudding, who dies not with a bang—not at some grand moment of ambition frustrated or fated reversal—but literally with a whimper: "Me little Mary hurts" (533). From Victoria Wren to Webb Traverse and from Enzian to his half brother Tchitcherine, however, Pynchon also presents figures who, in mythic stature and fate, rise to a tragic level. In their stories, readers may trace most of the features

Aristotle laid out in the *Poetics*: the pity and fear, the elevated language, the moral stature of the protagonist, the flaw, the reversal and recognition. Like Sophocles, whose greatest tragic protagonist he feminizes as *Lot 49*'s Oedipa Maas, Pynchon shows the source of a nation's anguish in one oblivious heart. Oedipa, like Oedipus, wanders an "infected city," herself the bacillus carried "to its far blood's branchings" (117).

The Encyclopedic Vision

Over thirty years ago, Edward Mendelson identified Pynchon as a writer of "encyclopedic" novels—fictions in which an author undertakes to treat her or his culture comprehensively.[8] Readers encounter Pynchon's encyclopedism in the guise of what Oedipa Maas, of *Lot 49*, calls "part of a plot, an elaborate, seduction, *plot*" (31). Pynchon seduces the reader with the promise of something like the big picture: read this book and you'll understand the age and its enormities. If in fact one does achieve considerable understanding, the insight takes an unexpected form. A Pynchon novel commonly stages for us the recognition of our hunger to know and understand. One learns, first, that the desire to know can be warped by the desire that the known take a certain congenial or at least comprehensible form. Beyond that painful recognition, however, lies something even more worth the knowing, which is the actual working of systems logic, whether the system be language or cosmos.

In the first part of his career, Pynchon develops wonderfully elaborate quest plots, predicated on recursivity. But none of Pynchon's novels ends with the grail possessed. Reified as V., the Tristero, the Rocket, the goal of each quest is knowledge that metastasizes and flees before the seeker. As Richard Powers remarks in his 1991 novel *The Gold Bug Variations*, "we lag behind ourselves, knowledge always hopelessly outstripped by information."[9] Thus the quest never ends, and in fact its goal becomes something like Derrida's "transcendental signified," whose "absence . . . extends the domain and the interplay of signification infinitely."[10] In *Lot 49*, Oedipa Maas rightly "wondered whether, at the end of this (if it were supposed to end), she too might not be left with only compiled memories of clues, announcements, intimations, but never the central truth itself, which must somehow each time be too bright for her memory to

hold; which must always blaze out, destroying its own message irrevers-
ibly, leaving an overexposed blank when the ordinary world came back"
(95). Like the knight of the grail quest romance, Oedipa (along with
Herbert Stencil of *V.* and Tyrone Slothrop of *Gravity's Rainbow*), must ask
the essential questions in the right way.

The quest becomes less perfectly self-sustaining in *Vineland*, which
marks a turning point, a graduation, as it were, from the old mythopoesis. *Vineland*'s Prairie Wheeler is a transitional figure—in her relatively
unproblematic mother search (a regendered Telemachiad), readers see
the attenuation of the quest plot that serves Pynchon so well in *V.*, *Lot
49*, and *Gravity's Rainbow*. In his later works, Pynchon may be thought
of as denying himself and his reader what Lyotard called the "solace of
good forms"—setting himself the task of engaging the world's complexi-
ties and the confusions of history without the safety net provided by the
quest diegesis. This is at once an explanation of the increasing difficulty
of Pynchon (some reviewers deplored the *longueurs* of *Against the Day*)
and a measure of his integrity. Even in *Inherent Vice* (2009), which seems
to embrace the conventions of detective novels, Pynchon foregoes the
easy gratifications of linear narrative.

Pynchon has been read across a wide spectrum of literary theory.
Certainly critics have been swift to test his postmodernism against the
doxa of poststructuralist thinking. The novels exemplify what Brian
McHale has identified as the "ontological" premise of postmodern literary art, which privileges the creation of worlds over representation of the
familiar terra (representation having entered poststructuralist crisis).[11]
Pynchon seemed always already to understand depthlessness and the
absconding signified, to doubt the pretensions of sign systems—speech,
writing, language, art—to mirror the real. His unwavering refusal of the
spotlight even becomes an ironic commentary on the much discussed
Death of the Author.

Yet one can still quite profitably read Pynchon against the critical economies of midcentury—those contemporaneous with his formative years
and early career. Indeed, to do so is to comply with Fredric Jameson's
familiar directive: "Always historicize!"[12] Names and movements would
include M. H. Abrams (with whom Pynchon studied at Cornell), Joseph
Campbell, the Chicago School (mentioned in the *Slow Learner* intro-

duction), and such New Critics as Cleanth Brooks, who shares his first name with the protagonist of Pynchon's preterite early story "Mortality and Mercy in Vienna" (uniquely "passed over" in the assembling of the *Slow Learner* collection), and R. W. B. Lewis, who recognized the importance of the American Adam archetype in the nation's literature (versions of this figure abound in Pynchon: Oedipa Maas, Tyrone Slothrop, Brock Vond, Mason and Dixon, the Traverses, and perhaps even Benny Profane).

Though little concerned with race, gender, and class, and too early for (or simply disinclined to embrace) deconstruction, Freudian and post-Freudian psychoanalysis, and postcolonial theory, Northrop Frye (1912–91) remains an especially good thinker to match with Pynchon. Both are brilliant humanists with an immense range of erudition. In *The Anatomy of Criticism* (which came out in 1957 and established itself as an especially important development in literary theory just as Pynchon, discharged from the navy, resumed his college education), Frye reintroduced the critical community to the strange genre known as "Menippean" satire—work characterized, from antiquity into modern times, by its ungainliness, its voluminous, encyclopedic ambitions, its scatology, its disgressiveness, and its descents into the fantastic. Frye named *The Golden Ass, Satyricon, Gargantua et Pantagruel, Candide, Gulliver's Travels,* and *Tristram Shandy* as representative examples. The importance of such historicizing for contemporary letters was considerable. Like the Molière character who delights to learn that he has been speaking "prose" all his life, a number of novelists—John Barth, Robert Coover, William Gaddis, and Joseph Heller, in addition to Pynchon—could congratulate themselves on being Menippean masters. In the successor generation, David Foster Wallace, William Vollmann, Richard Powers, and perhaps Mark Z. Danielewski have sipped as well at the Menippean fount.

As complement to the Menippean, Frye also sketched the attributes of the "encyclopaedic." Everything he says about "encyclopaedic form," moreover, finds its mirror in Pynchon's work: "In the mythical mode the encyclopaedic form is the sacred scripture, and in the other modes we should expect to find encyclopaedic forms which constitute a series of increasingly human *analogies* of mythical or scriptural revelation."[13]

Thus in *Gravity's Rainbow* "a rush of wind and fire" will take believers "to the chambers of the Rocket-throne," believers "who study the Rocket as Torah, letter by letter" (727). "So, yes yes this is a scholasticism here, Rocket state-cosmology" (726). In the post-Romantic imagination, says Frye, "the central episodic theme is the theme of the pure but transient vision, the aesthetic or timeless moment . . . The comparison of such instants with the vast panorama unrolled by history . . . is the main theme of the encyclopaedic tendency."[14] This visionary moment—commonly occulted by sobriety—takes various forms in Pynchon. In *Lot 49*, it is the epileptic's untranslatable epiphany—or simply that of an aged alcoholic: "She knew that the sailor had seen worlds no other man had seen if only because there was that high magic to low puns, because DT's must give access to DT's of spectra beyond the known sun, music made purely of Antarctic loneliness and fright" (129). This language and these tropes (he invokes the Antarctic with some frequency) figure repeatedly in Pynchon's novels. In *Gravity's Rainbow*, for example, a droll reflection on the insights available to those struck by lightning culminates as a "Polish undertaker in a rowboat" (663) joins their exclusive sodality and is last heard saying, "*Oh*, ho. Oh-ho-ho-*ho!*" (665). Here, too, Pynchon evokes "the charismatic flash no Sunday-afternoon Agfa plate could ever bear, the print through the rippling solution each time flaring up to the same annihilating white" (579). On a much larger scale, the Soviet operative Vaslav Tchitcherine experiences the mysterious and never explained Kirghiz Light. From a "single great episode of light" (165) to the "heavenwide blast" (779) of the 1908 Tunguska Event in Siberia, Pynchon invokes more such episodes of radiant brightness in his vast 2006 novel *Against the Day*. These mysterious phenomena anchor an epic meditation on the power of light itself—whether to obliterate or to illuminate.

Melville wrote only one truly encyclopedic novel (Blanchot speaks of *Moby-Dick*'s "offering itself as the written equivalent of the universe"), but Pynchon writes one after another.[15] Replicating the cultural universe in words, he realizes a Borgesian fantasy. He actually writes a succession of novels that are, as it were, volumes of a great and strange reference work—rather like the encyclopedia in Borges's story "Tlön, Uqbar, Orbis Tertius," which calls an imaginary world into existence.[16] Thus Pynchon regales readers of *Mason & Dixon* with everything—or what seems like everything—about British North America in the mid-eighteenth century. Readers of *Gravity's Rainbow* learn everything about the Faustian seductions of knowledge and power. In *Vineland* they contemplate everything about the 1960s and the *vingt ans après* of America's 1984. In *Lot 49* they explore eight hundred years of postal history. In *Against the Day* they survey the arrival, all across the world, of the twentieth century. All of this began with what one might call the elliptical inclusivity of *V.*, in which Pynchon assembles that century in a fragmented, faux-modernist guise. The technique novelizes what Frye describes as the specifically modernist "practice of cutting out predication, of simply juxtaposing images without making any assertions about their relationship."[17] Of course, the reader who reassembles the fragments discovers a principle that gives the lie to many a modernist illusion: the need for coherence creates an illusion of coherence. The need for myth creates a myth that is factitious. No malign female entity actually "explains" a chaotic and bloody age; neither Tristero nor Rocket anchors or legitimizes our burgeoning paranoia. Nor do the myths of the real world have anything like the universal validity they seemed to present to the moderns, fresh from their readings of Sir James George Frazer, Jane Harrison, and other mythographers. As the narrator of Oakley Hall's 1958 novel *Warlock* observes, "The human animal is set apart from other beasts by his infinite capacity for creating fictions."[18] A longtime admirer of *Warlock*, Pynchon observes and ironically participates in this mythopoesis.

One considers Pynchon's place in literary history, then, at almost exactly half a century since publication of his first novel, *V.*, in that American year of years, 1963. As noted previously, Pynchon made his presence felt roughly six months ahead of Lee Harvey Oswald and his violent self-insertion into history (through what Don DeLillo, twenty-five years later, would call "the seven seconds that broke the back of the American century").[19] In 1966, publication of *The Crying of Lot 49* coincided with Derrida's presentation of "Structure, Sign and Play in the Discourse of the Human Sciences" at the Languages of Criticism and the Sciences conference at Johns Hopkins University. Brian McHale notes this "synchronicity," along with what he calls a "signature" of the year 1966, the "pattern of overreaching and stalling out" announced at the end of that novel, "when the heroine is left suspended, stranded, waiting for the conspiracy she thinks she has uncovered to reveal itself—or not: the novel simply stops at this point, *stalls out,* leaving everything unresolved." According to McHale, "[t]his pattern" recurs in many of the "cultural practices and products of 1966, a recurrent pattern or shape, discernible in many cultural phenomena of that historical moment—in rock musicians' careers but also in their song lyrics, as well as in the fictional scenarios of contemporary novels."[20]

The year that saw the World Trade Center dedicated, 1973, also saw publication of *Gravity's Rainbow.* Its opening pages, an elaborate fantasy of escaping a great building that has been bombed, take on fresh meaning after 9/11; the same goes for the closing pages, in which an imagined missile drops toward another building full of people. Pynchon's great novel came out, in fact, in a year characterized by Andreas Killen as "a cultural watershed, a moment of major realignments and shifts in American politics, culture, and society."[21] *Vineland,* which looks back at the 1960s from the vantage of a Reagan-ridden 1984, bears the publication date 1990 but appeared in bookstores at the end of 1989, the year that saw the breaching of the Berlin Wall and the end, many would say, of the Cold War. *Mason & Dixon* appeared in 1997, halfway through the Clinton presidency. *Against the Day* appeared in 2006, three years into the second Iraq war. *Inherent Vice* came out in 2009, the year the United States's first black president took office.

Logging each succeeding Pynchon novel against its historical moment, one discerns intimations of concinnity. But do Pynchon's successive fictions in fact coincide with, comment on, or even anticipate events charged with millennial significance—or does the literary historian merely wish it so? This question—random vs. patterned—lies at the heart of the Pynchon aesthetic. The author devotes a long passage in his first novel to a simple but compelling catalog of the disasters that took place in a single year (as gleaned, the narrator observes, from an almanac). His point: that the random discloses no patterns. By the same token, just as postmodernism itself evolves from gauge of sixties paranoia to more subtle recognitions of the *kairos,* the matching of books and public events reveals significance only to those predisposed to entrail reading. But the symptomatic temptation—or desire—to see a pattern finds its mirror in hermeneutics itself. Just as humanity manufactures shapely narratives and other fictions of coherence about history and the human condition, so may readers find more to Pynchon's prescience than may be there. Even the most subtle readers stand ever ready to discover in texts the messages they consider most enlightened or congenial—or timely. This tendency has given us various avatars: atheistic Pynchon, religious Pynchon, Marxist Pynchon, Pynchon the American visionary, Pynchon the iconoclast, modern Pynchon, postmodern Pynchon, post-postmodern Pynchon, *u.s.w.* In good postmodern fashion, all of these are true.

Now Everybody

This discussion began with reflections on Pynchon's antecedents, the American and world writers the author read and admired and matched himself against—it would be fitting to conclude with those whom, however indirectly and at whatever distance, he mentors. At times he must figure as Shakespeare did for Goethe (in his conversations with Eckermann, the great German poet avowed himself fortunate not to have been born an Englishman—he would have chafed at the looming presence of such a master as Shakespeare).[22] But younger writers seem grateful for the path forged through a culture's tangled historical thicket—and for the inspiring example of a wonderfully flexible style in which to register their age and its confusion. They seek not to smash this literary rock but to come in under its shadow.

Nor ought readers to assume some inadequacy on the part of those content with their apostolic role. Karl Mannheim, borrowing a term from Wilhelm Dilthey, makes the valuable point that great artistic movements are characterized by the marriage of what we would now call their epistemic recognitions with the "entelechy" of a perfected style or aesthetic. Unless they want to grant only fifteen minutes of fame to every artistic generation, critics must be prepared to see the cachet of originality as something less than the aesthetic sine qua non it is often thought to be ("make it new," says Pound, as if anyone had ever told a really new story in truly fresh language). Mannheim argued for the legitimacy of certain artists' dispensing with the supposed need to disrupt artistic categories, to innovate, to take the principle of making it new as a universal directive. History, Mannheim suggested, contains abundant examples of artists who inherit and accept aesthetic principles that remain unexhausted, remain still in the process of full realization.[23] Indeed, what better climate in which to create than one in which aesthetic tradition is established but not yet edging over into mannerism?

Twenty years or so younger than the master, Richard Powers (b. 1957), William Vollmann (b. 1959), and David Foster Wallace (1962–2008) have seemed most obviously to be consolidating the Pynchon manner, extending the "encyclopedic" range of his subject matter. Admittedly Wallace, best known for his vast and magisterial *Infinite Jest* (1996), on occasion expressed discomfort at the inevitable comparisons of his work and that of Pynchon. The prolific Vollmann, on the other hand, seems completely undaunted by this terrible father. A 2005 National Book Award winner for *Europe Central,* he has authored an immense number of books, both fiction and nonfiction. Of special note is his series of novels on encounters between Native Americans and Europeans, *Seven Dreams,* of which four out of a projected seven volumes have appeared (they begin with *The Ice Shirt* [1990] and run, thus far, to 2600 pages). Part of an emergent apostolic succession, these writers affect the catalog, the anatomy, the grand Homeric list. Occasionally—notably in Powers—readers encounter the homage direct: the narrator of *Galatea* 2.2, for example, mentions having read *Gravity's Rainbow* in high school. The sensitive but feckless Franklin Todd, in *The Gold Bug Variations,* salutes Pynchon as his favorite living novelist. The protagonist of *Generosity: An Enhancement* falls asleep and "dreams himself into a Pynchon novel, with an international cartel trading in the arcane incunabula hidden in people's cells. His own sperm carries a sequence on the *Index Librorum Prohibitorum . . .*"[24] Possibly more polymath than Pynchon himself, Powers bridges C. P. Snow's "two cultures" in virtually every paragraph.[25]

The Summer 2005 issue of *Bookforum* provides space for a number of Pynchon's successors (and a handful of contemporaries, including DeLillo, Tom Robbins, Gerald Howard) to express their admiration and, to varying degrees, indebtedness. As represented here, the Tribe of Pyn includes not only Robert Polito (b. 1951); Kathryn Kramer (b. 1953); Carter Scholz (b. 1953); Jim Shepard (b. 1956); Andrew Hultkrans (b.

1966); and Erik Davis (b. 1967); but also Lydia Davis (b. 1947), much praised for her *Collected Stories* (2009); Jay Cantor (b. 1948), author of *Krazy Kat* (1988); Percival Everett (b. 1956), author of *Wounded* (2005); Lorrie Moore (b. 1957), author of *A Gate at the Stairs* (2009); George Saunders (b. 1958), author of *Pastoralia* (2000); Joanna Scott (b. 1960), author of *Tourmaline* (2002); Jeffrey Eugenides (b. 1960), author of *Middlesex* (2002); and Rick Moody (b. 1961), author of *Ice Storm* (1994). Other testimonials include those of Steve Erickson ("[f]or American literature in the last half of the twentieth century, Pynchon is the line in the sand that Faulkner was in the first half"); Trey Ellis ("Pynchon . . . describes the modern condition so accurately that all other novelists . . . owe him our creative lives"); and Emily Barton, who "in college . . . sang in a band named . . . Imipolex G" ("I couldn't write as I do without reckoning with his optimistic cynicism or his perverse understanding of history").[26]

Pynchon's place in literary history will depend, to some degree, on the achievement of those he inspires. It will also depend on the long-term viability of the postmodern aesthetic he helped to found in that extraordinary year, 1963. The genius of postmodernism may lie in its ability to alternate—as it has for some decades now—between the marginal and the mainstream. Frequently pronounced moribund or super-annuated by something clumsily interpellated as "post-postmodern," it seems, rather, to shape-shift in step with an age still confused about authority, referentiality in the sign, and the distinction between story and history, those geminate peas in the narrative pod. In film, in television, in politics and public discourse, in literature high and low, and even in children's entertainments, postmodernism seems increasingly a default mode, something woven into the very fabric of the cultural moment. Now and in the future, in any event, anyone wishing to ride the millennial interface will need to engage the thinking of Thomas Pynchon.

NOTES

INTRODUCTION

1. Thomas Pynchon, "To Richard Wilbur," in "Presentation to Thomas Pynchon of the Howells Medal for Fiction of the Academy," *Proceedings of the American Academy of Arts and Letters and the National Institute of Arts and Letters* 26 (1976): 43–46.

2. See Adrian Wisnicki, "A Trove of New Works by Thomas Pynchon? *Bomarc Service News* Rediscovered," *Pynchon Notes* 46–49 (2000–1): 9–34.

3. Thomas Pynchon, "Is It O.K. to Be a Luddite?" *The New York Times Book Review*, October 28, 1984, 41.

4. Edward Mendelson, "The Sacred, the Profane, and *The Crying of Lot 49*," in *Pynchon: A Collection of Critical Essays*, ed. Edward Mendelson (Englewood Cliffs, N.J.: Prentice Hall, 1978), 97–111.

5. Ralph Waldo Emerson, "The Sovereignty of Ethics," in *Lectures and Biographical Sketches* (Boston, New York: Houghton, Mifflin, ca. 1883), 186.

6. This letter, to Faith and Kirkpatrick Sale, is archived in the Harry Ransom Humanities Research Center at the University of Texas. See John Kraft, "Biographical Note," in *The Cambridge Companion to Thomas Pynchon*, ed. Brian McHale, Inger Dalsgaard, and Luc Herman (New York: Cambridge, 2011).

7. See James Boswell, *Life of Johnson* (London: Oxford University Press, 1953), 333.

CHAPTER ONE. *Prospero's Apprenticeship*

1. Michael Wood, "The Apprenticeship of Thomas Pynchon," *The New York Times Book Review*, April 15, 1984, http://www.nytimes.com/1984/04/15/ books/the-apprenticeship-of-thomas-pynchon.html (accessed July 28, 2010).

2. Christopher Lehmann-Haupt, "Books of the Times," review of *Slow Learner*, by Thomas Pynchon, *The New York Times*, March 29, 1984, http://www.nytimes .com/1984/03/29/books/books-of-the-times-085087.html, (accessed July 28, 2010).

3. Vincent King, "Giving Destruction a Name and a Face: Thomas Pynchon's 'Mortality and Mercy in Vienna,'" *Studies in Short Fiction* 35.1 (1998): 14n3.

4. Joseph Slade, *Thomas Pynchon* (New York: Peter Lang, 1990), 8.

5. Pynchon's juvenilia have been reproduced in Clifford Mead's *Thomas Pynchon: A Bibliography of Primary and Secondary Materials* (Elmwood Park, Illinois: Dalkey Archive Press, 1989), 156–67.

6. *The New York Times Magazine*, June 12, 1966, http://www.nytimes.com/ books/97/05/18/reviews/pynchon-watts.html (accessed August 1, 2010).

7. For a discussion of the relationship between the chapter in *V.* and the short story version, "Under the Rose," see my *Thomas Pynchon: The Art of Allusion* (Carbondale: Southern Illinois University Press, 1980), 65–74. For a linguistic analysis of "syntactic and lexical choices made by Pynchon when rewriting his early short story," see M. Angeles Martinez's "From 'Under the Rose' to *V.*: A Linguistic Approach to Human Agency in Pynchon's Fiction," *Poetics Today* 23.4 (December 2002): 633–54.

8. William Plater, *The Grim Phoenix: Reconstructing Thomas Pynchon* (Bloomington: Indiana University Press, 1978), 138.

9. Slade, 16–17, 126.

10. Tony Tanner, *Thomas Pynchon* (London: Methuen, 1982), 27.

11. I am indebted to John Krafft for this point.

12. Anne Mangel, "Maxwell's Demon, Entropy, Information: *The Crying of Lot 49*," *Tri-Quarterly* 20 (Winter, 1971): 206.

13. Igor Stravinsky, *An Autobiography* (New York: Norton, 1962), 73. The composer describes *L'Histoire du Soldat* and his sojourn in Switzerland on pages 72–77.

14. William H. Austin, *Music in the Twentieth Century* (New York: Norton, 1966), 267.

15. Leonard, Richard Anthony, *A History of Russian Music* (New York: Macmillan, 1957), 263.

16. Austin, 267.

17. Michel Serres, *Genesis* (1982), trans. Geneviève James and James Nielson (Ann Arbor: University of Michigan Press, 1995), 7, 119.

18. Rainer Maria Rilke, "Liebes-Lied" ["Love Song"], *New Poems*, sel. and trans. Edward Snow (New York: North Point Press, 2001), 10–11.

19. This phrase comes from the intriguing "Canzone for an Octopus," a poetic fragment by Pynchon, probably contemporaneous with this story. According to Clifford Mead in a private communication (8 June 2009), the poem is one of two Pynchon is known to have written while an undergraduate at Cornell. They surfaced in the papers of Arthur Mizener, with whom Pynchon had taken a class. The fragment is reproduced on the dust jacket of Mead's *Thomas Pynchon: A Bibliography of Primary and Secondary Materials* (Normal, Illinois: Dalkey Archive, 1989).

20. Gustave Flaubert, *Bouvard et Pécuchet: oeuvre posthume* (Paris: Bibliothèque Charpentier, 1903), 397.

CHAPTER TWO. *History and Myth*

1. Introduced and defined in *A Poetics of Postmodernism: History, Theory, Fiction*, historiographic metafiction blurs the boundaries between "story" and "history," revealing that history is always fictive—and not necessarily less fictive than historical fiction. Major practitioners include Pynchon, Barth, Coover, Doctorow, Fowles, and Eco.

2. As Herman and Krafft discovered in reviewing Pynchon's correspondence with Corlies Smith, the editor at Lippincott who worked with the author on the *V.* manuscript, the epilogue was in fact intended to be objective—that is, untainted by "Stencilization." See Luc Herman and John M. Krafft, "Fast Learner: The Typescript of Pynchon's *V.* at the Harry Ransom Center in Austin," *Texas Studies in Literature and Language* 49.1 (2007): 14.

3. Actually, as one learns in an article by Hanjo Berressem and Norbert Finzsch, White's metahistorical thinking dates back at least to the 1966 essay "The Burden of History," *History and Theory* 5 (1966): 111–34. See Hanjo Berressem and Norbert Finzsch, "Historiographic Metafiction/Metafictional Historiography: The *Mason & Dixon* Project," in *Approaches to Teaching Pynchon's The Crying of Lot 49 and Other Works*, ed. Thomas H. Schaub (New York: Modern Language Association, 2008), 124.

4. Hayden White, "Historical Pluralism," *Critical Inquiry* 12.3 (Spring 1986): 487.

5. John Keats to George and Thomas Keats, 21 or 27 December 1817, *The Letters of John Keats*, ed. Hyder E. Rollins, 2 vols. (Cambridge: Harvard University Press, 1958), 1:193.

6. F. Scott Fitzgerald, *The Crack-Up*, ed. Edmund Wilson (New York: New Directions, 1945), 69.

CHAPTER THREE. Streben nach dem Unendlichen

1. Thomas Pynchon to Thomas F. Hirsch, 8 January 1968, "Appendix: Pynchon's Reading for *Gravity's Rainbow*," in David Seed, *The Fictional Labyrinths of Thomas Pynchon* (Iowa City: University of Iowa Press, 1988), 240–41.

2. Steven Weisenburger, *A Gravity's Rainbow Companion: Sources and Contexts for Pynchon's Novel*, 2nd rev. ed. (Athens: University of Georgia Press, 2006), 380.

3. Ernst Klee and Otto Merk, *The Birth of the Missile*, trans. T. Schoeters (New York: Dutton, 1965), 32–33.

4. Siegfried Kracauer, *From Caligari to Hitler: A Psychological History of the German Film* (Princeton: Princeton University Press, 1947), v.

5. Kracauer, 81–95 and passim.

6. Kracauer, 83.

7. Peter Bogdanovich, *Fritz Lang in America* (New York: Praeger, 1969), 127.

8. Kracauer, 84.

CHAPTER FOUR. *Pynchon and the Sixties*

1. T. S. Eliot, *Four Quartets* (New York: Harcourt, 1971), 19.

2. Brian McHale, *Postmodernist Fiction* (New York: Methuen, 1987).

3. John Enck, "John Hawkes: An Interview," *Wisconsin Studies in Contemporary Literature* 6 (Summer 1965): 154.

4. Vladimir Nabokov, *The Real Life of Sebastian Knight* (London: Weidenfeld and Nicholson, 1941), 89.

5. Thomas Pynchon, "A Journey Into the Mind of Watts," *The New York Times Magazine*, 12 June 1966, 35.

6. Some years ago John Krafft noted the curious neglect of Pynchon's work on the part of "cultural historians of the 1960s" ("Thomas Pynchon," in *The 60s Without Apology*, ed. Sohnya Sayers, Anders Stephanson, Stanley Aronowitz, and Fredric Jameson [Minneapolis: University of Minnesota Press, 1984], 283). The situation was somewhat rectified in the myriad responses to *Vineland*, though

that novel's orientation to the 1960s was often grounds for reproach to an author thought to be unprofitably stuck in time. On the other hand, three articles in *Pynchon Notes*, ostensibly focused on a 1960s thematics in Pynchon, tend to be a little sporadic in their treatment. According to John Farrell, "The aura of expectation pervading *Lot 49*, with its pre-apocalyptic ending, held together the excitement and fear of a new politics" (150). Frederick Ashe locates this new politics as an intentional anachronism in *Gravity's Rainbow*. He argues (somewhat diffidently—he realizes the extravagance of the claim) that this novel "is in large part *about* the challenge issued by sixties youth to American power" (63). Eric Meyer, by the same token, suggests that the heteroglossia of *Gravity's Rainbow*, "the chaotic clash and clatter of competing codes that intersect in 'the Zone' of the text[,] reproduces the similarly dispersed array of forms-in-conflict that traversed the cultural field during the period of its production" (81). The novel's many contending voices, that is, are the voices in conflict during the 1960s.

7. Don DeLillo, *Mao II* (New York: Viking, 1991), 41.

8. Pynchon explains that in his early work he felt "an unkind impatience with fiction I felt then to be 'too autobiographical.'" Somewhere I had come up with the notion that one's personal life had nothing to do with fiction, when the truth, as everyone knows, is nearly the direct opposite" (*SL* 21).

9. In his review of García Márquez's *Death in the Time of Cholera*, Pynchon notes that "the predominant claim on the author's attention and energies comes from what is not so contrary to fact, a human consensus about 'reality' in which . . . varieties of magic have become, if not quite peripheral, then at least more thoughtfully deployed in the service of an expanded vision, matured, darker than before but no less clement." See "The Heart's Eternal Vow," *The New York Times Book Review* 10 April 1988, 49.

10. Quoted in Ross Wetzsteon, "The Professor of Desire," in *The Village Voice Anthology (1956–1980)*, ed. Geoffrey Stokes (New York: William Morrow, 1982), 320.

11. Thomas Pynchon, "Is It O.K. to Be a Luddite?" *The New York Times Book Review*, 28 October 1984, 41.

12. Edward Mendelson, "The Sacred, The Profane, And *The Crying of Lot 49*," in *Pynchon: A Collection of Critical Essays*, ed. Edward Mendelson (Englewood Cliffs, N.J.: Prentice Hall, 1978), 135.

13. Terrence Rafferty, "Long Lost," *The New Yorker* 19 February 1990, 108.

14. Virginia Woolf, *A Room of One's Own* (New York: Harcourt Brace, 1929), 79.

15. Salman Rushdie, "Still Crazy After All These Years," review of *Gravity's Rainbow*, by Thomas Pynchon, *The New York Times Book Review*, 14 January 1990, 37.

16. Bernard Duyfhuizen, "'God Knows, Few of Us Are Strangers to Moral Ambiguity': Thomas Pynchon's *Inherent Vice*" (review), *Postmodern Culture* 19.2 (January 2009): para. 6.

17. Zachary Leader, "Living on the Invisible Boundary," *The Times Literary Supplement* 2–8 February 1990, 115.

18. These terms are among those proposed by Ihab Hassan in his tabular differentiation of modernism and postmodernism. See *The Postmodern Turn: Essays in Postmodern Theory and Culture* (Columbus, Ohio: Ohio State University Press, 1987), 91–92. I am indebted to Spiros Papleacos for bringing this book to my attention.

19. James Joyce, *Finnegans Wake* (New York: Viking, 1958), 326.

20. Jean-Francois Lyotard, *The Postmodern Condition: A Report on Knowledge*, trans. Geoff Bennington and Brian Massumi (Minneapolis: University of Minnesota Press, 1984), 81.

21. Linda Hutcheon, *A Theory of Parody: The Teachings of Twentieth-Century Art Forms* (New York: Methuen, 1985), 6.

22. Rafferty, "Long Lost," 109.

23. Jean-François Lyotard, *The Postmodern Condition*, xxiv, 34–35, 37.

24. David Kipen, review of *Inherent Vice*, by Thomas Pynchon, *Publishers Weekly*, 6 July 2009, 38. The assumption that Pynchon takes some kind of holiday here recurs—largely without complaint—in a number of reviews. Zach Baron, in *The Village Voice*, characterized the novel as "[a] lark" ("Surf Noir: Thomas Pynchon's *Inherent Vice*," 4 August 2009, http://www.villagevoice.com/2009-08-04/books/surf-noir-thomas-pynchon-s-inherent-vice/), and Richard Lacayo, in *Time*, called it "second-tier Pynchon" ("Thomas Pynchon's Magical Mystery Tour," *Time*, 1 August 2009, http://www.time.com/time/arts/article/0,8599,1914149,00 .html). Similar remarks occur in Matt Steigbigel, *Playboy*, 4 August 2009, http://www.playboy.com/articles/books-thomas-pynchon-inherent-vice/index .html; Nicholas Lezard, *The Scotsman*, 8 August 2009, http://living.scotsman .com/books/Book-review-Inherent-Vice.5534825.jp; and Randy Boyagoda, *The Globe & Mail*, "Hard-Boiled or Highbrow?," 7 August 2009, http://www .theglobeandmail.com/books/inherent-vice-by-thomas-pynchon/ article1244614/. All of the above last accessed 20 August 2010.

25. The CD, called *Spiked!*, on the Catalyst label, appeared in 1994, almost thirty years after Jones's death.

26. A small anachronism: the narrator quotes from the television cartoon *Scooby-Doo!* which did not begin airing until September 1970; the Manson trial began the previous June.

27. Slavoj Žižek, "Class Struggle or Postmodernism? Yes, please!" in Slavoj Žižek, Judith Butler, and Ernesto Laclau, *Contingency, Hegemony, Universality: Contemporary Dialogues on the Left* (London: Verso, 2000), 90.

28. Richard Pearce-Moses, "A Glossary of Archival and Records Terminology," Society of American Archivists, 2005, http://www.archivists.org/glossary/term _details.asp?DefinitionKey=2704 (accessed 6 May 2011).

29. F. Scott Fitzgerald, *The Great Gatsby*, ed. Matthew J. Bruccoli (Cambridge: Cambridge University Press, 1991), 5.

30. Theodore Ziolkowski, "The Telltale Teeth: Psychodontia to Sociodontia," *PMLA* 91.1 (January 1976): 11.

31. Charles Bardsley, *Curiosities of Puritan Nomenclature*, 2nd ed. (London: Chatto and Windus, 1888).

32. See W. H. Auden, "As I Walked Out One Morning," in *Collected Poems*, ed. Edward Mendelson (New York: Random House, 2007), 134–35; Robert Frost, "The Gift Outright," in *The Poetry of Robert Frost: the Collected Poems*, ed. Edward Connery Lathem (New York: Henry Holt, 1969), 348; and "Obama Delivers Speech at NAACP Centennial Convention," *Washington Post*, 17 July 2009, http://www.washingtonpost.com/wp-dyn/content/article/2009/07/17/ AR2009071701596.html' (accessed 29 July 2010).

33. John Quincy Adams, *Memoirs of John Quincy Adams: Comprising Portions of His Diary from 1795 to 1848*, ed. Charles Francis Adams (Philadelphia: Lippincott, 1875), 7:164.

34. See Alfred Korzybski, "A Non-Aristotelian System and its Necessity for Rigour in Mathematics and Physics," in *Science and Sanity: An Introduction to Non-Aristotelian Systems and General Semantics* (New York: International Non-Aristotelian Library Publishing, 1933), 750.

CHAPTER FIVE. *The Luddite Vision*

1. Salutes to Pynchon's scientific acumen would continue in the reviews of *Mason & Dixon*. Pynchon "loves the intellectual purities of science and understands them better than any American novelist ever," declares Paul Gray in "Drawing the Line," *Time*, 5 May 1997, 98. Pynchon is "a literary encoder of scientific arcana," according to Louis Menand, "a novelist with a message that requires," among other things, "an advanced knowledge of thermodynamics . . .

and the differential calculus" ("Entropology," *The New York Times Review of Books,* 12 June 1997, 23).

2. Thomas Pynchon, "Is It O.K. to Be a Luddite?" *The New York Times Book Review,* 28 October 1984, 41.

3. John B. Henderson, "Chinese Cosmographical Thought: The High Intellectual Tradition," in *The History of Cartography,* vol. 2, bk. 2, *Cartography in the Traditional East and Southeast Asian Societies,* ed. J. B. Harley and David Woodward (Chicago: University of Chicago Press, 1987), 216.

4. Henry David Thoreau, *Walden,* ed. J. Lyndon Shanley (Princeton: Princeton University Press, 1971), 98.

5. "More than any other period of English history," writes Gordon S. Wood, "the century or so following the Restoration was the great era of conspiratorial fears and imagined intrigues . . . Everywhere people sensed designs within designs, cabals within cabals; there were court conspiracies, backstairs conspiracies, ministerial conspiracies, factional conspiracies, aristocratic conspiracies, and by the last half of the eighteenth century even conspiracies of gigantic secret societies that cut across national boundaries and spanned the Atlantic. Revolutionary Americans may have been an especially jealous and suspicious people, but they were not unique in their fears of dark malevolent plots and plotters" ("Conspiracy and the Paranoid Style: Causality and Deceit in the Eighteenth Century," *William and Mary Quarterly* 39 [July 1982]: 407). Though I see Pynchon as construing the paranoia of Mason and Dixon in ultimately positive terms, Wood's account of the eighteenth century's obsession with conspiracy reveals a kind of historiographical bonus in the author's conceptualization of characters ever ready to ascribe their sufferings (at the hands of the Royal Society, for example) to conscious and concerted vindictiveness among the mighty. It is a commonplace that writers of historical fiction frequently invite readers to recognize, in the past, a mirror of their own age, but the author of *Mason & Dixon* tempers any reflection, in his story, of twentieth-century paranoia with a recognition of sharp divergences in what one might call levels of innocence. Eighteenth-century paranoia, with its conviction of causality always traceable to human volition, was not without its charming, innocent side, and in this it contrasts with its late twentieth-century cousin. In the liner notes for *Spiked!* (Catalyst, 1994), a collection of the wacky, instrumentally challenged performances of Spike Jones, Pynchon characterizes the greater simplicity of the past as a "blessing and gift, finally, to us, adrift in our own difficult time, with moments of true innocence, like good cowbell solos, few and far between."

6. T. Coraghessan Boyle, "*Mason & Dixon,* by Thomas Pynchon," *The New York Times Book Review,* 18 May 1997, 9.

7. John Barth, *The Sot-Weed Factor*, 2nd ed. (Garden City, N.Y.: Doubleday, 1967), 220.

8. Quotations from "Mending Wall" are from *The Poetry of Robert Frost*, ed. Edward Connery Lathem (New York: Holt, Rinehart and Winston, 1969), 33–34.

9. Ted Mooney, "All Down the Line," *The Los Angeles Times Book Review*, 11 May 1997, 3.

CHAPTER SIX. *Pynchon, Genealogy, History*

1. Tiina Käkelä-Puumala, *Other Side of This Life: Death, Value, and Social Being in Thomas Pynchon's Fiction* (Helsinki: Yliopistopaino, 2007), 12.

2. Shawn Smith, *Pynchon and History: Metahistorical Rhetoric and Postmodern Narrative Form in the Novels of Thomas Pynchon* (New York: Routledge, 2005), 17.

3. Henry James, *The Selected Letters of Henry James*, ed. Leon Edel (New York: Farrar, Straus and Cuddahy, 1955), 202–3.

4. Here is the text of the letter, apparently faxed to the *Daily Telegraph* office on or before 6 December 2006:

Words for Ian McEwan
The Daily Telegraph
6 December 2006

Given the British genius for coded utterance, this could all be about something else entirely, impossible on this side of the ocean to appreciate in any nuanced way—but assuming that it really is about who owns the right to describe using gentian violet for ringworm, for heaven's sake, allow me a gentle suggestion. Oddly enough, most of us who write historical fiction do feel some obligation to accuracy. It is that Ruskin business about "a capacity responsive to the claims of fact, but unoppressed by them." Unless we were actually there, we must turn to people who were, or to letters, contemporary reporting, the Internet until, with luck, we can begin to make a few things of our own up. To discover in the course of research some engaging detail we know can be put into a story where it will do some good can hardly be classed as a felonious act—it is simply what we do. The worst you can call it is a form of primate behavior. Writers are naturally drawn, chimpanzee-like, to the color and the music of this English idiom we are blessed to have inherited. When given the choice we will usually try to use the more vivid and tuneful among its words. I cannot of course speak for Mr. McEwan's method of proceeding, but should be very surprised indeed if something of the sort, even for brief moments, had not occurred during his research for *Atonement*. Gentian violet! Come on. Who among us could have resisted that one?

Memoirs of the Blitz have borne indispensable witness, and helped later generations know something of the tragedy and heroism of those days. For Mr. McEwan to have put details from one of them to further creative use, acknowledging this openly and often, and then explaining it clearly and honorably, surely merits not our scolding, but our gratitude.

The *Daily Telegraph* reproduced this letter more than once in articles about various authors' weighing in to defend McEwan. Readers may still be able to link to a legible enlargement of Pynchon's fax in a 7 December 2007 *New York Times* story about this incident. See Sarah Lyall, "Novelists Defend One of Their Own Against a Plagiarism Charge," http://www.nytimes.com/2006/12/07/books/07pync.html?_r=1&oref=slogin (accessed 10 June 2008). See also Nigel Reynolds, "The Borrowers: 'Why McEwan Is No Plagiarist,'" *Daily Telegraph*, May 12, 2006, http://www.telegraph.co.uk/news/main.jhtml?xml=/news/2006/12/06/nwriters105.xml (accessed 18 April 2011).

5. Michel Foucault, "Nietzsche, Genealogy, History," trans. Trans. Donald E. Bouchard and Sherry Simon, in *The Foucault Reader*, ed. Paul Rabinow (New York: Pantheon, 1984), 76.

6. John Dugdale, "It's All About Bigging It Up," review of *Against the Day*, by Thomas Pynchon, *The Sunday Times*, December 10, 2006, http://entertainment.timesonline.co.uk/tol/arts_and_entertainment/books/article660437.ece (accessed March 10, 2009).

7. Bernard Duyfhuizen, "The Exact Degree of Fictitiousness," *Postmodern Culture* 17.2 (January 2007): para. 11. Duyfhuizen notes another "genealogical" dimension to this novel in its sketching of the Traverse-Becker lineage: "The genealogical connections track not only family DNA, but the transformation of Webb's anarchistic spirit through generations of decline to Frenesi's role as a government snitch. In the larger story of America that Pynchon's oeuvre presents, *Against the Day* redirects our attention to *Vineland* and to the commentary each Pynchon novel makes about the forks in the road America did not take and to our collective complicity in those decisions" (para. 6).

8. Michel Foucault, "Truth and Power," trans., Colin Gordon, in *Power*, ed. James B. Faubion, vol. 3 of *Essential Works of Foucault 1954–1984*, 3 vols., ed. Paul Rabinow (New York: New Press, 1997–2000), 132, 133.

9. Michel Foucault, *Discipline and Punish: The Birth of the Prison*, trans. Alan Sheridan (New York: Pantheon, 1977), 47, 228.

10. Norman Mailer, *Armies of the Night: History as a Novel/The Novel as History* (New York: New American Library, 1968), 176.

11. Henry Veggian, "Thomas Pynchon Against the Day," *Boundary 2* 35.1 (2008): 206.

12. Georg Lukács, *The Historical Novel*, trans. Hannah and Stanley Mitchell (London: Merlin Press, 1962), 168. Linda Hutcheon, *A Poetics of Postmodernism: History, Theory, Fiction* (New York: Routledge Kegan & Paul, 1988), ix.

13. Guy Debord, *The Society of the Spectacle*, trans. Donald Nicholson-Smith (New York: Zone, 1994), chap. 5, para. 134.

14. Thomas Pynchon, introduction to *1984*, by George Orwell (New York: Plume, 2003), xv.

15. Käkelä-Puumala, 47.

16. Heinz Ickstadt, "History, Utopia and Transcendence in the Space-Time of *Against the Day*," *Pynchon Notes* 54–55 (2008): 225.

17. John A. McClure, *Partial Faiths: Postsecular Fiction in the Age of Pynchon and Morrison* (Athens: University of Georgia Press, 2007), 7.

18. A putative religious valence in Pynchon has long exercised his critics. Among the most useful discussions of this subject is Edward Mendelson's "The Sacred, the Profane, and *The Crying of Lot 49*," first published in 1975 but most readily available in *Pynchon: A Collection of Critical Essays*, ed. Mendelson. Thomas Schaub presented a cogent counterargument in "Open Letter in Response to Edward Mendelson's 'The Sacred, the Profane, and *The Crying of Lot 49*,'" *Boundary 2* 4 (Fall 1976): 93–101.

Kathryn Hume has argued that *Against the Day* represents a new departure for Pynchon—she sees him as increasingly tolerant of political violence against plutocratic interests—and overtly religious. Though I disagree, ultimately, with the argument for Pynchon's "Catholic anarchism," I consider Hume's discussion of this novel especially original and refreshing. I have found my own thinking enormously stimulated by her analysis and by the e-mail exchanges we have had on the subject. See Kathryn Hume, "The Religious Vision of Pynchon's *Against the Day*," *Philological Quarterly* 86.1–2 (Winter–Spring 2007): 164.

19. Don DeLillo, *Ratner's Star* (New York: Knopf, 1976), 432.

20. Thomas Pynchon, introduction to *The Teachings of Don B.: Satires, Parodies, Fables, Illustrated Stories, and Plays of Donald Barthelme*, ed. Kim Herzinger (New York: Turtle Bay, 1992), xx.

21. See Tom LeClair, "Lead Zeppelin: Encounters with the Unseen in Pynchon's New Novel," review of *Against the Day*, by Thomas Pynchon, *Bookforum* 13, no. 4 (December–January 2007): 17.

22. Dwight Eddins, *The Gnostic Pynchon* (Bloomington: Indiana University Press, 1990), 8.

23. Rabindranath Tagore, *Stray Birds* (New York: Macmillan, 1916), 17.

24. Ralph Waldo Emerson, "The Sovereignty of Ethics," in *Lectures and Biographical Sketches* (Boston, New York: Houghton, Mifflin, ca. 1883), 186.

25. Thomas Pynchon, introduction to *Stone Junction*, by Jim Dodge (New York: Grove, 1998), xi.

26. John Ruskin, cited in Pynchon's letter, "Words for Ian McEwan."

27. Pynchon, introduction to *The Teachings of Don B.*, xvii.

28. Smith, *Pynchon and History*, 181.

29. William Pfaff, "The Fallen Hero," *The New Yorker*, May 8, 1989, 105.

30. Thomas Pynchon, "Is It O.K. to Be a Luddite?" *The New York Times Book Review*, October 28, 1984, 41.

31. Thomas Pynchon, foreword to *1984*, by George Orwell (New York: Plume, 2003), xv, xvi.

32. Pynchon, introduction to *Stone Junction*, xiii.

CHAPTER SEVEN. *The Historiographer Historicized*

1. Karl Mannheim, *Essays on the Sociology of Knowledge*, trans. Paul Kecskemeti (New York: Oxford, 1952), 293.

2. Steven Weisenburger, "Thomas Pynchon: A Recovered Autobiographical Sketch," *American Literature* 62.4 (December 1990): 692–97. This document is no longer publically available.

3. *Investigation on the Assassination of President John F. Kennedy, Hearings Before the President's Commission on the Assassination of President Kennedy*, appendix 13 (Washington, D.C.: GPO, 1964), 688.

4. Don DeLillo, "American Blood: The JFK Assassination," *Rolling Stone*, December 8, 1983, 24.

5. Oscar Wilde, *The Artist as Critic: Critical Writings of Oscar Wilde*, ed. Richard Ellmann (New York: Random House, 1969), 235.

6. Jane Austen, *Northanger Abbey*, in *The Novels of Jane Austen*, ed. R. W. Chapman, vol. 5., *Northanger Abbey and Persuasion*, 3rd ed. (New York: Oxford, 1933), 38.

7. Thomas Pynchon, foreword to *1984*, by George Orwell (New York: Plume, 2003), xx.

8. See Edward Mendelson, "Gravity's Encyclopedia," in *Essays on Thomas Pynchon*, ed. George Levine and David Leverenz (Boston: Little, Brown, 1976), 161–95.

9. Richard Powers, *The Gold Bug Variations* (New York: Morrow, 1991), 593.

10. Jacques Derrida, *Writing and Difference*, trans. Alan Bass (Chicago: University of Chicago Press, 1978), 280.

11. See Brian McHale, *Postmodernist Fiction* (New York: Methuen, 1987).

12. Fredric Jameson, *The Political Unconscious: Narrative as a Socially Symbolic Act* (London: Methuen, 1981), ix.

13. Northrop Frye, *Anatomy of Criticism: Four Essays* (Princeton: Princeton University Press, 1957), 322, 56. Note the similar account at p. 315.

14. Frye, 61.

15. Maurice Blanchot, *Faux Pas*, trans. Charlotte Mandell (Stanford University Press, 2001), 239.

16. See Jorge Luis Borges, "Tlön, Uqbar, Orbis Tertius," trans. James E. Irby, in *Labyrinths, Selected Stories and Other Writings*, ed. Irby and Donald A. Yates (New York: New Directions, 2007), 3–18.

17. Frye, 61.

18. Oakley Hall, *Warlock* (New York: Viking, 1958), 388. Pynchon wrote a brief appreciation of this novel a few years after it came out. See "A Gift of Books," *Holiday*, December 1965, 164–65.

19. Don DeLillo, *Libra* (New York: Viking, 1988), 181.

20. Brian McHale, "1966 Nervous Breakdown; or, When Did Postmodernism Begin?" *Modern Language Quarterly* 69:3 (September 2008): 412, 393, 407.

21. Andreas Killen, *1973 Nervous Breakdown: Watergate, Warhol, and the Birth of Post-Sixties America* (New York: Bloomsbury, 2006), 51.

22. Johann Peter Eckermann, *Conversations with Goethe* (Leipzig, 1836), trans. John Oxenford (London: J. M. Dent, 1930), 31–32. Cited in Walter Jackson Bate, *The Burden of the Past and the English Poet* (Cambridge, Mass.: Harvard University Press, 1970), 5–6.

23. Mannheim, 298, 310.

24. Richard Powers, *Generosity: An Enhancement* (New York: Farrar, Straus and Giroux, 2009), 169.

25. See Sir Charles Percy Snow, *The Two Cultures; and, A Second Look: An Expanded Version of "The Two Cultures and the Scientific Revolution"* (New York: Cambridge University Press, 1964).

26. These remarks appear as boxed text in a special section, "Pynchon from A to V," *Bookforum* (June/July/August/September 2005), 36, 38, 40.

BOOKS, PAMPHLETS, AND SPECIAL PERIODICAL ISSUES ON THOMAS PYNCHON

In compiling this list, I am indebted to the bibliographical updates in *Pynchon Notes*, to its coeditor, John Krafft, to Otto Sell's online bibliography, http://www.ottosell.de/pynchon/lit2.htm, and to Michel Ryckx's Web site, Vheissu.org.

MONOGRAPHS

Arich-Gerz, Bruno. *Lesen-Beobachten. Modell einer Wirkungsästhetik mit Thomas Pynchons* Gravity's Rainbow [*Reading-Observing. A Model of Reader-Response Criticism Based on Thomas Pynchon's* Gravity's Rainbow]. Konstanz: UVK, 2001.

Battesti, Anne. *Thomas Pynchon: L'approche et l'esquive* [*Thomas Pynchon: Approach and Avoid*]. Paris: Belin, 2003.

Berressem, Hanjo. *Pynchon's Poetics: Interfacing Theory and Text.* Urbana: University of Illinois Press, 1993.

Brownlie, Alan W. *Thomas Pynchon's Narratives: Subjectivity and Problems of Knowing.* New York: Peter Lang, 2000.

Chambers, Judith. *Thomas Pynchon.* New York: Twayne, 1992.

Clerc, Charles. *Mason & Dixon & Pynchon.* Lanham, Md.: University Press of America, 2000.

Collado-Rodríguez, Francisco. *Orden del caos: Literatura y posthumanidad en la narrativa de Thomas Pynchon* [*Order out of Chaos: Literature and Posthumanism in the Fiction of Thomas Pynchon*]. Valencia, Spain: Universidad de Valencia, 2004.

Colville, Georgiana M. M. *Beyond and Beneath the Mantle: On Thomas Pynchon's* The Crying of Lot 49. Amsterdam: Rodopi B.V., 1988.

Cooper, Peter L. *Signs and Symptoms: Thomas Pynchon and the Contemporary World.* Berkeley: University of California Press, 1983.

Cowart, David. *Thomas Pynchon: The Art of Allusion.* Carbondale: Southern Illinois University Press, 1980.

D'Amico, Maria Vittoria. *Le matrici dell'apprendista: I racconti di Thomas Pynchon* [*The Learner's Matrix: The Stories of Thomas Pynchon*]. Bari: Adriatica, 1992.

Dugdale, John. *Thomas Pynchon: Allusive Parables of Power.* New York: St. Martin's Press, 1990.

Eddins, Dwight. *The Gnostic Pynchon.* Bloomington: Indiana University Press, 1990.

Fowler, Douglas. *A Reader's Guide to* Gravity's Rainbow. Ann Arbor, Mich.: Ardis Press, 1980.

Grant, J. Kerry. *A Companion to* The Crying of Lot 49. 2nd ed. Athens: University of Georgia Press, 2008.

———. *A Companion to* V. Athens: University of Georgia Press, 2000.

Hägg, Samuli. *Narratologies of* Gravity's Rainbow. Joensuu: University of Joensuu Press, 2005.

Hite, Molly. *Ideas of Order in the Novels of Thomas Pynchon.* Columbus: Ohio State University Press, 1983.

Hohmann, Charles. *Thomas Pynchon's* Gravity's Rainbow*: A Study of Its Conceptual Structure and of Rilke's Influence.* New York: Peter Lang, 1987.

Hume, Kathryn. *Pynchon's Mythography: An Approach to* Gravity's Rainbow. Carbondale: Southern Illinois University Press, 1987.

Hurley, Patrick J. *Pynchon Character Names: A Dictionary.* Jefferson, N.C.: McFarland, 2008.

Käkelä-Puumala, Tiina. *Other Side of This Life: Death, Value, and Social Being in Thomas Pynchon's Fiction.* Helsinki: Yliopistopaino: 2007.

Kharpertian, Theodore D. *A Hand to Turn the Time: The Menippean Satires of Thomas Pynchon.* Rutherford, N.J.: Fairleigh Dickinson University Press, 1989.

Kihara, Yoshihiko. *Thomas Pynchon: Museifu-shugi-teki-kiseki no Uchu* [*Thomas Pynchon: The Universe of Anarchist Miracle*]. Kyoto: Kyoto University Press, 2001.

Kolbuszewska, Zofia. *Poetics of Chronotope in the Novels of Thomas Pynchon*. Lublin: Learned Society of the Catholic University of Lublin, 2000.

Kopp, Manfred. *Triangulating Thomas Pynchon's Eighteenth-Century World: Theory, Structure, and Paranoia in* Mason & Dixon. Essen: Blaue Eule, 2004.

Lalo, Alexei. *Thomas Pynchon and His America: Enigmas, Parallels, Cultural Contexts* [in Russian]. Minsk: RIVSH-BGU, 2001.

Liu, Fengshan. *The World behind Fantasy: A Study of Thomas Pynchon's Fiction.* Beijing: Foreign Language Teaching and Research Press, 2011.

Mackey, Douglas. *The Rainbow Quest of Thomas Pynchon*. San Bernardino, Calif.: Borgo Press, 1980.

Madsen, Deborah L. *The Postmodernist Allegories of Thomas Pynchon*. New York: St. Martin's Press, 1991.

Mattessich, Stefan. *Lines of Flight: Discursive Time and Countercultural Desire in the Work of Thomas Pynchon*. Durham: Duke University Press, 2002.

McHoul, Alec W. and David Wills. *Writing Pynchon: Strategies in Fictional Analysis.* Urbana: University of Illinois Press, 1990.

Mead, Clifford. *Thomas Pynchon: A Bibliography of Primary and Secondary Materials.* Elmwood Park, Ill.: Dalkey Archive Press, 1989.

Newman, Robert. *Understanding Thomas Pynchon*. Columbia: University of South Carolina Press, 1986.

Moore, Thomas. *The Style of Connectedness:* Gravity's Rainbow *and Thomas Pynchon.* Columbia: University of Missouri Press, 1987.

Park, Eunjung. *A Study on Thomas Pynchon: Empire and the Postmodern* [in Korean]. Seoul: Daesun, 2000.

Plater, William M. *The Grim Phoenix: Reconstructing Thomas Pynchon.* Bloomington: Indiana University Press, 1978.

Pöhlmann, Sascha. *Pynchon's Postnational Imagination*. Heidelberg: Winter, 2010.

Price, Victoria H. *Christian Allusions in the Novels of Thomas Pynchon*. New York: Peter Lang, 1989.

Schaub, Thomas H. *Pynchon: The Voice of Ambiguity*. Urbana: University of Illinois Press, 1981.

Seed, David. *The Fictional Labyrinths of Thomas Pynchon*. London: Macmillan, 1988.

Siegel, Mark Richard. *Pynchon: Creative Paranoia in* Gravity's Rainbow. Port Washington, New York: Kennikat Press, 1978.

Sigvardson, Joakim. *Immanence and Transcendence in Thomas Pynchon's* Mason & Dixon: *A Phenomenological Study*. Stockholm: Almqvist & Wiksell International, 2002.

Slade, Joseph W. *Thomas Pynchon.* New York: Warner, 1974. Reprint, New York: Peter Lang, 1994.

Smith, Shawn. *Pynchon and History: Metahistorical Rhetoric and Postmodern Narrative Form in the Novels of Thomas Pynchon.* New York: Routledge, 2005.

Stark, John O. *Pynchon's Fictions: Thomas Pynchon and the Literature of Information.* Athens: Ohio University Press, 1980.

Tanner, Tony. *Thomas Pynchon.* London: Methuen, 1982.

Thomas, Samuel. *Pynchon and the Political.* New York: Routledge, 2007.

Trainini, Marco. *A silent extinction: Saggio su* L'arcobaleno della gravità *di Thomas Pynchon* [*A Silent Extinction: An Essay on* Gravity's Rainbow *by Thomas Pynchon*]. Milan: Arcipelago Edizioni, 2010.

Weisenburger, Steven C. *A* Gravity's Rainbow *Companion: Sources and Contexts for Pynchon's Novel,* 2nd rev. ed. Athens: University of Georgia Press, 2006.

Witzling, David. *Everybody's America: Thomas Pynchon, Race, and the Cultures of Postmodernism.* New York: Routledge 2008.

Zadworna-Fjellestad, Danuta. Alice's Adventures in Wonderland *and* Gravity's Rainbow*: A Study in Duplex Fiction.* Stockholm: Almqvist and Wiksell International, 1986.

COLLECTIONS

Abbas, Niran, ed. *Thomas Pynchon: Reading from the Margins.* Fairleigh Dickinson University Press, 2003.

Alfano, Giancarlo, and Mattei Carratello, eds. *La dissoluzione onesta: Scritti su Thomas Pynchon* [*Honest Dissolution: Writings on Thomas Pynchon*]. Naples: Cronopio, 2003.

Asada, Akira, et al. *Yuriika* [*Eureka*] 21.2 (February 1989): 53–245.

Berressem, Hanjo, and Leyla Haferkamp, eds. "Site-Specific: From Aachen to Zwölfkinder Pynchon/Germany" (papers from Site Specific Pynchon/Germany Conference, Köln, 2002). Special issue, *Pynchon Notes* 54–55 (Spring–Fall 2008): 1–304.

Bianchi, Petra, Arnold Cassola, and Peter Serracino Inglott. *Pynchon Malta and Wittgenstein.* Valletta: Malta University Publishers, 1995.

Bloom, Harold, ed. *Thomas Pynchon* (Bloom's Major Novelists). New York: Chelsea, 2003.

———. *Thomas Pynchon* (Bloom's Modern Critical Views). New York: Chelsea, 2003.

————. *Thomas Pynchon's* Gravity's Rainbow. New York: Chelsea, 1986.

Cassidy, Eric, and Dan O'Hara, eds. "Thomas Pynchon: Schizophrenia and Social Control: Papers from the Warwick Conference." Special issue, *Pynchon Notes* 34–35 (Spring–Fall 1994): 1–224.

Chamerois, Gilles, ed. *Reading Thomas Pynchon's Latest Novel* Against the Day. Special issue, *Graat* 3 (2008).

Claro, Christophe, et al., eds. *Face à Pynchon* [*Facing Pynchon*]. Paris: Le Cherche Midi, 2008.

Clerc, Charles, ed. *Approaches to* Gravity's Rainbow. Columbus: Ohio State University Press, 1983.

Copestake, Ian, ed. *American Postmodernity: Essays on the Recent Fiction of Thomas Pynchon.* New York: Peter Lang, 2003.

Dalsgaard, Inger, Luc Herman, and Brian McHale, eds. *The Cambridge Companion to Thomas Pynchon.* New York: Cambridge, 2011.

Ghosh, Shubha, ed. *Thomas Pynchon and the Law.* Special issue, *Oklahoma City University Law Review* 24.3 (1999).

Green, Geoffrey, Donald J. Greiner, and Larry McCaffery, eds. *The* Vineland *Papers: Critical Takes on Pynchon's Novel.* Normal, Ill.: Dalkey Archive Press, 1994. Reprint, with additional essays, of special issue of *Critique* 32.2 (Winter 1990): 67–144.

Herman, Luc, ed. "Approach and Avoid: Essays on *Gravity's Rainbow,* Papers from International Pynchon Week, Antwerp, 1998." Special issue, *Pynchon Notes* 42–43 (Spring–Fall 1998): 1–342.

————. *Yang* 28.1 (January–March 1992).

Hinds, Elizabeth Jane Wall, ed. *The Multiple Worlds of Pynchon's* Mason & Dixon: *Eighteenth-Century Contexts, Postmodern Observations.* Rochester, N.Y.: Camden House, 2005.

Horvath, Brooke, and Irving Malin, eds. *Pynchon and* Mason & Dixon. Newark: University of Delaware Press, 2000.

Ickstadt, Heinz, ed. *Ordnung und Entropie: Zum Romanwerk von Thomas Pynchon* [*Order and Entropy: On the Novels of Thomas Pynchon*]. Hamburg: Rowohlt, 1994.

Levine, George, and David Leverenz, eds. *Mindful Pleasures: Essays on Thomas Pynchon.* Boston: Little Brown, 1976.

Mangen, Anne, and Rolf Gaasland, eds. *Blissful Bewilderment: Studies in the Fiction of Thomas Pynchon.* Oslo: Novus, 2002.

Mendelson, Edward, ed. *Pynchon: A Collection of Critical Essays.* Englewood Cliffs, N.J.: Prentice Hall, 1978.

O'Donnell, Patrick, ed. *New Essays on* The Crying of Lot 49. Cambridge, UK: Cambridge University Press, 1991.

Orbit: Writing Around Pynchon. Electronic journal founded 2011, edited by Martin Paul Eve, Douglas Haynes, and Samuel Thomas.

Pearce, Richard, ed. *Critical Essays on Thomas Pynchon.* Boston: G. K. Hall, 1981.

Pöhlmann, Sascha, ed. *Against the Grain: Reading Pynchon's Counternarratives.* Amsterdam: Rodopi, 2010.

Pynchon Notes. Periodical published since 1979, edited by John Krafft, Bernard Duyfhuizen, Khachig Tölölyan. Every issue a new book on Pynchon.

Schaub, Thomas H., ed. *Approaches to Teaching* The Crying of Lot 49 *and Other Works.* New York: Modern Language Association, 2008.

Siegert, Bernhard, and Markus Krajewski, eds. *Thomas Pynchon. Archiv—Verschwörung—Geschichte* [*Thomas Pynchon: Archive—Conspiracy—History*]. Weimar: Vdg-Verlag, 2003.

Vanderbeke, Dirk, and Bruno Arich-Gerz, eds. *Into the Zone 2000.* Special issue, *Pynchon Notes* 50–51 (Spring–Fall 2002): 1–207.

Werli, Antonio, et al., eds. "Pynchon Dossier." Special issue, *Ciclocosmia* 1 (September 2008): 33–119.

WORKS CITED

Adams, John Quincy. *Memoirs of John Quincy Adams: Comprising Portions of His Diary from 1795 to 1848.* Vol. 7. Edited by Charles Francis Adams. Philadelphia: Lippincott, 1875.

Angeles Martinez, M. "From 'Under the Rose' to *V.*: A Linguistic Approach to Human Agency in Pynchon's Fiction." *Poetics Today* 23.4 (December 2002): 633–54.

Ashe, Frederick. "Anachronism Intended: *Gravity's Rainbow* in the Sociopolitical Sixties." *Pynchon Notes* 28–29 (Spring–Fall 1991): 59–75.

Auden, W. H. *Collected Poems.* Edited by Edward Mendelson. New York: Random House, 2007.

Austen, Jane. *Northanger Abbey.* In *The Novels of Jane Austen.* 3rd ed. Vol. 5. Edited by R. W. Chapman. New York: Oxford, 1933.

Austin, William H. *Music in the Twentieth Century.* New York: Norton, 1966.

Bardsley, Charles. *Curiosities of Puritan Nomenclature.* 2nd ed. London: Chatto and Windus, 1888.

Baron, Zach. "Surf Noir: Thomas Pynchon's *Inherent Vice.*" *The Village Voice,* August 4, 2009, http://www.villagevoice.com/2009-08-04/books/surf-noir -thomas-pynchon-s-inherent-vice/ (accessed 20 August 2010).

Barth, John. *The Sot-Weed Factor.* 2nd ed. Garden City, N.Y.: Doubleday, 1967.

Bate, Walter Jackson. *The Burden of the Past and the English Poet.* Cambridge, Mass.: Harvard University Press, 1970.

Berressem, Hanjo, and Norbert Finzsch. "Historiographic Metafiction/
   Metafictional Historiography: The *Mason & Dixon* Project." In *Approaches
   to Teaching Pynchon's* The Crying of Lot 49 *and Other Works*, edited by
   Thomas Schaub, 121–29. New York: Modern Language Association,
   2008.

Blanchot, Maurice. *Faux Pas*. Translated by Charlotte Mandell. Palo Alto:
   Stanford University Press, 2001.

Bogdanovich, Peter. *Fritz Lang in America*. New York: Praeger, 1969.

Borges, Jorge Luis. "Tlön, Uqbar, Orbis Tertius." Translated by James E. Irby.
   In *Labyrinths, Selected Stories and Other Writings*, edited by James E. Irby and
   Donald A. Yates, 3–18. New York: New Directions, 2007.

Boyagoda, Randy. "Hard-Boiled or Highbrow?" *The Globe & Mail*, August 7,
   2009, http://www.theglobeandmail.com/books/inherent-vice-by-thomas
   -pynchon/article1244614/ (accessed 20 August 2010).

Boyle, T. Coraghessan. "*Mason & Dixon*, by Thomas Pynchon." *The New York
   Times Book Review*, May 18, 1997, 9.

Cowart, David. *Thomas Pynchon: The Art of Allusion*. Carbondale: Southern
   Illinois University Press, 1980.

Debord, Guy. *The Society of the Spectacle*. Translated by Donald Nicholson-Smith.
   New York: Zone, 1994.

DeLillo, Don. "American Blood: The JFK Assassination." *Rolling Stone*,
   December 8, 1983, 21–22, 24, 27–28, 74.

———. *Libra*. New York: Viking, 1988.

———. *Mao II*. New York: Viking, 1991.

———. *Ratner's Star*. New York: Knopf, 1976.

Derrida, Jacques. *Writing and Difference*. Translated by Alan Bass. Chicago:
   University of Chicago Press, 1978.

Dugdale, John. "It's All About Bigging It Up." Review of *Against the Day*,
   by Thomas Pynchon. *The Sunday Times*, December 10, 2006, http://
   entertainment.timesonline.co.uk/tol/arts_and_entertainment/books/
   article660437.ece (accessed 18 April 2011).

Duyfhuizen, Bernard. "The Exact Degree of Fictitiousness": Thomas Pynchon's
   Against the Day." Review of *Against the Day*, by Thomas Pynchon. *Postmodern
   Culture* 17.2 (January 2007).

———. "'God Knows, Few of Us Are Strangers to Moral Ambiguity': Thomas
   Pynchon's *Inherent Vice*." Review of *Inherent Vice*, by Thomas Pynchon.
   Postmodern Culture 19.2 (January 2009).

Eckermann, Johann Peter. *Conversations with Goethe*. Translated by John
   Oxenford. Leipzig, 1836. Reprint, London: J. M. Dent, 1930.

Eddins, Dwight. *The Gnostic Pynchon.* Bloomington: Indiana University Press, 1990.

Eliot, T. S. *Four Quartets.* New York: Harcourt, 1971.

Emerson, Ralph Waldo. "The Sovereignty of Ethics." In *Lectures and Biographical Sketches,* 175–206. Boston, New York: Houghton, Mifflin, ca. 1883.

Enck, John. "John Hawkes: An Interview." *Wisconsin Studies in Contemporary Literature* 6 (Summer 1965): 141–55.

Farrell, John. "The Romance of the '60s: Self, Community and the Ethical in *The Crying of Lot 49.*" *Pynchon Notes* 30–31 (Spring–Fall 1992): 139–56.

Fitzgerald, F. Scott. *The Crack-Up.* Edited by Edmund Wilson. New York: New Directions, 1945.

———. *The Great Gatsby.* Edited by Matthew J. Bruccoli. Cambridge, UK: Cambridge University Press, 1991.

Flaubert, Gustave. *Bouvard et Pécuchet: Oeuvre posthume.* Paris: Bibliothèque Charpentier, 1903.

Foucault, Michel. *Discipline and Punish: The Birth of the Prison.* Translated by Alan Sheridan. New York: Pantheon, 1977.

———. "Nietzsche, Genealogy, History." Translated by Donald E. Bouchard and Sherry Simon. In *The Foucault Reader,* edited by Paul Rabinow, 76–100. New York: Pantheon, 1984.

———. "Truth and Power." Translated by Colin Gordon. In *Power,* edited by James B. Faubion, 111–33. Vol. 3 of *Essential Works of Foucault 1954–1984,* edited by Paul Rabinow. New York: New Press, 2000.

Frost, Robert. *The Poetry of Robert Frost.* Edited by Edward Connery Lathem. New York: Holt, Rinehart and Winston, 1969.

Frye, Northrop. *Anatomy of Criticism: Four Essays.* Princeton: Princeton University Press, 1957.

Gardner, John. *On Moral Fiction.* New York: Basic Books, 1978.

Gray, Paul. "Drawing the Line." Review of *Mason and Dixon,* by Thomas Pynchon. *Time,* May 5, 1997, 98.

Hall, Oakley. *Warlock.* New York: Viking, 1958.

Hassan, Ihab. *The Postmodern Turn: Essays in Postmodern Theory and Culture.* Columbus: Ohio State University Press, 1987.

Henderson, John B. "Chinese Cosmographical Thought: The High Intellectual Tradition." In *The History of Cartography,* vol. 2, bk. 2, edited by J. B. Harley and David Woodward, 203–27. Chicago: University of Chicago Press, 1987.

Herman, Luc, and John M. Krafft. "Fast Learner: The Typescript of Pynchon's *V.* at the Harry Ransom Center in Austin." *Texas Studies in Literature and Language* 49.1 (2007): 1–20.

Howard, Gerald, et al. "Pynchon from A to V." *Bookforum* (June/July/August/ September 2005): 29–40.

Hume, Kathryn. *Pynchon's Mythography: An Approach to* Gravity's Rainbow. Carbondale: Southern Illinois University Press, 1987.

———. "The Religious Vision of Pynchon's *Against the Day.*" *Philological Quarterly* 86.1–2 (Winter–Spring 2007): 163–87.

Hutcheon, Linda. *A Poetics of Postmodernism: History, Theory, Fiction.* New York: Routledge Kegan & Paul, 1988.

———. *A Theory of Parody: The Teachings of Twentieth-Century Art Forms.* New York: Methuen, 1985.

Huyssen, Andreas. *After the Great Divide: Modernism, Mass Culture, Postmodernism (Theories of Representation and Difference).* Bloomington: Indiana University Press, 1986.

Ickstadt, Heinz. "History, Utopia and Transcendence in the Space-Time of *Against the Day.*" *Pynchon Notes* 54–55 (2008): 216–44.

Jameson, Fredric. *The Political Unconscious: Narrative as a Socially Symbolic Act.* London: Methuen, 1981.

Joyce, James. *Finnegans Wake.* New York: Viking, 1958.

Käkelä-Puumala, Tiina. *Other Side of This Life: Death, Value, and Social Being in Thomas Pynchon's Fiction.* Helsinki: Yliopistopaino: 2007.

Keats, John. To George and Thomas Keats, 21 or 27 December 1817. In *The Letters of John Keats,* edited by Hyder E. Rollins, 1:193. Cambridge: Harvard University Press, 1958.

Killen, Andreas. *1973 Nervous Breakdown: Watergate, Warhol, and the Birth of Post-Sixties America* (New York: Bloomsbury, 2006).

King, Vincent. "Giving Destruction a Name and a Face: Thomas Pynchon's 'Mortality and Mercy in Vienna.'" *Studies in Short Fiction* 35.1 (1998): 13–21.

Kipen, David. Review of *Inherent Vice,* by Thomas Pynchon. *Publishers Weekly,* July 6, 2009, 38.

Klee, Ernst, and Otto Merk. *The Birth of the Missile.* Translated by T. Schoeters. New York: Dutton, 1965.

Korzybski, Alfred. "A Non-Aristotelian System and Its Necessity for Rigour in Mathematics and Physics." In *Science and Sanity: An Introduction to Non-Aristotelian Systems and General Semantics,* 747–62. New York: International Non-Aristotelian Library Publishing, 1933.

Kracauer, Siegfried. *From Caligari to Hitler: A Psychological History of the German Film.* Princeton: Princeton University Press, 1971.

Krafft, John M. "Thomas Pynchon." In *The '60s without Apology,* edited by

Sohnya Sayers, Anders Stephanson, Stanley Aronowitz, and Fredric Jameson, 283–86. Minneapolis: University of Minnesota Press, 1984.

Lacayo, Richard. "Thomas Pynchon's Magical Mystery Tour." *Time*, August 1, 2009, http://www.time.com/time/arts/article/0,8599,1914149,00.html (accessed 20 August 2010).

Leader, Zachary. "Living on the Invisible Boundary." *Times Literary Supplement* February 2–8, 1990, 115.

LeClair, Tom. "Lead Zeppelin: Encounters with the Unseen in Pynchon's New Novel." Review of *Against the Day*, by Thomas Pynchon. *Bookforum* 13, no. 4 (December/January 2007): 17, 58.

Lehmann-Haupt, Christopher. "Books of the Times." Review of *Slow Learner*, by Thomas Pynchon. *The New York Times*, March 29, 1984, http://www.nytimes .com/1984/03/29/books/books-of-the-times- 085087.html (accessed 28 July 2010).

Leonard, Richard Anthony. *A History of Russian Music.* New York: Macmillan, 1957.

Levine, George and David Leverenz, eds. *Mindful Pleasures: Essays on Thomas Pynchon.* Boston: Little, Brown, 1976.

Lyall, Sarah. "Novelists Defend One of Their Own against a Plagiarism Charge." *The New York Times*, December 7, 2006 http://www.nytimes.com/ 2006/12/07/books/07pync.html?_r=1&oref=slogin (accessed 20 March 2011).

Lezard, Nicholas. Review of *Inherent Vice*, by Thomas Pynchon. *The Scotsman*, August 8, 2009, http://living.scotsman.com/books/Book-review-Inherent -Vice.5534825.jp (accessed 20 August 2010).

Lukács, Georg. *The Historical Novel.* Translated by Hannah and Stanley Mitchell. London: Merlin Press, 1962.

Lyotard, Jean-François. *The Postmodern Condition: A Report on Knowledge.* Translated by Geoff Bennington and Brian Massumi. Minneapolis: University of Minnesota Press, 1984.

Mailer, Norman. *Armies of the Night: History as a Novel/The Novel as History.* New York: New American Library, 1968.

Mangel, Anne. "Maxwell's Demon, Entropy, Information: *The Crying of Lot 49.*" *Tri-Quarterly* 20 (Winter 1971): 201–3, 206–7.

Mannheim, Karl. *Essays on the Sociology of Knowledge.* Translated by Paul Kecskemeti. New York: Oxford, 1952.

McClure, John A. *Partial Faiths: Postsecular Fiction in the Age of Pynchon and Morrison.* Athens: University of Georgia Press, 2007.

McHale, Brian. "1966 Nervous Breakdown; or, When Did Postmodernism
    Begin?" *Modern Language Quarterly* 69:3 (September 2008):391–413.
———. *Postmodernist Fiction.* New York: Methuen, 1987.
Mead, Clifford. *Thomas Pynchon: A Bibliography of Primary and Secondary Materials.*
    Elmwood Park, Ill.: Dalkey Archive Press, 1989.
Meixner, John A. "The All-Purpose Quest." *Kenyon Review* 25 (Autumn 1963):
    729–35.
Menand, Louis. "Entropology." Review of *Mason & Dixon,* by Thomas Pynchon.
    The New York Times Review of Books June 12, 1997, 23–25.
Mendelson, Edward. "Gravity's Encyclopedia." In *Essays on Thomas Pynchon,* ed-
    ited by George Levine and David Leverenz, 161–95. Boston: Little, Brown,
    1976.
Mendelson, Edward, ed. *Pynchon: A Collection of Critical Essays.* Englewood Cliffs,
    N.J.: Prentice-Hall, 1978.
Mendelson, Edward. "The Sacred, the Profane, and *The Crying of Lot 49.*" In
    Pynchon: A Collection of Critical Essays, edited by Edward Mendelson, 97–111.
    Englewood Cliffs, N.J.: Prentice-Hall, 1978.
Meyer, Eric. "Oppositional Discourses, Unnatural Practices: *Gravity's Rainbow*
    and the '60s." *Pynchon Notes* 24–25 (Spring–Fall 1989): 81–104.
Mooney, Ted. "All Down the Line." Review of *Mason & Dixon,* by Thomas
    Pynchon. *The Los Angeles Times Book Review,* May 11, 1997, 3–4.
Nabokov, Vladimir. *The Real Life of Sebastian Knight.* London: Weidenfeld and
    Nicholson, 1941.
Newman, Charles. *The Post-Modern Aura: The Act of Fiction in an Age of Inflation.*
    Evanston, Ill.: Northwestern University Press, 1985.
"Obama Delivers Speech at NAACP Centennial Convention." *Washington Post,*
    July 17, 2009, http://www.washingtonpost.com/wp- dyn/content/article/
    2009/07/17/AR2009071701596.html (accessed 29 July 2010).
Pearce-Moses, Richard. "A Glossary of Archival and Records Terminology."
    Society of American Archivists, 2005, http://www.archivists.org/glossary/
    term_details.asp?DefinitioDefi=2704 (accessed 30 August 2010).
Pfaff, William. "The Fallen Hero." *The New Yorker,* May 8, 1989, 105–15.
Plater, William. *The Grim Phoenix: Reconstructing Thomas Pynchon.* Bloomington:
    Indiana University Press, 1978.
Powers, Richard. *Generosity: An Enhancement.* New York: Farrar, Straus and
    Giroux, 2009.
———. *The Gold Bug Variations.* New York: Morrow, 1991.
Pynchon, Thomas. *Against the Day.* New York: Penguin, 2006.

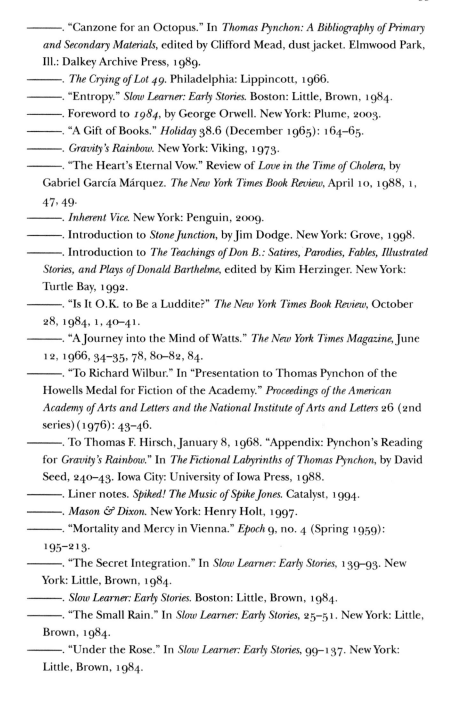

———. "Canzone for an Octopus." In *Thomas Pynchon: A Bibliography of Primary and Secondary Materials,* edited by Clifford Mead, dust jacket. Elmwood Park, Ill.: Dalkey Archive Press, 1989.

———. *The Crying of Lot 49.* Philadelphia: Lippincott, 1966.

———. "Entropy." *Slow Learner: Early Stories.* Boston: Little, Brown, 1984.

———. Foreword to *1984,* by George Orwell. New York: Plume, 2003.

———. "A Gift of Books." *Holiday* 38.6 (December 1965): 164–65.

———. *Gravity's Rainbow.* New York: Viking, 1973.

———. "The Heart's Eternal Vow." Review of *Love in the Time of Cholera,* by Gabriel García Márquez. *The New York Times Book Review,* April 10, 1988, 1, 47, 49.

———. *Inherent Vice.* New York: Penguin, 2009.

———. Introduction to *Stone Junction,* by Jim Dodge. New York: Grove, 1998.

———. Introduction to *The Teachings of Don B.: Satires, Parodies, Fables, Illustrated Stories, and Plays of Donald Barthelme,* edited by Kim Herzinger. New York: Turtle Bay, 1992.

———. "Is It O.K. to Be a Luddite?" *The New York Times Book Review,* October 28, 1984, 1, 40–41.

———. "A Journey into the Mind of Watts." *The New York Times Magazine,* June 12, 1966, 34–35, 78, 80–82, 84.

———. "To Richard Wilbur." In "Presentation to Thomas Pynchon of the Howells Medal for Fiction of the Academy." *Proceedings of the American Academy of Arts and Letters and the National Institute of Arts and Letters* 26 (2nd series) (1976): 43–46.

———. To Thomas F. Hirsch, January 8, 1968. "Appendix: Pynchon's Reading for *Gravity's Rainbow.*" In *The Fictional Labyrinths of Thomas Pynchon,* by David Seed, 240–43. Iowa City: University of Iowa Press, 1988.

———. Liner notes. *Spiked! The Music of Spike Jones.* Catalyst, 1994.

———. *Mason & Dixon.* New York: Henry Holt, 1997.

———. "Mortality and Mercy in Vienna." *Epoch* 9, no. 4 (Spring 1959): 195–213.

———. "The Secret Integration." In *Slow Learner: Early Stories,* 139–93. New York: Little, Brown, 1984.

———. *Slow Learner: Early Stories.* Boston: Little, Brown, 1984.

———. "The Small Rain." In *Slow Learner: Early Stories,* 25–51. New York: Little, Brown, 1984.

———. "Under the Rose." In *Slow Learner: Early Stories,* 99–137. New York: Little, Brown, 1984.

———. *V.* New York: Lippincott, 1963.

———. *Vineland.* New York: Little, Brown, 1990.

———. "Words for Ian McEwan."

Rafferty, Terrence. "Long Lost." *The New Yorker,* February 19, 1990, 108–12.

Reynolds, Nigel. "The Borrowers: 'Why McEwan Is No Plagiarist.'" *Daily Telegraph,* May 12, 2006, http://www.telegraph.co.uk/news/main.jhtml ?xml=/news/2006/12/06/nwriters105.xml (accessed 18 April 2011).

Rilke, Rainer Maria. *New Poems.* Selected and translated by Edward Snow. New York: North Point Press, 2001.

Rushdie, Salman. "Still Crazy After All These Years." Review of *Vineland,* by Thomas Pynchon. *The New York Times Book Review,* January 14, 1990, 1, 36–37.

Sayers, Sohnya, Anders Stephanson, Stanley Aronowitz, and Fredric Jameson, eds. *The '60s Without Apology.* Minneapolis: University of Minnesota Press, 1984.

Schaub, Thomas, ed. *Approaches to Teaching Pynchon's* The Crying of Lot 49 *and Other Works.* New York: Modern Language Association, 2008.

———. "Open Letter in Response to Edward Mendelson's 'The Sacred, the Profane, and *The Crying of Lot 49.'*" *Boundary* 2 4 (Fall 1976): 93–101.

Seed, David. *The Fictional Labyrinths of Thomas Pynchon.* Iowa City: University of Iowa Press, 1988.

Serres, Michel. *Genesis.* Translated by Geneviève James and James Nielson. Ann Arbor: University of Michigan Press, 1995.

Shakespeare, William. *Hamlet.* In The *Complete Works of Shakespeare,* edited by David Bevington, 5th ed., 1097–149. New York: Longman, 2004.

Slade, Joseph. *Thomas Pynchon.* New York: Warner Paperback Library, 1974. Reprint, New York: Peter Lang, 1990.

Smith, Shawn. *Pynchon and History: Metahistorical Rhetoric and Postmodern Narrative Form in the Novels of Thomas Pynchon.* New York: Routledge, 2005.

Snow, Sir Charles Percy. *The Two Cultures; and A Second Look: An Expanded Version of "The Two Cultures and the Scientific Revolution."* New York: Cambridge University Press, 1964.

Steigbigel, Matt. Review of *Inherent Vice,* by Thomas Pynchon. *Playboy,* August 4, 2009, http://www.playboy.com/articles/books-thomas-pynchon-inherent -vice/index.html (accessed 20 August 2010).

Stravinsky, Igor. *An Autobiography.* New York: Norton, 1962.

Tagore, Rabindranath. *Stray Birds.* New York: Macmillan, 1916.

Tanner, Tony. *Thomas Pynchon.* London: Methuen, 1982.

Thoreau, Henry D. *Walden.* Edited by J. Lyndon Shanley. Princeton: Princeton University Press, 1971.

U.S. President's Commission on the Assassination of President John F. Kennedy. *Investigation on the Assassination of President John F. Kennedy. Hearings before the President's Commission on the Assassination of President Kennedy.* 26 vols. Washington, D.C.: GPO, 1964.

Veggian, Henry. "Thomas Pynchon Against the Day." *Boundary 2* 35.1 (2008): 197–215.

Weisenburger, Steven. *A Gravity's Rainbow Companion: Sources and Contexts for Pynchon's Novel.* 2nd rev. ed. Athens: University of Georgia Press, 2006.

———. "Thomas Pynchon: A Recovered Autobiographical Sketch." *American Literature* 62.4 (December 1990): 692–97.

Wetzsteon, Ross. "The Professor of Desire." In *The Village Voice Anthology (1956–1980),* edited by Geoffrey Stokes, 319–31. New York: William Morrow, 1982.

White, Hayden. "The Burden of History." *History and Theory* 5 (1966): 111–34.

———. "Historical Pluralism." *Critical Inquiry* 12.3 (Spring 1986): 480–93.

———. *Metahistory: The Historical Imagination in Nineteenth Century Europe.* Baltimore: Johns Hopkins University Press, 1973.

Wilde, Oscar. *The Artist as Critic: Critical Writings of Oscar Wilde.* Edited by Richard Ellmann. New York: Random House, 1969.

Wisnicki, Adrian. "A Trove of New Works by Thomas Pynchon? *Bomarc Service News* Rediscovered." *Pynchon Notes* 46–49 (2000–1): 9–34.

Wood, Gordon S. "Conspiracy and the Paranoid Style: Causality and Deceit in the Eighteenth Century." *William and Mary Quarterly* 39 (1982): 401–41.

Wood, Michael. "The Apprenticeship of Thomas Pynchon." *The New York Times Book Review,* April 15, 1984, http://www.nytimes.com/1984/04/15/books/the-apprenticeship-of-thomas- pynchon.html (accessed 28 July 2010).

Woolf, Virginia. *A Room of One's Own.* New York: Harcourt Brace, 1929.

Yeats, William Butler. *The Poems.* Rev. ed. Edited by Richard J. Finneran. New York: Macmillan, 1989.

Ziolkowski, Theodore. "The Telltale Teeth: Psychodontia to Sociodontia." *pmla* 91.1 (January 1976): 9–22.

Žižek, Slavoj. "Class Struggle or Postmodernism? Yes, Please!" In *Contingency, Hegemony, Universality: Contemporary Dialogues on the Left,* by Slavoj Žižek, Judith Butler, and Ernesto Laclau, 90–135. London: Verso, 2000.

INDEX

Abish, Walter, 84, 111; *How German Is It*, 84

Abrams, M. H., 3, 199

Adams, Henry, 26, 31, 87, 168, 174, 190, 192; "The Dynamo and the Virgin," 46; *The Education of Henry Adams*, 46–47, 162–65

Adams, John Quincy, 131–32

Adonais (Shelley), 180

Aeneid (Virgil), 164–65

Aerospace Accident and Maintenance Review, 3

Aerospace Safety, 3

A-4. *See* V-2

Against the Day (Pynchon), 18–21, 159–88; assassinations and disasters in, 170–71; augury of 9/11 in, 181; Chums of Chance in, 20, 177, 190, 193; elision of year 1922 in, 186–87; as "genealogy," 160, 161, 164, 174, 185, 187, 216n7; geographical range of, 18–19, 180; and gnosticism, 177–80; history in, 18, 20, 21, 182; Iceland spar and doubling in, 20–21,

125, 172–74, 178, 194; light and day in, 180–83; math and mathematicians in, 176; power as theme in, 160–61, 165; railroads in, 171; and religious feeling, 175–77, 217n18; title of, 18, 183; Tunguska event, 172, 177, 181, 201; World War I in, 170, 171–72, 174, 185–86, 188; mentioned, 24, 60, 92, 93, 103, 104, 105, 115, 121, 122, 125, 129, 130, 131, 133, 134, 135, 137, 190, 193, 194, 201, 202, 203

Allen, Woody, 116, 167

"All's Fair in Oven War." *See Simpsons, The*

Althusser, Louis, 56, 142

American Adam, 16, 118, 187, 200

American Dream, 16, 84, 148

Anatomy of Criticism (Frye), 45, 200–202

ancients and moderns, 83, 194–95

Appleton, Victor, 20

Approach: The Naval Aviation Safety Review, 3

Arbella, 127, 131

Aristotle, 155; *Poetics*, 197–98

Arkwright, Richard, 137

Armies of the Night: History as a Novel/The Novel as History (Mailer), 161

Army, U.S. xi–xii

Arnould, Joseph, 125

"Ash Wednesday" (Eliot), 191

"As I Walked Out One Evening" (Auden), 131

Auden, W. H., 122; "As I Walked Out One Evening," 131

Augustine, Saint, *Confessions*, 10

Austen, Jane, *Northanger Abbey*, 195

Babbitt (Lewis), 28

Bach, Johann Sebastian, 59, 115

Bachofen, Johann Jakob, 47

Bacon, Sir Francis, xiii, 16

Baltimore, 1st Baron (George Calvert), 150

Bardsley, Charles, *Curiosities of Puritan Nomenclature*, 130–31

Barker, Pat, Regeneration trilogy, 185

Barnes, Djuna, 33

Barth, John, 83, 92, 123, 162, 200; "The Literature of Exhaustion," 83; *The Sot-Weed Factor*, 154

Barthelme, Donald, 4, 83, 176; *The Teachings of Don B.*, Pynchon's introduction to, 4, 169, 176, 185

Baudelaire, Charles, 39

Baudrillard, Jean, 23, 134

Beats, 26, 99, 100, 134, 192

Beckett, Samuel, 82

Been Down So Long It Looks Like Up to Me (Fariña), 3, 25, 191

Beethoven, Ludwig van, 57, 76, 122

"Belle Dame Sans Merci, La" (Keats), 110

Berkeley, George (Bishop of Cloyne), 23

Berkeley, University of California at, 88, 89–90

Birth of the Missile, The (Klee and Merk), 66

black humor, 84

Bladerunner, 59

Blake, William, 6, 142, 149, 166, 179

Blanchot, Maurice, 201

Bloom, Harold, 112, 116

Boeing, Pynchon's employment with, 3

Bohr, Niels, 11–12

Boltzmann, Ludwig, 33

Bomarc Service News, 3

Bonanza, 88

Bone, James, 3–4

Book of Daniel, The (Doctorow), 84

Bordando el Manto Terrestre (Varo), and cognitive education of Oedipa Maas, 9

Borges, Jorge Luis, 193, 201; "Tlön, Uqbar, Orbis Tertius," 201

Bostic, Earl, 39

Boswell, James, 23

"*Boule de Suif*" (de Maupassant), 130

Bourdieu, Pierre, 56

Boyle, Robert, 137

Boyle, T. Coraghessan, 153

Braun, Wernher von, 58

Brecht, Bertolt, 57

Brooks, Cleanth, 200

Buffon, Georges-Louis Leclerc de, 137

"Burnt Norton" (Eliot), 82

Busch, Wilhelm, 76

Bush, George W., 92, 128

Butler, Octavia, *Kindred*, 162

Byron, George Gordon, 189, 191; *Don Juan*, 164

Calcutta, Black Hole of, 142

Calvert, George. *See* Baltimore, 1st Baron

Calvinism, 62, 102

canonicity, Pynchon's, 195

"Canzone for an Octopus" (Pynchon), 37, 209n19

Carlyle, Thomas, 46

Cartwright, Edmund, 137

Castle of Otranto, The (Walpole), 140

Catch-22 (Heller), 84, 200

Cervantes, Miguel de, 148, 189

Chatfield, Ernle, 124–25

Ciboulette (Hahn), 186

Clausius, Rudolf, 33, 57

"Clean, Well-Lighted Place, A" (Hemingway), 38

Clinton, Bill, 92, 128

colonialism and postcolonialism, 56, 77, 142, 167, 182, 185, 195, 196, 197, 200

Columbus, Christopher, 14

Confessions (St. Augustine), 10

Conrad, Joseph, 20, 27, 59, 124; *Heart of Darkness*, 142

Conroy, Pat, 165

conspiracy. *See* paranoia

Coover, Robert, 200; *The Public Burning*, 84

Cornell University, 2–3, 10, 38, 59, 109, 112, 191, 199

Cornell Writer, 27

Crack-Up, The (Fitzgerald), 55

Critias (Plato), 133

Cromer, Evelyn Baring, 40–41

Crying of Lot 49, The (Pynchon), 9–11; compared with *Vineland*, 119–20; *The Courier's Tragedy* in, 193–94, 197; German cultural references in, 60–61, 73; Oedipa as Fisher King, 91; and *Oedipus Rex*, 198; paranoia in, 5, 9–10, 87–88, 91; as reflection of the sixties, 88–93, 202–3; religious yearning in, 11, 104; as spiritual autobiography, 10, 14, 90,

112; visionary moments in, 198–99, 201; mentioned, xi, xii, 4, 5, 13, 16, 21, 22, 26, 28, 32, 38, 39, 54, 59, 85, 93, 97, 98, 105, 108, 112, 115–16, 119, 121, 123, 126, 128, 131, 132, 133, 134, 136, 139, 141–42, 157, 165, 168, 174, 179, 180, 188

Crystal Palace, 79

Curiosities of Puritan Nomenclature (Bardsley), 130

Dampier, William, 31

Danielewski, Mark Z., 200

D'Annunzio, Gabriele, 42

Deadly Sins (Pynchon and others), 4

de Bergerac, Cyrano, 146

Debord, Guy, *Society of the Spectacle*, 165

Deleuze, Gilles, 115

DeLillo, Don, 28, 165, 194, 202, 205; *Libra*, 194; *Mao II*, 93; *Ratner's Star*, 176

de Maupassant, Guy, 148; "*Boule de Suif*," 130

Derrida, Jacques, 91–92, 157, 202; mentioned, xiii

"Design" (Frost), 87

Dewey, George, 124

"Diatribe of a Mad Housewife." See *Simpsons, The*

Dickinson, Emily, 95, 148, 193; "Tell All the Truth but Tell It Slant," 169–70

Diderot, Denis, *Encyclopédie, ou diction- naire raisonné des sciences, des arts et des métiers*, 137

Dilthey, Wilhelm, 204

Discipline and Punish (Foucault), 160–61

Dixon, Franklin W., 20

Dixon, Jeremiah, 85, 125. See also *Mason & Dixon*

Doctorow, E. L., *The Book of Daniel*, 84

Dodge, Jim, *Stone Junction*, Pynchon's introduction to, 4, 184, 188

Don Juan (Byron), 164
Donne, John, xii, 31
Dora concentration camp, 67, 76, 197
Dos Passos, John, 121, 165
Dr. Mabuse der Spieler (Lang), 66, 69, 70–72; mentioned, 78
Dubliners (Joyce), 112
Dugdale, John, 160
Duino Elegies (Rilke), 186
Duyfhuizen, Bernard, 109
"Dynamo and the Virgin, The" (Adams), 46

"Easter, 1916" (Yeats), 190
Eckermann, Johann Peter, 204
Eddins, Dwight, *The Gnostic Gospels*, 178–79
Education of Henry Adams, The (Adams), 46–47, 162–65
Eighteenth Brumaire of Louis Bonaparte, The, (Marx), 173
Eisenhower, Dwight David, 92, 120
Eliot, T. S.: "Ash Wednesday," 191; "Burnt Norton," 82; *The Waste Land*, 27, 28, 46, 171, 174, 186; mentioned, 6, 8, 38, 46, 163, 166, 190
Emerson, Ralph Waldo, 110, 183; mentioned, 19, 92, 115, 168, 193
Emerson, William, 145, 147; "The Sovereignty of Ethics," 110, 184
Emile (Rousseau), 162
Encyclopédie, ou dictionnaire raisonné des sciences, des arts et des métiers (Diderot), 137
Engels, Friedrich, 62
entropy (information theory), 32–33
entropy (thermodynamics), 5; in "Entropy," 30–35, 37; in *V.*, 7, 75, 87, 106, 163; mentioned, 94, 125, 147, 149, 166, 182
"Entropy" (Pynchon), 30–39; as "Beat

story," 192; mentioned, 4, 14, 103, 166
Epoch, 26
Ericson, Leif, 14–15, 113
Eschenbach, Wolfram von, 76
Essays on the Sociology of Knowledge (Mannheim), 190, 204–5
Ethiopia, xi

Fariña, Richard, *Been Down So Long It Looks Like Up to Me*, 3, 25, 191
fascism: in *The Crying of Lot 49*, 60; in *Gravity's Rainbow*, 74, 75; in *Inherent Vice*, 22, 128–29; in *V.*, 7, 42, 75, 76, 79, 87; in *Vineland*, 121, 128; mentioned, 98, 102, 105
Fashoda crisis, 7, 29, 40, 41, 86
Faulkner, William, 24, 33, 158, 162, 167, 191, 192, 206
Faust (Goethe), 58, 60
Faust and Faustian desire, 58, 60, 78, 93, 104, 117, 140, 161, 202
feng shui, 143
Fichte, Johann Gottlieb, 62
Fielding, Henry, 153; *Tom Jones*, 148
Finnegans Wake (Joyce), 113, 114
Fisher King, 91, 100
Fitzgerald, F. Scott, 38, 126–27, 138, 191, 192; *The Crack-Up*, 55; *The Great Gatsby*, 126–27, 138
Flaubert, Gustave, 38
Ford, John, 130, 148
Forrest Gump, (Groom), 90
Forrest Gump, (Zemeckis), 90
Forster, E. M., 165
Foucault, Michel, 143, 165, 167; *Discipline and Punish*, 160–61; "Nietzsche, Genealogy, History," 160; "Truth and Power," 160; mentioned, xiii
Frankenstein (Shelley), 140

Franklin, Benjamin, in *Mason & Dixon*, 138, 147; mentioned, 15, 137
Frau im Mond, Die (Lang), 65–66; mentioned, 78
French and Indian Wars, 150
French Revolution, 96
Freud, Sigmund, 56, 73–74; mentioned, xiii, 142
Frolic of His Own, A (Gaddis), 124
From Caligari to Hitler (Kracauer), 66, 69, 72–73
Frost, Robert: "Design," 87; "The Gift Outright," 131; "Mending Wall," 155–56. See also *Mason & Dixon*
Frye, Northrop, *Anatomy of Criticism*, 45, 200–202
Fukuyama, Francis, 172–73
Fussell, Paul, *The Great War and Modern Memory*, xii

Gaddis, William, 124, 200; *A Frolic of His Own*, 124
Galatea 2.2 (Powers), 205
García Márquez, Gabriel, 4, 94; *Love in the Time of Cholera*, 4
Gardner, John, 165; *On Moral Fiction*, 83
Garfield, John, 126
Garnett, Tay, *The Postman Always Rings Twice*, 126
Gauss, Carl Friedrich, 57, 176
Generosity: An Enhancement (Powers), 205
Genesis, book of, 151, 174
genocide, 7, 24, 74, 76, 84, 85, 97
German Southwest Africa, 7, 57, 74, 77, 95, 97, 115
Gibbon, Edward, 154
Gibbs, Willard, 33
"Gift Outright, The" (Frost), 131
Gilligan's Island, 127, 129–30, 134, 187
Glorious Revolution, 150

Gnostic Gospels, The (Pagels), 179
gnosticism, in *Against the Day*, 177–80; in *Gravity's Rainbow*, 70
Gnostic Pynchon, The (Eddins), 178–79
Goethe, Johann Wolfgang von, 57, 76, 204; *Faust*, 58, 60
Goetzke, Bernhardt, 69, 72
Gold Bug Variations, The (Powers), 198
Gore, Albert Arnold, 128
Gothic, 195. See also *Mason & Dixon*
Gramsci, Antonio, 56
Graves, Robert, 8, 14, 87, 107, 174, 190; *The White Goddess*, 47
Gravity's Rainbow (Pynchon), 11–13; and film of the Weimar era, 65–73, 193; German culture in, 58–81 passim; paranoia in, 5, 43, 96; scientific paradigms in, 11–12; and the sixties, 86; Slothrop *qua* Tannhäuser, 62–65; voyage of the *Anubis*, 81; mentioned xii, 3, 6, 9, 18, 22, 25, 27, 36, 37, 42, 44, 88, 93, 95, 97, 99, 100, 104, 105, 108, 109, 113, 115, 116, 121, 122, 123, 125, 126, 128, 129, 130, 131, 132–33, 134, 136–37, 139–40, 143, 145, 148, 152, 165, 168, 170, 174–75, 176, 178, 179, 180, 184, 186, 187, 188, 189, 190, 193, 195, 196–97, 199, 201, 202, 203, 205
Great Gatsby, The (Fitzgerald), 126–27, 138
Great War and Modern Memory, The (Fussell), xii
Gridley, Charles, 124
Groddeck, Georg, 172
Groom, Winston, 90
Guattari, Félix, 115
Gunpowder Plot, 150

Hahn, Reynaldo, *Ciboulette*, 186
Hall, Oakley, *Warlock*, 202

Hamlet (Shakespeare), 126, 129, 149, 169, 192
"Hänsel and Gretel," 76–77
Hardy, Thomas, 38
Hardy, Thomas Masterman, 124
Hardy Boys, 20
Harlot's Ghost (Mailer), 188
Harrison, Jane, 47
Hassan, Ihab, 212n18
Hathaway, Baxter, 3
Hawkes, John, 83
Hawthorne, Nathaniel, 103, 162; "Young Goodman Brown," 103
Haydn, Franz Joseph, 122, 133
Heart of Darkness (Conrad), 142
Hegel, Georg Wilhelm Friedrich, 57, 62, 79, 170
Heine, Heinrich, 57, 76
Heisenberg, Werner, 11, 57
Heller, Joseph, *Catch-22*, 84, 200
Hemingway, Ernest, 31, 157, 166, 191; "A Clean, Well-Lighted Place," 38; "The Killers," 38; "The Snows of Kilimanjaro," 38
Henderson, John B., 144
Hereros, 7, 74, 97, 113, 196
Herman, Pee-wee, 115
Herodotus, 46, 154
Hersey, John, 170
Hiaasen, Carl, 123
Hiroshima, 51, 180, 181
Hirsch, Thomas F., 57
historical fiction, xiv, 153, 154, 155, 159–60, 161–62, 173, 185
history and historiography, 23–24, 45–46, 128, 134–35, 164, 170; in *Inherent Vice*, 22, 122–23; in *Mason & Dixon*, 15–18, 140, 141, 152–55; and millenarianism, 103–5; and story, 15, 152–55, 162; in *V.*, 6–8, 40–56, 104; in *Vineland*, 13, 14–15, 116–17; men-

tioned, xiv, 1, 13. See also *Against the Day*: World War I in
Hitler, Adolph, 67, 69, 70, 71, 75, 180
holocaust, 7, 74, 97
Hoover, J. Edgar, 87
How German Is It (Abish), 84
Hume, Kathryn, 217n18; *Pynchon's Mythography*, 117
Hutcheon, Linda, 44, 115, 162
Huyssen, Andreas, 164

Ickstadt, Heinz, 173
inanimate, the, 7–8, 49, 50, 51, 52–54, 75, 101, 106, 112
Industrial Revolution, 17
Infinite Jest (Wallace), 205
Inflationzeit (German economy after Great War), 71, 72, 76, 80
influenza, Spanish, 33, 34, 172
Inherent Vice (Pynchon), 21–22, 121–35; American Dream in, 21; catalogs in, 21; doubling in, 125–26; and *Gilligan's Island*, 127, 129–30, 135; and *The Great Gatsby*, 126–27; history in, 22, 122–23; nautical lore in, 124–25; 1960s in, 21; and Plato's cave, 132–33; postmodern features of, 123–24; quest plot in, 123–24; teeth in, 129; title of, 124, 125; mentioned, 98, 105, 108, 165, 199, 203
"Is It O.K. to Be a Luddite?" (Pynchon): and *Against the Day*, 187; and *Mason & Dixon*, 139–140; mentioned, 4, 5, 18, 25, 92, 93, 101
Israel Potter (Melville), 138

Jackson, Melanie (Pynchon's spouse), 3
James, E. O., 47
James, Henry, 20, 72, 160, 161, 169, 191
James, William, 115

Jameson, Fredric, 23, 164, 199
Japan and Japanese culture,
   100–101
Jellicoe, John, 124–25
Jesuits. See *Mason & Dixon*: Society of
   Jesus in
Job, book of, 141
Johnson, Samuel, 1, 23, 141, 154
Jones, Spike, 4, 122, 192. See also
   Spiked! The Music of Spike Jones
"Journey into the Mind of Watts, A"
   (Pynchon), 84; mentioned, 4, 10, 28
Joyce, James: compared with Pynchon,
   111–14, 121, 189; *Finnegans Wake*,
   113, 114; *A Portrait of the Artist as a
   Young Man*, 112, 113; *Ulysses*, 113,
   114, 186; mentioned, 12, 46
Jung, Carl Gustav, 73, 126
Jutland, Battle of, 124–25

kabbala, 175, 178
Käkelä-Puumala, Tiina, 159, 172
Kant, Immanuel, 62, 170
Keats, John, 55; "La Belle Dame Sans
   Merci," 110
Kennedy, John F., assassination of, 85.
   See also Warren Commission
Kennedy, Robert, assassination of, 87
Kenner, Hugh, 129
Kepler, Johannes, 137
Kerouac, Jack, 26; *On the Road*, 192
Killen, Andreas, 203
"Killers, The" (Hemingway), 38
Kindred (Butler), 162
King, Martin Luther, Jr., 87
King, Vincent, 26–27
Kipling, Rudyard, 18
Klee, Ernst, *The Birth of the Missile*, 66
Klein-Rogge, Rudolf, 66, 67–69, 71, 72
Kollwitz, Käthe, 57
Korzybski, Alfred, 132

Kracauer, Siegfried, 70; *From Caligari to
   Hitler*, 66, 69, 72–73
Krupp conglomerate, 80
Ku Klux Klan, xii

Lacan, Jacques, mentioned, xiii
Lang, Fritz: *Dr. Mabuse der Spieler*, 66, 69,
   70–72; films of in *Gravity's Rainbow*,
   65–73; *Die Frau im Mond*, 65–66; *M*,
   70, 78; *Metropolis*, 66–68, 72, 78; *Der
   Müde Tod*, 66, 69, 72; *Die Nibelungen*,
   66, 68, 72, 78; mentioned, 57
language, and representation, 82–83
Larkin, Philip, xi
Last Man, The (Shelley), 174
Last Puritan, The (Santayana), 23
Lavoisier, Antoine-Laurent de, 137
Lawrence, D. H., 6, 142, 166, 179
League of Nations, 81
Lehmann-Haupt, Christopher, 26
Leibniz, Gottfried Wilhelm, 62, 137
Leonard, Elmore, 123
Lévy, Bernard-Henri, 134
Lewis, R. W. B., 200
Lewis, Sinclair, *Babbitt*, 29
Ley, Willy, *Rockets, Missiles, and Space
   Travel*, 65
L'Histoire du Soldat (Stravinsky), 33,
   34–35
Libra (DeLillo), 194
Linnaeus, Carl, 137
literary awards, Pynchon's history with,
   1
"Literature of Exhaustion, The"
   (Barth), 83
Lodge, David, *Nice Work*, 121
Lolita (Nabokov), 3, 84
Lombroso, Cesare, 106
Lotion (rock group), mentioned, 4
Love in the Time of Cholera (García
   Márquez), 4

"Low-lands" (Pynchon), 28–29; mentioned, 3, 4, 130
Luddism, 139–40, 158
Ludwig II, 70
Lukács, Georg, 161
Luther, Martin, 62
Lyotard, Jean-François, xiii, 114, 117; *The Postmodern Condition*, 83, 199

M (Lang), 70, 78
Machiavelli, Niccolò, 33, 193
Mailer, Norman, 94, 191, 192; *Armies of the Night: History as a Novel/The Novel as History*, 161; *Harlot's Ghost*, 188
Mandeville, John, 155
Mangel, Anne, 31, 32–33
Manila Bay, Battle of, 124
Mannheim, Karl, *Essays on the Sociology of Knowledge*, 190, 204–5
Manon Lescaut (Puccini), 29, 194
Manson, Charles, 123, 187
Mao II (DeLillo), 93
Mary (queen of England), 150
Marx, Karl, 21; *The Eighteenth Brumaire of Louis Bonaparte*, 173; mentioned, 57, 62, 79
Mason, Charles, 85, 125. See also *Mason & Dixon*
Mason & Dixon (Pynchon), 15–18, 136–58; and American destiny, 15; and American religion, 15–16; and American Revolution, 15; boundaries in, 150–58, passim; colonialism in, 142, 146–47; Enlightenment in, 15, 17–18, 140, 143, 149, 175; Frost's "Mending Wall" and, 155–56; Gothicism and *The Ghastly Fop* in, 139, 140, 153, 177, 178; history vs. story in, 15, 152–55; and Luddism, 17, 140–41, 158; paranoia in, 16–17; Society of Jesus in, 16, 143, 146, 149,

150; and subjunctivity, 15; symbolism of the Line, 138, 140, 144–45, 151, 155; Thoreau echoed in, 145–46; time and space in, 145–49; mentioned, 3, 22, 24, 85, 93, 112, 121, 122, 125, 128, 130, 135, 164, 165, 168, 174, 175, 176, 190, 196, 202, 203
McCarthy, Cormac, *No Country for Old Men*, 133
McClure, John A., 175
McConkey, James, 3
McEwan, Ian. See "Words for Ian McEwan"
McHale, Brian, on postmodernism, 82–83, 199; on the year 1966, 202–3
Measure for Measure (Shakespeare), 27
Melville, Herman, 124, 189, 193, 201; *Israel Potter*, 138; *Moby-Dick*, 160, 201
Mendelson, Edward, 10–11, 104, 198
"Mending Wall" (Frost), 155–56
Menippean satire, 197, 200
Meritorious Price of Our Redemption, The (William Pynchon), 193
Merk, Otto, *The Birth of the Missile*, 66
Metahistory (White), 45–46, 56, 209n3
Metropolis (Lang), 66–68, 72; mentioned, 78
Middle of the Journey, The (Trilling), 98
Midsummer Night's Dream, A (Shakespeare), 167
millennium, 14
Miller, Henry, 33
Milton, John, *Paradise Lost*, 63
Mizener, Arthur, 3, 209n19
Moby-Dick (Melville), 160, 201
modernism, 38, 43, 46, 47, 54, 82–83, 87, 111, 112, 113–14, 117, 130, 156–57, 163, 187
Monty Python, 150
Moore, Marianne, 132

"Mortality and Mercy in Vienna"
    (Pynchon), 26–27; mentioned, 4,
    14, 23, 103, 200
Motif-Index of Folk-Literature
    (Thompson), 166–67
Mozart, Wolfgang Amadeus, 33, 174
Müde Tod, Der (Lang), 66, 69, 72
Münchhausen, Karl Friedrich
    Hieronymus, 155
Mussolini, Benito, 7, 42, 75
Mussorgsky, Modest, 33, 39
myth. *See* Pynchon, Thomas: and myth

Nabokov, Vladimir, 83; *Lolita*, 3, 84;
    The Real Life of Sebastian Knight, 83;
    mentioned, 59, 82, 84, 97, 174
Nagasaki, 180, 181
Narrenschiff, Das, 76, 81
"Nearer, My Couch, to Thee"
    (Pynchon), 4
Nelson, Horatio, 124
Neumann, Erich, 47
New Criticism, 157, 200
Newman, Charles, *The Post-Modern Aura*,
    83
Newton, Isaac, 137, 145
Nibelungen, Die (Lang), 66, 68, 72; men-
    tioned, 78
Nicaea, Council of, 178
Nice Work (Lodge), 121
Nietzsche, Friedrich, 160
"Nietzsche, Genealogy, History"
    (Foucault), 160
9/11, 181, 203
1984 (Orwell), Pynchon's introduction
    to, 36, 165, 187, 195
Nixon, Richard, 86, 98, 118, 121, 128,
    134
Nobody's Cool (album by Lotion), men-
    tioned, 4
No Country for Old Men (McCarthy), 133

Nordhausen, Germany, 63, 67, 76
Norris, Frank, 168
Northanger Abbey (Austen), 195
novel, Austen's definition of, 195

Obama, Barack, 128; mentioned, 92,
    128, 203
O'Brian, Patrick, 124, 130
Oedipus, 91
On Beauty and Being Just (Scarry), 195
On Moral Fiction (Gardner), 83
On the Road (Kerouac), 192
Orientalism (Said), 56
Orwell, George, 36, 88, 97, 142, 165,
    187; *1984*, Pynchon's introduction
    to, 36, 165, 187, 195
Oswald, Lee Harvey, 87, 194, 202

Pagels, Elaine, *The Gnostic Gospels*, 179
Pakula, Alan J., *The Parallax View*, 87–88
"Pale Horse, Pale Rider" (Porter), 34
Paradise Lost (Milton), 63
Parallax View, The (Pakula), 87–88
paranoia, 5–6; and conspiracy in the
    eighteenth century, 214n5; in *The
    Crying of Lot 49*, 9–10, 87–88; in
    Gravity's Rainbow, 43; in *Mason &
    Dixon*, 149–50, 155; in *V.*, 43–44, 56;
    in *Vineland*, 88, 99; mentioned, 160,
    166, 202, 203
Parker, Robert B., 123
Peace Corps, xi
Peenemünde, 65, 66, 67, 180
Percy, Walker, 165
Perry Mason, 88
Pfaff, William, 185
Picasso, Pablo, 33
Planck, Max, 12
Planetary Motion, Kepler's Laws of,
    137
Plater, William, 26, 30

Plato, 132–33, 182; *Critias*, 133;
  Timaeus, 133
Poetics (Aristotle), 197–98
Poirier, Richard, xii
Pollack, Sydney, *Three Days of the Condor*,
  88
Porter, Katherine Anne, "Pale Horse,
  Pale Rider," 34
Portrait of the Artist as a Young Man, A
  (Joyce), 112, 113
Postman Always Rings Twice, The
  (Garnett), 126
Post-Modern Aura, The (Newman), 83
Postmodern Condition, The (Lyotard), 83,
  199
postmodernism, 20, 23, 24, 38, 39, 45,
  46, 47, 54, 83–84, 94, 111–12, 113,
  114–15, 117, 123–24, 130, 152, 153,
  156, 162, 163, 164, 174, 178, 186,
  187, 192, 194, 199, 203
Pound, Ezra, 92, 163, 204
Powers, Richard: *Generosity: An
  Enhancement*, 205; *The Gold Bug
  Variations*, mentioned, 31, 198, 200;
  homages to Pynchon, 205
Prelude, The (Wordsworth), 10
Priestley, Joseph, 137
*Protestant Ethic and the Spirit of Capitalism,
  The* (Weber), 102
psychoanalysis, 73, 141–42, 200. *See also*
  Freud, Sigmund; Jung, Carl Gustav
Public Burning, The (Coover), 84
Puccini, Giacomo, *Manon Lescaut*, 29,
  194
Puritanism, 94, 101–3, 159, 193
Purple and Gold, 27
Pynchon, Jackson (son), 3, 25
Pynchon, Thomas Ruggles, Jr.: ca-
  reer parallels with Joyce, 111–14,
  121; continuity in the work of,
  93–96, 166–67; depictions of African

Americans, 196–97; and encyclopedism, 197, 198, 200; ethnic speech
in the work of, 95, 195–6; Ford
Foundation grant application of,
191–92, 194; Germany and German
culture in the work of, 57–81; "going
over," being "turned," as recurrent
themes, 105–6, 135; history and
historiography in the thinking of,
23–24, 61–62, 116–17, 134–35,
159–60, 161–62, 165, 173, 185; and
imaginary works of literature, 193;
Japan and Japanese culture in the
work of, 59–60; life, 2–4, 25–26, 59;
literary awards, 1; literary history,
place in, 189–206; and modernism,
38, 187, 191, 202; and myth, xiii, 8,
16, 24, 45, 46–49, 56,
60, 63, 87, 91, 102, 107, 111,
117, 118, 121, 163, 202; and postmodernism, 20, 23, 24, 38, 39, 174,
178, 186, 187, 192, 199, 204, 206;
and realism, 22–23; and religion,
175–77, 217n18; science, art, and
antirationalism in, 6, 136, 141–42,
143, 149; and sixties ethos, 82–135,
210–11n6; and spiritual autobiography, 10, 14, 90, 112; teeth in the
works of, 129; as tragedian, 197–98;
and younger writers, 205–6. *See also*
titles of individual works
Pynchon, Thomas Ruggles, Sr. (father),
  2
Pynchon, William (ancestor), 193
Pynchon Notes, 1
Pynchon's Mythography (Hume), 117

quest, as plot feature in Pynchon's work,
  4–5, 8, 43, 44–45, 56, 94,
  113, 123–24, 137, 154, 157, 174,
  198–99

Rabbit novels and novella (Updike), 90, 91

racism, 24, 30, 74, 76, 84–85, 90, 91, 120, 167

Rafferty, Terrence, 105, 117

Rathenau, Walter, 79, 80

Ratner's Star (DeLillo), 176

Reagan, Ronald, 88, 97, 98, 121, 134, 135, 203

Real Life of Sebastian Knight, The (Nabokov), 83

Reed, Ishmael, 162

Regeneration trilogy (Barker), 185

Revelation of St. John, 181

Richardson, Samuel, 164

Rilke, Rainer Maria, 78; *Duino Elegies*, 186; mentioned, 36, 57, 76, 193, 195

Robeson, Paul, 131

Rockets, Missiles, and Space Travel (Ley), 65

Romans, book of, 183

Rosenberg, Ethel and Julius, 84

Roth, Philip, 167, 192

Rousseau, Henri, 33; *Emile*, 162

Rousseau, Jean Jacques, 137, 162

Rover Boys, 20, 193

Royal Society, 15, 16, 139, 149. See also *Mason & Dixon*

Ruby, Jack, 87

Rushdie, Salman, 108

Ruskin, John, 184

Sacre du Printemps, Le (Stravinsky), 34, 166

Sade, Donatien Alphonse François (Marquis de Sade), 33

Said, Edward, Orientalism, 56

Sajak, Pat, 116

Sales, Nancy Jo, 3

Salinger, J. D., 26, 170

Santayana, George, *The Last Puritan*, 23

Sarajevo, 29, 41

Scarry, Elaine, *On Beauty and Being Just*, 195

Schacht, Hjalmar, 79

Schelling, Friedrich Wilhelm Joseph von, 62

Schiehallion, 141

Schopenhauer, Arthur, 62

Schwarzenegger, Arnold, 134

Scott, Walter, 162

2 Peter, 183

"Secret Integration, The" (Pynchon), 26; racism in, 84–85; mentioned, 4, 108, 196

Seed, David, xiii

Serres, Michel, xiii, 35

Shakespeare, William, 169, 204; *Hamlet*, 126, 129, 149, 169, 192; *Measure for Measure*, 27; *A Midsummer Night's Dream*, 167; *Twelfth Night*, 167

Shambhala, 20

Shelley, Mary, 193; *Frankenstein*, 140; *The Last Man*, 174

Shelley, Percy Bysshe, 31; *Adonais*, 180

"Shrink Flips, The" (Pynchon), 4

Simpsons, The, Pynchon's appearances on, 4

Slade, Joseph, 26, 27, 31

Slatoff, Walter, 3

Slow Learner (Pynchon), 25–39; Pynchon's introduction to, 191–93, 194, 195, 199–200; mentioned, 3, 94, 109, 110, 112, 116, 119, 140. See *also* titles of individual stories

"Small Rain, The" (Pynchon), 27–28; mentioned, 4, 29, 38, 145

Smith, Adam, 137

Smith, John, 155

Smith, Shawn, 159, 185

Smollett, Tobias, 148

Snow, Charles Percy, *The Two Cultures; and A Second Look: An Expanded Version of The Two Cultures and the Scientific Revolution*, 6, 205
"Snows of Kilimanjaro, The" (Hemingway), 38
Society of the Spectacle (Debord), 165
Socrates, 24
Sophocles, 46, 198
Sot-Weed Factor, The (Barth), 154
"Sovereignty of Ethics, The" (Emerson), 110, 184
Sower, Parable of the, 28
Spanish-American War, 124
Spengler, Oswald, 163, 185
Spiked! The Music of Spike Jones, Pynchon's liner notes for, 214n5; mentioned, 4, 192
Spohr, Ludwig, 57
Stagecoach (Ford), 130, 148
Star Trek, 85, 166
Steinbeck, John, 121
Sterne, Laurence, 162, 189; *Tristram Shandy*, 162, 200
Stinnes, Hugo, 79, 80
Stockhausen, Karlheinz, 60
Stone Junction (Dodge), Pynchon's introduction to, 4, 184, 188
Stradonitz, Friedrich August Kekulé von, 57, 79
Stravinsky, Igor, 33–35, 39, 54; *L'Histoire du Soldat*, 33, 34–35; *Le Sacre du Printemps*, 34, 166
Stuart, Charles Edward, 150
Styron, William, 170
Suez crisis of 1956, 42, 86
Suso, Heinrich, 76
Swift, Jonathan, 140, 167, 189, 190
Symmes, John Cleves, 140

Tacitus, 76
Tagore, Rabidranath, 183

Tanner, Tony, 26, 31
Tannhäuser story, 76. See also *Gravity's Rainbow*
Tchernobyl, 181
Teachings of Don B., The (Barthelme), Pynchon's introduction to, 4, 169, 176, 185
Tea Party, 128
"Tell All the Truth but Tell It Slant" (Dickinson), 169–70
thermodynamics, 5, 33, 34, 35, 125
Thomas, Dylan, 38
Thompson, Hunter S., 99
Thompson, Stith, *Motif-Index of Folk-Literature*, 166–67
Thoreau, Henry David, 145–46
Three Days of the Condor (Pollack), 88
Timaeus (Plato), 133
Time Machine, The (Wells), 149, 182
"Tlön, Uqbar, Orbis Tertius" (Borges), 201
Tolstoy, Leo, 162
Tom Jones (Fielding), 148
Tom Swift novels, 20, 193
Tosca (Puccini), 115, 194
Tractatus Logico-Philosophicus (Wittgenstein), 186
Trafalgar, Battle of, 124
tragedy, elements of in Pynchon's work, 197–98
Treaty of Versailles (1919), 80
Trilling, Lionel, *The Middle of the Journey*, 98
Tristram Shandy (Sterne), 162, 200
Trotha, Adrian Dietrich Lothar von, 74, 81
"Truth and Power" (Foucault), 160
Tuchmann, Barbara W., 21, 173
Turner, Frederick Jackson, 122, 187
Twelfth Night (Shakespeare), 167
Two Cultures; and A Second Look: An Expanded Version of The Two Cultures

and the Scientific Revolution (Snow), 6, 205

Ulysses (Joyce), 113, 114, 186
"Under the Rose" (Pynchon), 29; and *V.*, 40, 41; mentioned, 4, 143, 171
Updike, John, 166; *Rabbit* novels and novella, 90, 91
Utgarthaloki (Norse myth), 76, 80

V. (Pynchon), 6–8, 40–56, 86–87; art and artists in, 54–55; catalog of disasters in, 170, 203; decadence in, 53–54; entropy in, 49, 51–53; fascism in, 52, 53, 75; female characters in, 48–49; myth in, 46–49, 56; paranoia in, 43–44, 86; point of view in, 40, 43; and White Goddess, 14, 87, 107; mentioned, xi, xiii, 3, 4, 9, 18, 22, 24, 59, 60, 62, 74, 81, 88, 93, 97, 103, 106, 108, 110, 112, 115, 119, 122, 125, 130, 136, 139, 145, 164, 165, 170, 171, 174, 186, 189, 190, 194, 196, 198, 199, 202
Varo, Remedios, 180; *Bordando el Manto Terrestre* as parable of cognition, 9
Vaucanson, Jacques de, 17
Veggian, Henry, 161
Venus, transits of. See *Mason & Dixon*
Victoria (queen of England), 44
Vineland (Pynchon), 13–15, 93–121; compared with *The Crying of Lot 49*, 119–20; and drugs in America, 98–100; Emerson quotation in, 19; entropy in, 101; ethnic speech in, 195–96; Faustian myth in, 60, 117; feminism in, 107, 118; film in, 116; history in, 13, 14–15, 116–17, 120–21; Japan and Japanese culture in, 100–101; limits of postmodernist aesthetic in, 111–12, 114–15, 117; myth of the Fall in, 105, 106–7; para-

noia in, 88, 94, 96–97; Puritanism in, 101–3; quest in, 13–14, 96, 97–98, 100, 101, 108, 123; views of the 1960s in, 13, 88; Viking reference in title of, 14–15, 118; mentioned, xiv, 22, 59, 61, 75, 85, 92, 93, 124, 125, 128, 129, 134, 135, 137, 140, 165, 174, 176, 184, 187, 188, 189, 199, 203
Virgil, 190; Aeneid 164–65
Virginia Resolutions of 1769, 145
Vollman, William, 200, 205
Vonnegut, Kurt, 14, 84, 121
v-2, 11, 12, 66, 95, 103

"*Wachet Auf*" (Bach), 115
Wagner, Richard, allusions to *Tannhäuser* in *Gravity's Rainbow*, 62–65; mentioned, 57, 76
Walden (Thoreau), 145–46
Wallace, David Foster, 200; *Infinite Jest*, 205
Walpole, Horace, *The Castle of Otranto*, 140
Warlock (Hall), 202
Warren Commission, 87, 194
Washington, George, 15, 138
Waste Land, The (Eliot), 27, 28, 31, 46, 171, 174, 186
Watt, James, 137
Watts riots of 1965. See "Journey into the Mind of Watts"
Weber, Max, 62; *The Protestant Ethic and the Spirit of Capitalism*, 102
Weimar Republic, 65, 72, 73, 78
Weisenburger, Steven, 65, 191
Wells, H. G., 38; *The Time Machine*, 149, 182
West, Nathanael, 31, 108
White, Hayden, *Metahistory*, 45–46, 56, 209n3
White Goddess, the, 8, 14, 87, 107

White Goddess, The (Graves), 47
Whitman, Walt, 166, 189
Wiener, Norbert, 26
Wilbur, Richard, Pynchon letter to, 2
Wilde, Oscar, 195
Winthrop, John, 127
Wittgenstein, Ludwig, *Tractatus Logico-Philosophicus*, 186
Wood, Michael, 26
Woolf, Virginia, 108; mentioned, 46, 93
"Words for Ian McEwan" (Pynchon), 160, 184, 215–16n4
Wordsworth, William, 182; *The Prelude*, 10
"World (This One), The Flesh (Mrs. Oedipa Maas), and The Testament of Pierce Inverarity" (Pynchon), 4
World Trade Center, 181, 203
World War I, 18, 20, 21, 29, 33–34, 41, 43, 50, 54, 61, 75, 80, 86, 93, 95, 170, 185. See also *Against the Day*

World War II: in *Gravity's Rainbow*, 58–81 passim; mentioned, 11, 12, 21, 42, 43, 50, 54, 75, 76, 82, 86, 88, 95, 114, 121, 137, 170, 180, 181
Wouk, Herman, 170

X, Malcolm, 87

Yankovic, Weird Al, 133
Yeats, William Butler, 6, 94, 110, 141, 163; "Easter, 1916," 190
Yerby, Frank, 161–62
"Young Goodman Brown" (Hawthorne), 103

Zapruder film, 87
Zemeckis, Robert, 90
Ziolkowski, Theodore, 129
Žižek, Slavoj, xiii, 123
Zwingli, Ulrich, 62

CPSIA information can be obtained at www.ICGtesting.com
Printed in the USA
LVOW061045210712

290955LV00003B/6/P